# 365 Days of Self-Discovery

## A Daily Guided Writing Journal

**Hagit Elmakiyes**

# 365 Days of Self-Discovery

## A Daily Guided Writing Journal

Original version edited by: Tali Cohen-Zion

Translated from the Hebrew by:
Adva Webber, Tanya Rosenblit

English edited by: Nancy Peled

Illustrated by: Yael Hertzog

Cover design and layout: Gali Gonen



**6 Harimon Street, Pardes Hanna, Israel**

ISBN: 9798804430567

Hagit@masabemilim.co.il
A Journey Through Words



Printed in Israel, 2020

**Note:**

The writing exercises in this journal are not considered therapy of any kind, nor are they a replacement for emotional / spiritual / psychological treatment.

Implementing the exercises in this book is the sole responsibility of the writer.

Let the words flow through you like the water flowing in the stream. Place no claim over your words. Do not hang on to them. They are not yours. They never were. Remember that all reach their destination and unite somewhere with the sea.

Do not ask them to slow down. Do not hasten them forward. Allow them to move freely as they are. Let the words pass through you, peaceful and pleasant, temperamental and raging, sweet or bitter. Be a river whose only designation is to carry.

Let the words flow through you like the water flowing in the stream. Place no claim over your words. Do not ask them to slow down. Do not hasten them forward. Allow them to move freely as they are. Let the words pass through you peaceful and pleasant, temperamental and raging, sweet or bitter. They are not yours. They never were. Remember that all reach their destination and unite somewhere with the sea. Do not hang on

## Be a River

Let the words flow through you,
Like the water flowing in the stream.
Build no dam over your words,
Do not ask them to slow down,
Do not urge them on.
Allow them to move freely,
As they are.

Let the words pass through you,
Peaceful and pleasant,
Temperamental and raging,
Sweet or bitter.
They are not yours,
They never were.

Do not let your words overflow,
Do not hold onto them.

Learn from the river:
Its only purpose is
To carry the water.

Be
A river

# Introduction

This writing journal was born from my search for the perfect writing space. I wanted a personal journal for myself, where I could express my feelings, impressions and thoughts, as well as record inspirational writing I found in the poems, stories and reflections of great writers.

The exercises in this journal were created and collected over twelve years, during which I conducted intuitive writing workshops, accompanying women and men on their personal writing journeys. Over the years, I have repeatedly encountered people's need for a daily writing space. I have come to realize that even if the love of writing is deeply entrenched in our bones, without a regulated framework, it remains absent from our lives.

In light of this, I wanted to create for you, and for myself, an instrument that offers a daily guided writing space. Every day of the year has its own page, with an exercise that encourages you to take an inner stroll through words, stories, poems, thoughts or any other way you choose to express yourself. The purpose of this is to prompt inspiration and awaken your passion - for words and for life. Consistently filling the journal will keep the writing flame alight.

Ever since I was a little girl, I have held a pencil or a pen in my hand. As a child, my "Dear Diary" was a refuge, an attentive listener and even a tool for survival. The pain I experienced faded away on the paper that absorbed it; and after the pain, wonderful words always arrived to give me the strength to continue on the journey of my life.

Since then, many rivers of ink have flowed through my pens, but I still feel deep gratitude to the writing that was always there for me. Writing is a significant and inseparable part of my life. It is an accessible utensil for my contemplations, my self-expression, for learning about myself, and discovering new places within.

Writing is a meditative tool that enables me to be present with all that comes to me from my soul, and keeps me alert to all that is happening inside of me. It allows me to cleanse the screen that stands between me and myself.

For many years, I have religiously filled countless notebooks and journals. I write when I wake up, to clear the night away and become inspired for the new day. I write before I fall asleep, to summarize the day and take a bird's eye view of it. I write when I am in an emotional tempest, when I need clarity, when I experience a momentous event and seek to turn it into a milestone that is engraved in my memory. I write to release and to forget.

In truth, I lose myself in writing, in order to know myself.

Each time I put pen to paper, I set forth on an inner journey to the unknown. At times, it is a short visit to a familiar place, while at other times, I am like Alice in Wonderland, falling down the rabbit hole. During the writing process, I never know where I am going or where I may end up. Sometimes, I don't even know where I am. However, one thing is clear: I will never emerge from my writing the same woman who initially put her pen to paper.

*365 Days of Self-Discovery* was born out of great love for writing and acknowledgement of its power as a tool for healing, expression and creativity, as a way for us to know ourselves more deeply, and thus for creating change. It is a space that invites you to write to come closer to who you are, in a cyclical, gentle and structured process.

I wish you a wonderful and fascinating journey on your way to yourself.

**With love,**
**Hagit**

## Before You Begin your Journey

Writing is one of the most intimate places a person has. Writing is the realm of "alone". At times, it is an escape to solitude, but mostly it has a powerful togetherness, the merging of a person with him-or-her-self.

How many times in your life have you allowed yourself to take a pen and a notebook and simply write from your heart, just for yourself? Not a poem or a story, not a great novel, not an academic outpouring or a piercing political article. To simply write, to bring out what comes up inside you. In this moment.

Intuitive writing, and writing in general, is an excellent method for connecting us to ourselves, to our inner truth and our natural flow, by the simplest means we possess. We do not need to travel anywhere, or make a great effort, or possess much time or money - we do not even need a large space. All we need is the will to commit and to write. And most importantly: to love.

Many writers are constrained by the magic of writing, as if writing were the Holy of Holies. Many of us will not take a pen in hand, unless we have the inspiration, the muse, or the desire to write a novel overnight, turning us into authors or poets to be included in the "canon".

We are used to living within the constraints of strict writing rules and we don't allow ourselves the space or the right to write ourselves spontaneously, associatively, raw - as we are in this moment.

When we write, we usually address our writing automatically to someone else, a potential reader or an external critic. We long to be understood. After many years inside a strict educational system with exact writing rules, we grow accustomed to writing for others, and too little for ourselves. Thus most of the time, we don't even dare.

Intuitive writing is the path to breaking boundaries, defying rules, eliminating laws. To flow with our primal thoughts, those that are pure, that have evaded our inner censor. This is the place from which a simple, authentic creation is born, made from the materials of our lives. For that, we must look inward and explore what is inside of us, rather than look outside.

Deeply engrained in us is the craving to write, which is part of our longing for expression and creativity. But over the years, we have built obstacles, barriers and excuses around that desire.

If we just agree to reconnect to our beginnings - our core and intuition- if we just agree to make room for writing in our lives, we can rediscover ourselves amongst the letters, amidst the words, in between the sentences and the lines. We can also express our unique voices in poems and stories.

The journal you are holding in your hands aims to create a space that enables exactly this type of writing. To explore, discover, reflect, wonder, accept and love all that passes through us, without judgement. This space is first and foremost meant for you - whether writing is a part of your life or whether you have never even thought you could write.

To help you make the most of this space, I will provide suggestions and writing principles that will allow you to break free from everything you have learned till now in response to the question: "How should I write?"
All that you need to do is trust the process and abide by the principles. The results will speak directly from your heart to the paper.

## Commitment and Perseverance

To enable a deep, authentic, writing experience, we must commit to it and persevere. Many people (and I am one of them) are apprehensive when we hear the word "commitment". This term tends to close in on us, so we feel we are losing our freedom. But this response is actually deceptive, as it is only through deep commitment to ourselves that we are able to attain complete inner freedom. The commitment to the process of writing does not require much time. Even ten minutes a day is enough. Fill one page in the journal - that is all we must do. The commitment is to be dedicated to the process for one year, from the minute you begin. Just one exercise - every day.

In this way we can continuously experience, over a period of time, the magic and power of writing that will lead us to internal reflection, to becoming better acquainted with ourselves, and even, perhaps, to creating the changes in our lives we wish for and dream about. Self-discipline and commitment to the process generates meaning, and in doing so, provides us with a genuine sense of freedom.

## A Room of Your Own

I recommend that you create a writing "womb" for yourself: a set time and space that is comfortable for you to write in. Writing can take place on the patio, with your morning coffee, or in the study at night, before you go to bed. I recommend always writing in the same place, somewhere you feel protected, and have all the comfort and privacy to write in the time frame you have fixed for yourself, without interruptions.

In her book, *A Room of One's Own*, Virginia Woolf emphasizes the materialistic conditions that are essential for writing. She believed that the fountains of creation are not an uncontrollable force. External circumstances, such as a suitable room, privacy, and silence, are very important and make creation possible. This is an opportunity for you to create or define a "room of your own" and preserve its boundaries for the sake of the process.

Intuitive writing and the experience you will undergo in this journal, will stimulate your writing glands (and your general creativity) and take writing outside the boundaries of this book, in such a way that you may find yourself writing beyond your expectations and outside your set space. When you do have a "room of your own", do not hesitate to break out of its boundaries every now and then, and write anywhere and anytime you desire. You may even choose to draw, dance, sculpt, play music or go for a stroll. Anything you do will be worthy.

## A Journey through Words Over the Four Seasons

You may start this journal any day of the year. It is divided into four portals, one for each season. Every section contains three months of intuitive writing exercises, according to the spirit of the season. Every season has its own rhythm and energy. Each season is part of the cycle of change of the universe - and humanity.

Look around you at the flow of nature, and you will see that cyclicity everywhere:
Autumn is a time of renewal, creation and realization. It is the season for sowing seeds in the ground.
In Winter, nature stands still, gathering inward. Work and growth occur in the dark.
In Spring, we discern the appearance of buds, heralding the

flowering to come.
Summer is the season when the fruit of last year's labor ripens. This is a good time to rest, let go, and recharge for the new cycle that will begin again in the fall.

Autumn, Winter, Spring and Summer. This journal proposes a way to get closer to ourselves through words and the spirit of the season. Every season is an invitation to synchronize with the laws of nature, to become familiar with its cyclicity, and reconnect with ourselves. Every month holds a special energy, a fundamental theme for reflection and expression. Every day, there is a new invitation for observation, investigation and creation.

## Start writing

Open your journal on today's date. Read the exercise and start writing whatever comes to you from within. Release your words on the paper, with no censorship.

It is important to internalize the simple idea that is the basis of the exercises in this journal: there are no mistakes; no "right" or "wrong", no one way to understand the instructions, and no one way to follow them. Anything you write will be absolutely correct, accurate and excellent, and this is the approach I recommend you adopt: the main thing is – write.

Make sure that your hand keeps moving. Do not stop to think or read what you have written, certainly not to edit, style or condense what is coming out from within. In fact, do not stop at all until the page in front of you is filled. That way, you allow yourself full expression of the most raw and pure primal thoughts that come forth from within. Write them as they are. Online. Do not try to control the process. Do not even try to understand what you are writing. Simply write.

Do not erase, do not write in an orderly, structured fashion; do not be consistent. You don't even have to complete a sentence, if new sentences appear. The only commitment you have is to yourself, not to an external reader. Remember, the journal is personal and it is yours.

Fragmented text is also just fine. No teacher will read it or mark a red "X" on the page. Sometimes your thoughts will be faster than your hand, but don't try keeping up with the "old" thought or insisting on its expression. Instead, let the pen move on to the new thought that arises, in the moment.

Do not overthink it; do not be "logical" or consistent. There is no logic in intuition. There is only truth. Be committed to your truth in each new moment. Be devoted to it.
Allow your hand to write you. The more you are open and the more you practice the more surprised you'll be to find how independent your hand can be and how it has a life of its own. Allow it this life.

Writing is listening. There is something in you that wants to be written, more than you want to write. Listen to it. Agree to write it.

Let go of the need for punctuation, correct grammar, or spelling. Any concern about commas or full stops might interrupt the flow. Allow yourself to write in illegible script, or in different sizes. Relax, make spelling mistakes, have fun. You can write in any form you want: vertically, horizontally, in a circle that creates a mandala, big or small letters, with a pen or a pencil.

The only instruction is that you write you, and nothing but you.

If the space provided is not enough for you, you may add pages to the journal or move outside of its boundaries. In fact, I encourage you to write beyond this journal, whenever you like.

If you skipped a day, that's perfectly fine! You can complete the writing exercise another day or you can let it go completely. Whatever happens, remember: what's important is the process, not the product.

**I wish you a meaningful journey of discovery, pleasure and joy!**

**Putting a pen to a blank page**

**Is like taking off your shoes when you come home**

# Autumn

## SEEDS OF CHANGE

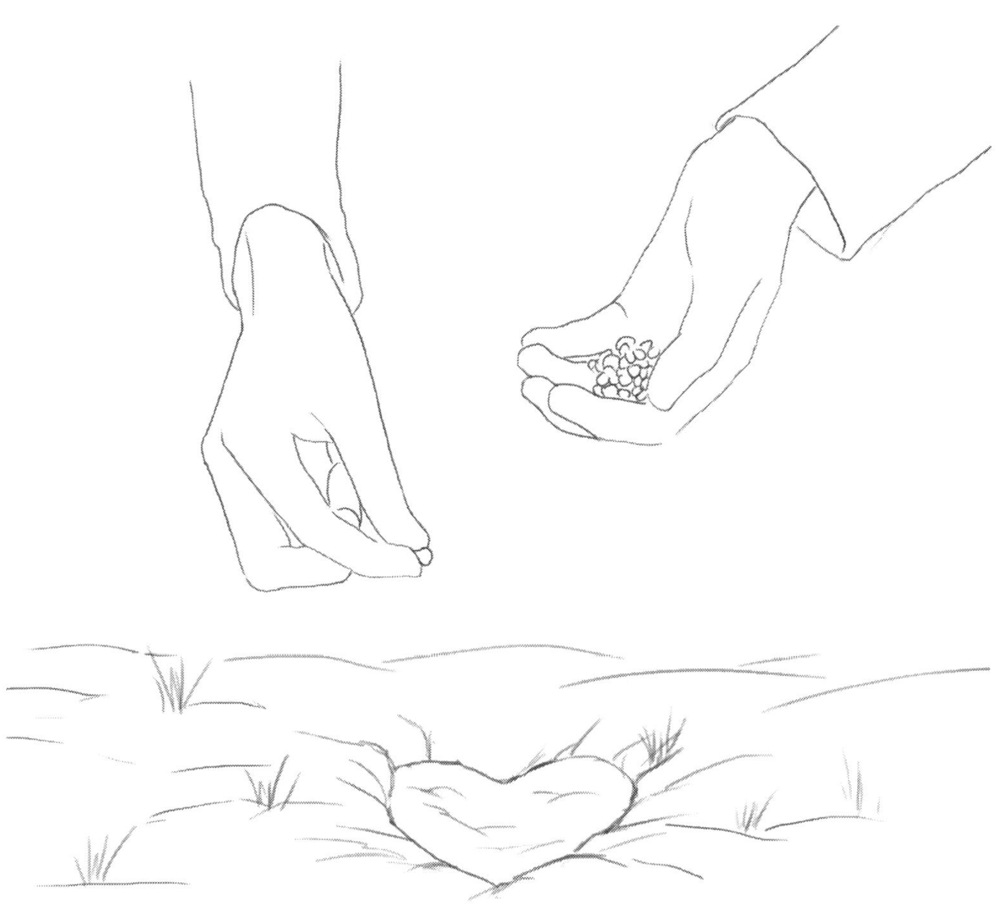

## Writing in Autumn

The fall season is when the new year actually begins, setting the stage for the year to come, a time of creation, for us as in nature. At this time we can make use of the energy inherent in this new season to sow our own seeds of change.

This season guides us to turn inwards and reflect. Looking back over the past year we should ask: are we where we want to be? Do we express our values every day? Do we fulfill ourselves? Is there something we can cast off to make room for something new? What should we change?

Hidden in these questions lies a wonderful opportunity to observe the thoughts, activities, and people around us, and the way we fill our lives, from a new angle. This is the time to clear away what has become irrelevant, in order to replenish ourselves. To do that, we must till the soil, let it breathe, and allow it to regenerate, so it can absorb the new seeds that hold the potential for a whole new life.

Indeed after introspection, this time of year encourages us to discard anything in our lives that no longer serves us, as a tree sheds its leaves. It is the best time to create hope that fall will bring us change, progress and growth.

**This portal invites you, through your words, to sow seeds of change. To write in order to cast off, change and reflect.**

# September

## Writing to Let Go

Let the words flow through you, Like the water flowing in the stream Place no dam over your words, Do not ask them to slow down, Do not hasten them forward Allow them to move freely As they are. Let the words pass through you, Peaceful and pleasant Temperamental and raging Sweet or bitter. They are not yours, They never were. Remember that all they want Is to reach their

## September 1st

With the sea. Do not over flow, Do not hang on words. Learn from the river: Its only designation is To carry water

# Going on a Journey

Imagine that you are embarking on the greatest journey of your life at this very moment. Where are you really going? Where do you hope to end up?

Start with the words **I am going on a journey**, and let the pen simply lead you on a new path through writing. Observe the words and see where they take you. Allow yourself to move ahead without knowing where you are going to end up. Whenever you feel stuck, you can return again and again to the key words and restart your journey.

Bon voyage!

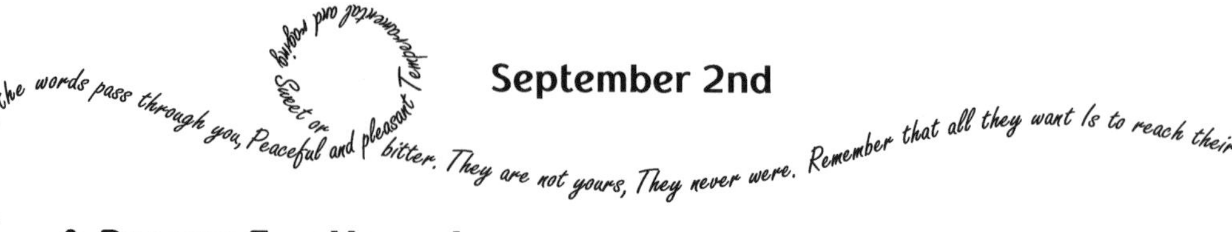
Let the words flow through you, Like the water flowing in the stream Place no dam over your words, Do not ask them to slow down, Do not hasten them forward Allow them to move freely As they are. Let the words pass through you, Peaceful and pleasant Temperamental and raging Sweet or bitter. They are not yours, They never were. Remember that all they want Is to reach their

**September 2nd**

## A Prayer For Your Journey

Write your own traveler's prayer, a text that contains provisions for your special journey, a text you can go back to any time you like, should you need a reminder or encouragement. Allow yourself to pray deeply. You can direct your prayer to God, to the universe, or to yourself, personally, whatever feels right to you. Simply deliver a prayer in your own words for a safe journey on the road that stretches out ahead.

What do you wish for yourself on that road? What would you like to take with you as provisions for the journey? Maybe you wish to write a message that will accompany you on your way – your values, beliefs, or insights.

Write to yourself in the second person, as if the text is written from a higher place within you. Start with the words **As you begin your journey...**

# September 3rd

*With the sea. Do not over flow, Do not hang on words. Learn from the river: Its only designation is To carry water*

## Where Do I Come From?

Close your eyes for a few moments, breathe deeply, and become one with a peaceful place deep within you. When you are still, ask yourself: where do I come from? Where do I belong? Try to understand where you have come from right now – physically, emotionally and spiritually.

Try to hold on to the question, without rushing to find answers. Continue your inner stroll to the rhythm of your deep breathing. If an answer arises, examine it a moment, then release it and allow a new answer to take its place in your consciousness. Now return to the question.

After this short meditation, write about where you have come from. Start with the words **I come from...**

Begin with whatever thoughts arose during your moments of silence, and accept any additional answers that may be revealed to you as you write.

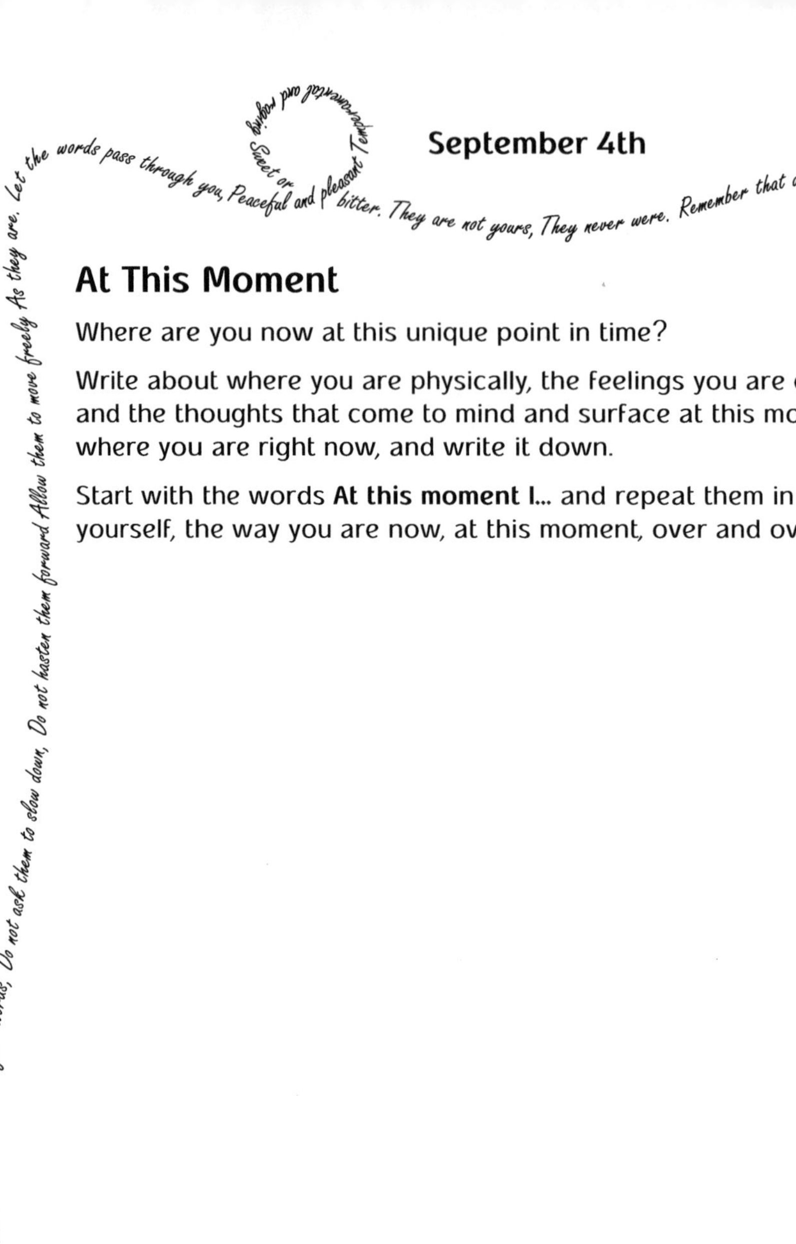
Let the words flow through you, Like the water flowing in the stream Place no dam over your words, Do not ask them to slow down, Do not hasten them forward Allow them to move freely As they are. Let the words pass through you, Peaceful and pleasant Temperamental and raging Sweet or bitter. They are not yours, They never were. Remember that all they want Is to reach their

## At This Moment

Where are you now at this unique point in time?

Write about where you are physically, the feelings you are experiencing, and the thoughts that come to mind and surface at this moment. Observe where you are right now, and write it down.

Start with the words **At this moment I...** and repeat them in order to write yourself, the way you are now, at this moment, over and over again.

## September 5th

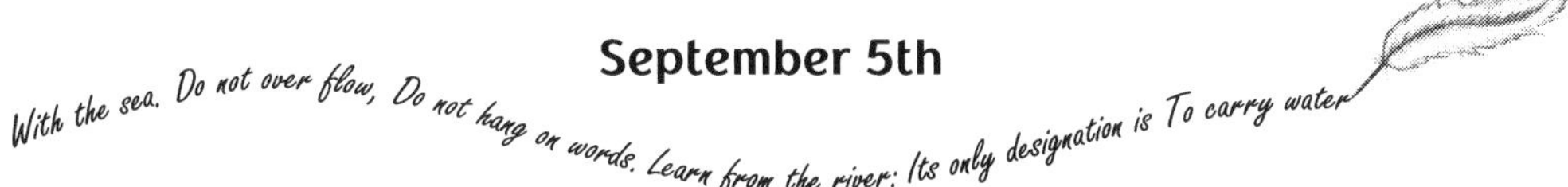
With the sea. Do not over flow, Do not hang on words. Learn from the river: Its only designation is To carry water

# It is Time to Leave Behind

In "Enchanted Bird" poet Zelda lists all the things which we should prepare to leave behind.

This exercise is inspired by her poem. Write a text that starts with the words **It's time to leave behind...**

What should you say goodbye to?

"You have to begin to leave behind the brilliance in heaven and the colors of the earth ... to bid goodbye to the words -all the words I have ever heard or read."

"Enchanted Bird". *The Spectacular Difference: Selected Poems of Zelda,* Edited and translated by Marcia Falk. Hebrew Union College Press, 2004, p 137.

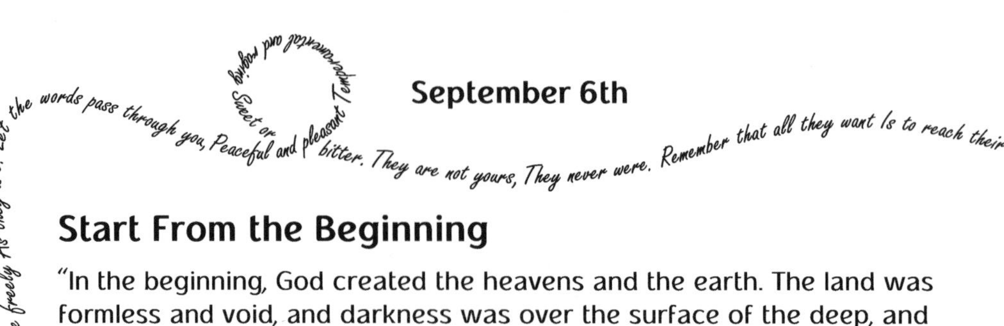
Let the words flow through you, Like the water flowing in the stream Place no dam over your words, Do not ask them to slow down, Do not hasten them forward Allow them to move freely As they are. Let the words pass through you, Peaceful and pleasant Temperamental and raging Sweet or bitter. They are not yours, They never were. Remember that all they want Is to reach their

## September 6th

# Start From the Beginning

"In the beginning, God created the heavens and the earth. The land was formless and void, and darkness was over the surface of the deep, and the Spirit of God was hovering over the waters. And God said: 'Let there be light"; and there was light."' (Genesis 1:1–3)

God created the world with words. He spoke the word, and the world came into being. Write a text that connects you to the idea of creation and formation.

Remember times when you experienced yourself creating and forming the reality of your life through your words. Do you remember such an experience? Write about it. Start your writing with the words that created reality for you.

With the sea. Do not over flow, Do not hang on words. Learn from the river: Its only designation is To carry water

## Return to Myself

Today is the birthday of **Rabbi Avraham Yitzchak HaCohen Kook**, religious leader and philosopher born in 1865.

"The essential answer is that one returns to him- or- her- self," he wrote in one of his books of wisdom.

In this exercise, inspired by Rabbi Kook, ask yourself: is there something in you to which you wish to return? Is there something you abandoned long ago, and now wish to reclaim in order to return to yourself?

Perhaps an old dream, a simple joy or an authentic spirit.

Return to yourself by writing to yourself. Where do you wish to return? To what? Start with the words **When I return to myself...** or **On the way to myself...** and write everything that surfaces, throughout this journey of return to yourself.

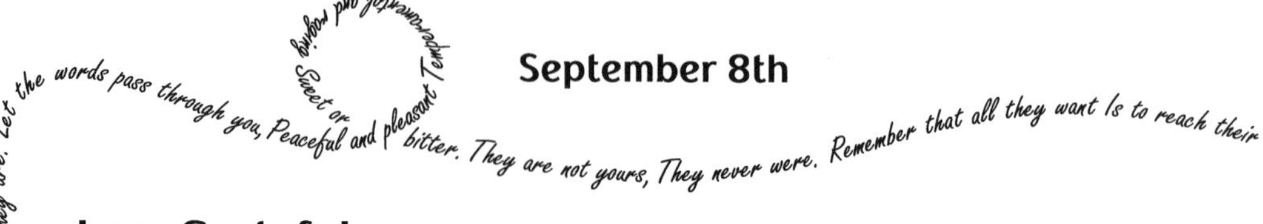
Let the words flow through you, Like the water flowing in the stream Place no dam over your words, Do not ask them to slow down, Do not hasten them forward Allow them to move freely As they are. Let the words pass through you, Peaceful and pleasant Temperamental and raging Sweet or bitter. They are not yours, They never were. Remember that all they want Is to reach their

**September 8th**

## I am Grateful

At the beginning of this journey, take the time to look around and be grateful for everything – everything that exists, the good and the less worthy, for everything that you have produced, and everything you have received throughout your life. Just be grateful.

In this exercise, you cherish what is. Write a text that is all about gratitude for what is present in your life in this moment. Start with the words **Thank you for...** or **I am grateful...**

## September 9th



# Release Parts of Yourself in Ink

Today is the birthday of author **Leo Tolstoy**, born in 1828.

Tolstoy profoundly understood the possibilities of release concealed in the act of writing. "One ought only to write when one leaves a piece of one's own flesh in the inkpot, each time one dips one's pen," he wrote.

In this exercise, inspired by Tolstoy, ask yourself whether writing is a space of release for you. Write what you release every time you write, what you leave in the inkwell while writing, and whether you consent to leave parts of yourself on the paper.

"True life is lived when tiny changes occur." **Leo Tolstoy**

Let the words flow through you, Like the water flowing in the stream Place no dam over your words, Do not ask them to slow down, Do not hasten them forward Allow them to move freely As they are. Let the words pass through you, Peaceful and pleasant

Temperamental and raging
Sweet or bitter. They are not yours, They never were. Remember that all they want Is to reach their

## September 10th

# Writing to Cast Off

Fall is a good time to shed our leaves, to peel off old layers, as in the cycle of nature. We also should leave behind all that has grown old, that "has run its course", to make room for the new. Write about the "leaves" you wish to shed this fall. What will you let go?

Write in the present tense, as if you are discarding something right now.

Start with the words **I am casting off...**

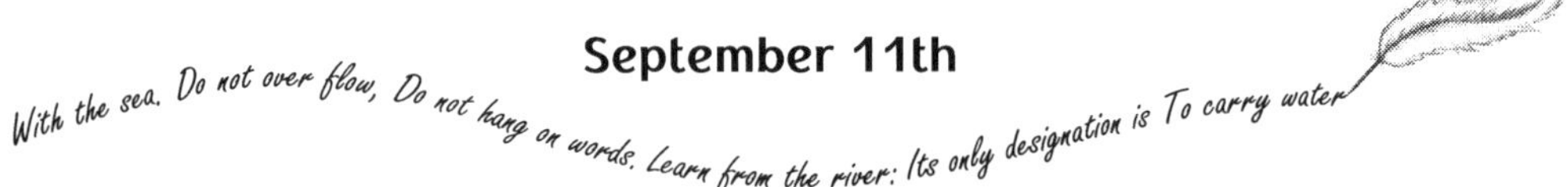
With the sea. Do not over flow, Do not hang on words. Learn from the river: Its only designation is To carry water

## The Last Leaf

Today is the birthday of the author **O. Henry**, born in 1862.

This is an exercise inspired by his story "The Last Leaf", about a young woman who is lying on her deathbed looking out at an ivy vine whose leaves are falling, and decides that when the last leaf falls, she will die.

Write about your "last leaf", the one that will enable you to kill something inside of you when it is gone, and lead to your rebirth. Specify with as much detail as possible the one thing that you find hardest to leave behind forever.

Write your difficulty with letting it go, and explain why you no longer need it.

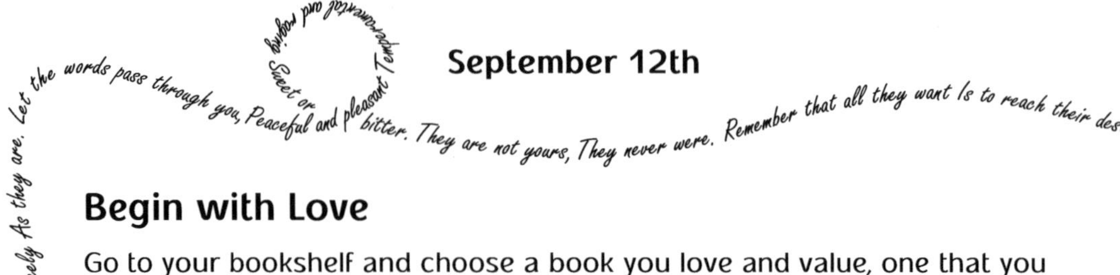
Let the words flow through you, Like the water flowing in the stream Place no dam over your words, Do not ask them to slow down, Do not hasten them forward Allow them to move freely As they are. Let the words pass through you, Peaceful and pleasant Temperamental and raging Sweet or bitter. They are not yours, They never were. Remember that all they want Is to reach their dest

## September 12th

# Begin with Love

Go to your bookshelf and choose a book you love and value, one that you are always happy to read again. Open it to the first page, and copy the opening sentence.

Now let this sentence lead you freely to write the next sentence and the next, until there is an entirely new text before you - a story, a poem or anything that begs to be written from your soul.

*With the sea. Do not over flow, Do not hang on words. Learn from the river: Its only designation is To carry water*

## Emotional Writing

Close your eyes and breathe deeply. Look inside; what emotion do you feel at this moment?

Let this feeling become present, and write it here. Describe it as it is, with no embellishment. Approach the writing process as an opportunity for its simplest expression.

As you know, a feeling is fleeting, not permanent. Allow it to express itself completely, leaving it behind through writing. Do not try to hold onto it. After you finish writing, close your eyes and check to see if a new feeling comes to you. If so, write this feeling as well.

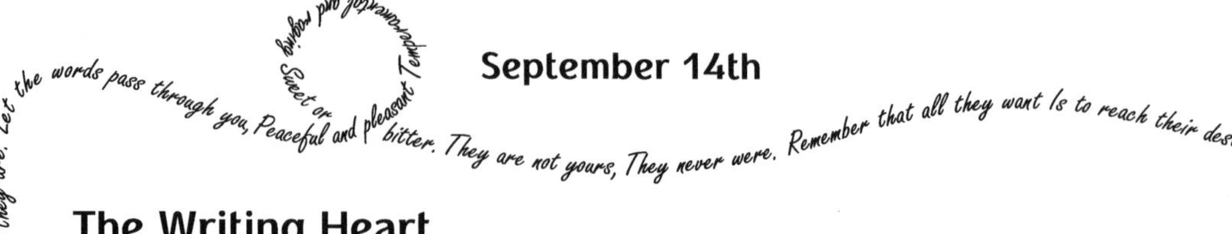
Let the words flow through you, Like the water flowing in the stream Place no dam over your words, Do not ask them to slow down, Do not hasten them forward Allow them to move freely As they are. Let the words pass through you, Peaceful and pleasant Temperamental and raging Sweet or bitter. They are not yours, They never were. Remember that all they want Is to reach their dest

**September 14th**

## The Writing Heart

Sit comfortably. Close your eyes. Take deep breaths and focus your attention on your heart. Listen to it. Listen to the words that are coming from your heart and allow yourself to write them down. Be the conduit that carries the wisdom of your heart to the paper. Do not attempt to control or navigate the words. Just listen and write your heart as it is. Let it write itself. What is it saying?

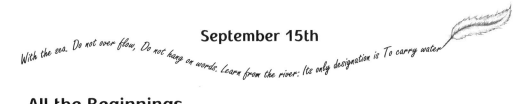

# September 15th

With the sea. Do not over flow, Do not hang on words. Learn from the river: Its only designation is To carry water

## All the Beginnings

If you were writing an imaginary book, how would it begin?

In this exercise, we will remain at the beginning. Write all sorts of possible beginnings for this imaginary book, without going forward. Write more and more beginnings for your book.

In order to do this, you can use an event from your past, or something that happened just this morning, a sentence you have heard randomly that continues to echo inside your head, or any other idea that comes to mind.

Don't spend too much time on one beginning. The more possibilities for beginnings you have, the better. Write all your beginnings.

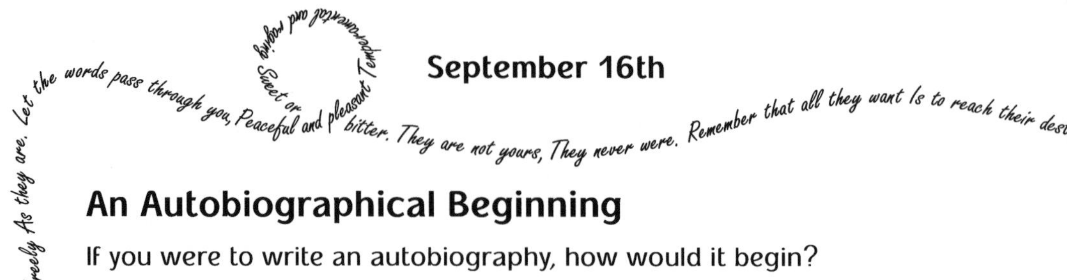
Let the words flow through you, Like the water flowing in the stream Place no dam over your words, Do not ask them to slow down, Do not hasten them forward Allow them to move freely As they are. Let the words pass through you, Peaceful and pleasant Temperamental and raging Sweet or bitter. They are not yours, They never were. Remember that all they want Is to reach their dest

## September 16th

# An Autobiographical Beginning

If you were to write an autobiography, how would it begin?

Write a beginning for the story of your life. You can start at any point in time, or any place, you choose – move, explore, and allow your beginning to develop. The most important thing is to begin.

## September 17th

*With the sea. Do not over flow, Do not hang on words. Learn from the river: Its only designation is To carry water*

# I Have to

Write a text that starts with the words **I have to...** Write everything that these words trigger, and do not stop writing, not even for one moment, until you fill the entire page. You can return to the words **I have to** any time you want or need to.

Uncover from within: what it is that you really "have to" do or be?

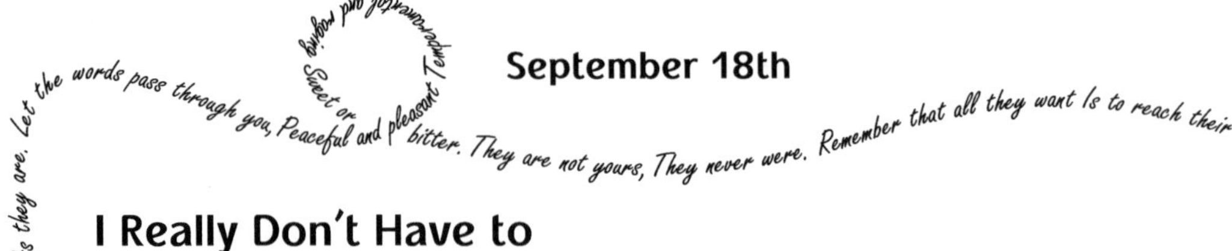
Let the words flow through you, Like the water flowing in the stream Place no dam over your words, Do not ask them to slow down, Do not hasten them forward Allow them to move freely As they are. Let the words pass through you, Peaceful and pleasant Temperamental and raging Sweet or bitter. They are not yours, They never were. Remember that all they want Is to reach their

**September 18th**

# I Really Don't Have to

Write a text that starts with the words **I really don't have to...**

Write everything that these words trigger, and do not stop writing, not even for one minute, until you fill the entire page. Go back to these words any time you need to, so you can discover what it is that you "really don't have to" do or be. This is an opportunity to abandon all the responsibilities you don't really need.

# September 19th

## Avoidance

Are you avoiding something in your life? Write the word **avoidance** and explore its presence, or lack of presence, in your life.

What is it you are avoiding? Perhaps there is more than one such thing? If so, write them all down, with no criticism or judgement. Do not avoid looking at them.

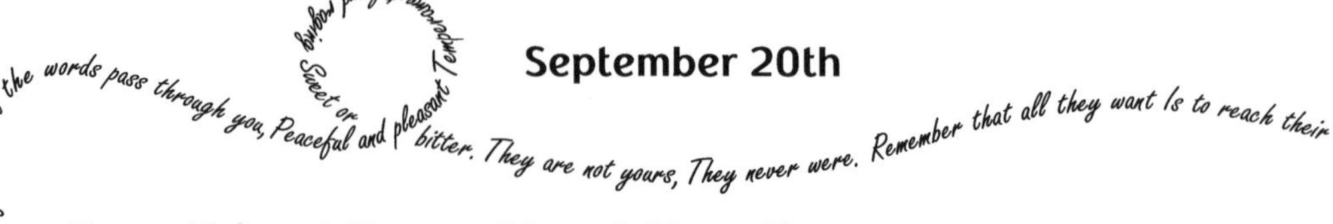
Let the words flow through you, Like the water flowing in the stream Place no dam over your words, Do not ask them to slow down, Do not hasten them forward Allow them to move freely As they are.
Let the words pass through you, Peaceful and pleasant Temperamental and raging Sweet or bitter. They are not yours, They never were. Remember that all they want Is to reach their

## September 20th

# Everything I Know About Myself

Write anything that you want to share about yourself, as if you are the only person you can speak about.

Begin with the words **Everything I know about myself...** Allow yourself to be exposed. Don't hold back.

# September 21st



## I am Ready

Today is the birthday of the musician, poet and author, **Leonard Cohen**, born in 1934.

In his last song Cohen wrote: "Hineni, Hineni, I'm ready, my Lord". "Hineni" in Hebrew means "I am".

Roll the word **ready** on your tongue, turn it over in your mind, and let it slide down your pen onto your journal. What does this word arouse in you? Do you feel ready? If so, what are you ready for in your life?

Here you may write to someone close to you, to God, or even to yourself. Start with the words **I am ready...** and write intuitively. Allow your writing to carry you to new realms, realms for which you did not realize you were ready.

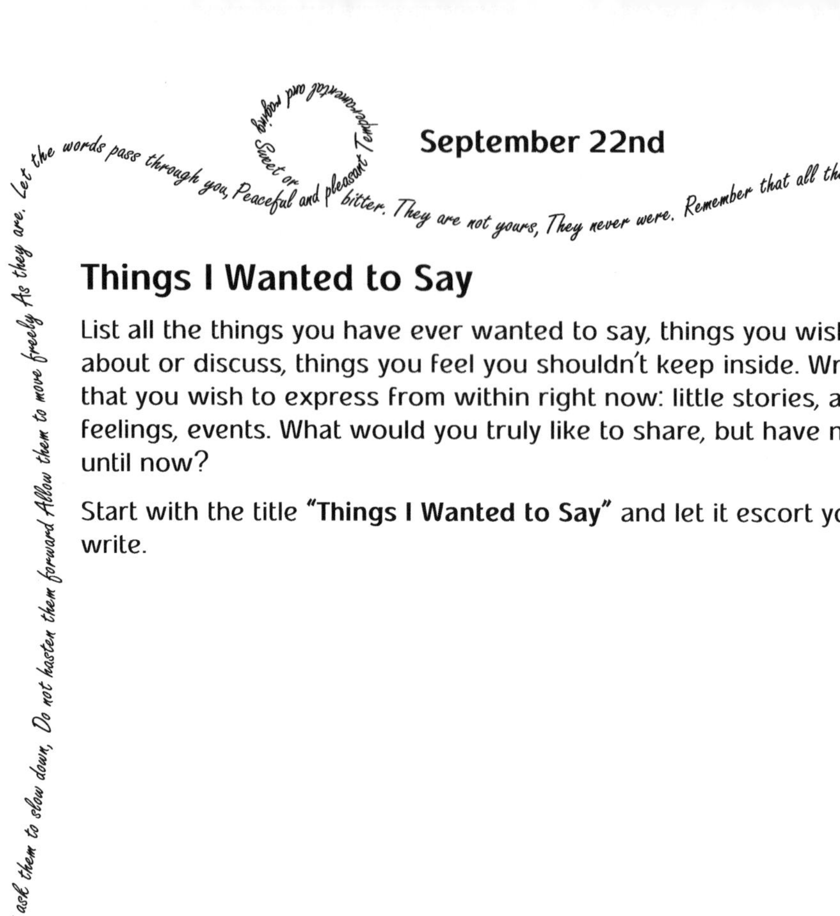

September 22nd

## Things I Wanted to Say

List all the things you have ever wanted to say, things you wish to write about or discuss, things you feel you shouldn't keep inside. Write all that you wish to express from within right now: little stories, anecdotes, feelings, events. What would you truly like to share, but have not dared to until now?

Start with the title **"Things I Wanted to Say"** and let it escort you as you write.

With the sea. Do not over flow, Do not hang on words. Learn from the river: Its only designation is To carry water

## I Wanted to Tell You

Many times, we do not say what is truly on our mind, whether these are words of anger and disappointment, or words of respect, appreciation and love. When these feelings arise, for whatever reason, we do not stop to express them.

Write to someone with whom you would be happy to share what is in your heart. This is the time to communicate what you have to say and unburden yourself. Is there someone you wish to tell just how much you love and appreciate them, but haven't until now? Dare to say it here.

Address this person, starting with the words **I wanted to tell you...**

"The truth will set you free." **John** 8:31-32

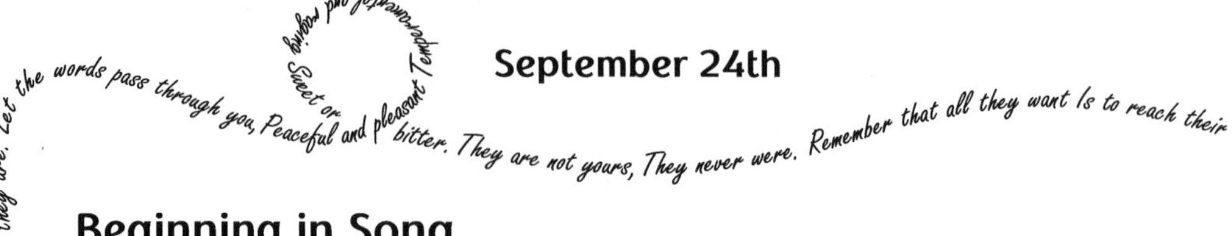
Let the words flow through you, Like the water flowing in the stream Place no dam over your words, Do not ask them to slow down, Do not hasten them forward Allow them to move freely As they are. Let the words pass through you, Peaceful and pleasant Temperamental and raging Sweet or bitter. They are not yours, They never were. Remember that all they want Is to reach their

**September 24th**

## Beginning in Song

Close your eyes, take several deep breaths and focus inward. Let a song play within you. The moment the song appears welcome it and hum it.

Now write the opening line of the song, and let it carry you to writing a new song. A song of your own.

## September 25th

With the sea. Do not over flow, Do not hang on words. Learn from the river: Its only designation is To carry water

## The Giving Tree

Today is the birthday of writer and illustrator **Shel Silverstein**, the author of *The Giving Tree*, born in 1930.

This exercise is inspired by his famous book on the power of giving.

Write a text that expresses the things that you naturally give to the world: describe your trunk, your leaves and your fruit. Describe the shade, the happiness and the tranquility. See yourself as the giving tree that shares everything it has with the world. How does that make you feel?

Begin with the words **I give to the world...**

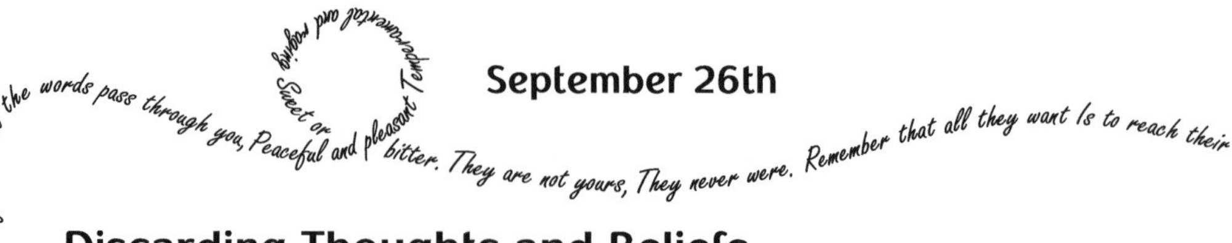
Let the words flow through you, Like the water flowing in the stream Place no dam over your words, Do not ask them to slow down, Do not hasten them forward Allow them to move freely As they are. Let the words pass through you, Peaceful and pleasant Temperamental and raging Sweet or bitter. They are not yours, They never were. Remember that all they want Is to reach their

### September 26th

## Discarding Thoughts and Beliefs

Write a list of beliefs, opinions and thoughts you hold on to whose time has come to discard. Fill the page with expressions that have become rooted deep inside of you over the years, for as far back as you can remember.

Love hurts. Life is only suffering. Perhaps you alone are enough to make your way in this life.

Consider what beliefs you hold that you can relinquish now.

When you finish writing, reread the sentences expressing your beliefs. Are you ready to reassess them, or even consider letting them go altogether?

Observe. Write. Let go.

## September 27th

# Forgiveness

"Sorry seems to be the hardest word," sings **Elton John** in one of his most beautiful songs.

Think about a person or a thing that deserves your forgiveness. Asking for forgiveness from yourself is very important too.

Start with the words **I forgive**, and continue writing the requests for forgiveness that arise from your soul.

Allow yourself to sincerely ask forgiveness. And give yourself permission to forgive.

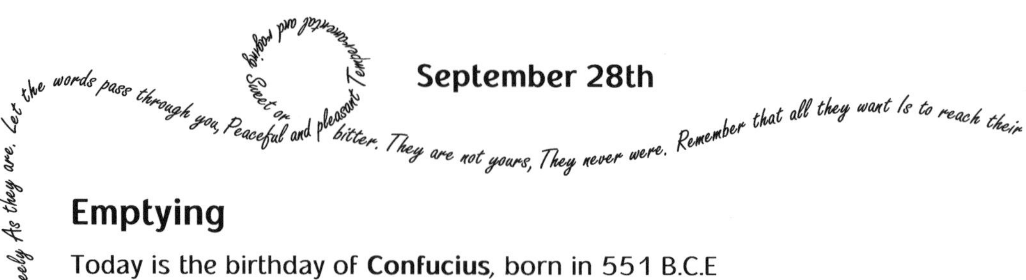
Let the words flow through you, Like the water flowing in the stream Place no dam over your words, Do not ask them to slow down, Do not hasten them forward Allow them to move freely As they are. Let the words pass through you, Peaceful and pleasant Temperamental and raging Sweet or bitter. They are not yours, They never were. Remember that all they want Is to reach their

## September 28th

# Emptying

Today is the birthday of **Confucius**, born in 551 B.C.E

"There is no one emptier than he who fills himself," taught Confucius, in praise of emptiness and simplicity. He believed the less we have, the fuller we are.

Autumn is an appropriate time for genuine emptying.

In the past year, you may have filled yourself and your surroundings with objects, thoughts, opinions and stories. Do you agree to empty yourself of them and clear space within yourself? Begin with the verb **"To empty"** (or any of its forms.) Write what you would be happy to empty, physically and mentally.

## September 29th

*With the sea. Do not over flow, Do not hang on words. Learn from the river: Its only designation is To carry water*

# Close One Door, Open Another

Today is the birthday of the author **Miguel de Cervantes**, the creator of *Don Quixote*, born in 1547.

"When one door shuts, another opens," wrote Cervantes. How do you experience this sentence in your own life?

Write about a door that closed for you, after which another immediately opened. What was behind the new door?

Write a text that expresses this process. Begin with **When I closed the door...**

If you are facing the closing of such a door at present, imagine what might open for you instead. Free your imagination and describe where the opening of a new door will lead you.

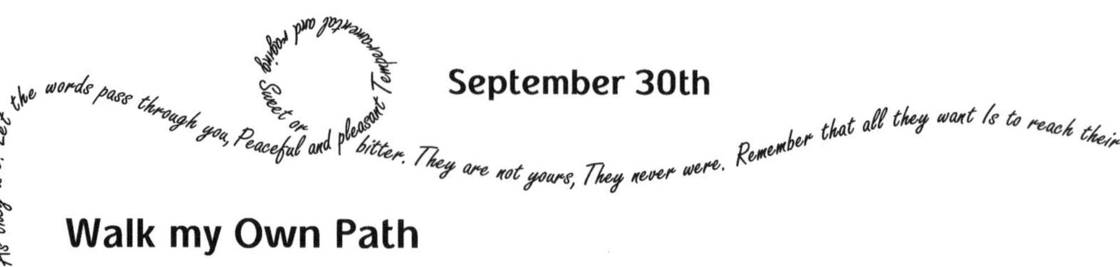
Let the words flow through you, Like the water flowing in the stream Place no dam over your words, Do not ask them to slow down, Do not hasten them forward Allow them to move freely As they are. Let the words pass through you, Peaceful and pleasant Temperamental and raging Sweet or bitter. They are not yours, They never were. Remember that all they want Is to reach their

## September 30th

# Walk my Own Path

Today is the birthday of philosopher and poet **Jalāl Ad-Dīn Rūmī**, born in 1207.

"When a man starts walking, the road appears before him," he wrote.

This exercise, inspired by Rūmī, encourages you to create your own path. Close your eyes. Imagine yourself walking on a road you have never walked before. Imagine where it is, what it is made of, its width, and the landscape surrounding it. It is a road that exists only within you, inside your soul, and it begins the minute you choose to step on it. All you need to do is give yourself permission to start walking, and it will reveal itself before you. Do you consent to walk your own path?

Describe your steps, the road signs, the views. Allow your pen to be your guide. You can use Rumi's sentence and start with the words **When I start to walk...**

With the sea. Do not over flow, Do not hang on words. Learn from the river: Its only designation is To carry water

"Come, come, whoever you are.
Wanderer, worshiper, lover of leaving. It doesn't matter.
Ours is not a caravan of despair.
Come, even if you have broken your vows a thousand times.
Come, yet again, come, come."

*Rumi and His Sufi Path of Love*. Edited by M Fatih Citlak and Huseyin Bingul, Tughra Books, 2007, p. 81

# October

## Writing to change

Let the words flow through you, Like the water flowing in the stream Place no dam over your words, Do not ask them to slow down, Do not hasten them forward Allow them to move freely As they are. Let the words pass through you, Peaceful and pleasant Temperamental and raging Sweet or bitter. They are not yours, They never were. Remember that all they want Is to reach their

# October 1st

## Seeds of Change

**Writing creates change**. This refrain has escorted me for years on end. Change is the nature of life itself, because life is always in motion. The power of writing to create change excites me again and again, every time.

In this exercise, give yourself permission to sow seeds of change. Write a list of all the changes you would be happy to bring into your life now, in every aspect: the physical, emotional, mental and spiritual.

Write changes that will encourage you and make you happy, changes that will bring you closer to yourself and the values you believe in. Don't think of what is possible or relevant; don't fear that you might have to commit to those changes. Just let yourself write everything you would like to change in your life.

"Nothing is permanent, except change." **Heraclitus**

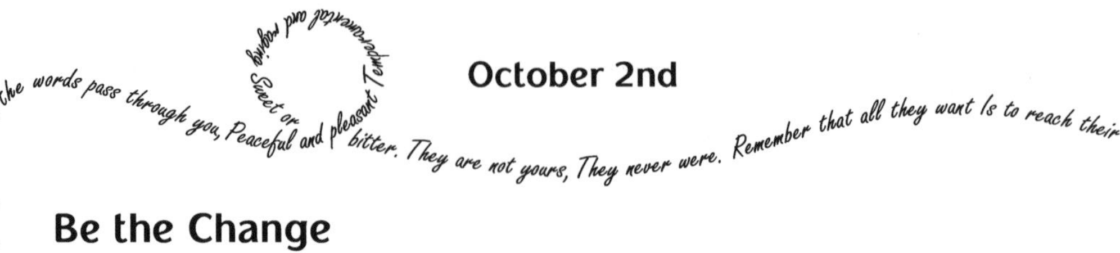
Let the words flow through you, Like the water flowing in the stream Place no dam over your words, Do not ask them to slow down, Do not hasten them forward Allow them to move freely As they are. Let the words pass through you, Peaceful and pleasant Temperamental and raging Sweet or bitter. They are not yours, They never were. Remember that all they want Is to reach their

**October 2nd**

## Be the Change

This is the birthday of **Mahatma Gandhi**, born in 1869.

"If we could change ourselves, the tendencies in the world would also change," he wrote.* "As a man changes his own nature, so does the attitude of the world change towards him... We need not wait to see what others do."

In this exercise, inspired by Gandhi, consider: what does it mean to "change your own nature"? Write how **you** can be the change you wish to create. What must you be or express, in order to bring change to the world?

* *Collected Works of Mahatma Gandhi*. Publications Division, Ministry of Information and Broadcasting, Government Of India, 1958; 1994, Vol. 13. p.241

# October 3rd

## One Small Change

Select one "seed", a value that you wish to sow and nurture this year, a small change you wish to create.

What do you wish to sow in the soil of your heart, and let grow in your life? Perhaps happiness, courage, or truthfulness? Or maybe it's hope, faith, creativity? What about freedom, or peace?

Focus on just one thing. Develop this seed, elaborate on your desire for it to come into your life, describe the sensations it generates inside you when you imagine it becoming a tangible fruit.

Write about the process of sowing the seed, and when you are done, write a poem about that sowing, a poem that is a heartfelt prayer describing the process. Start with the words **I am sowing...**

To accompany your writing, you can sow a seed in the garden or a pot, to symbolize your process.

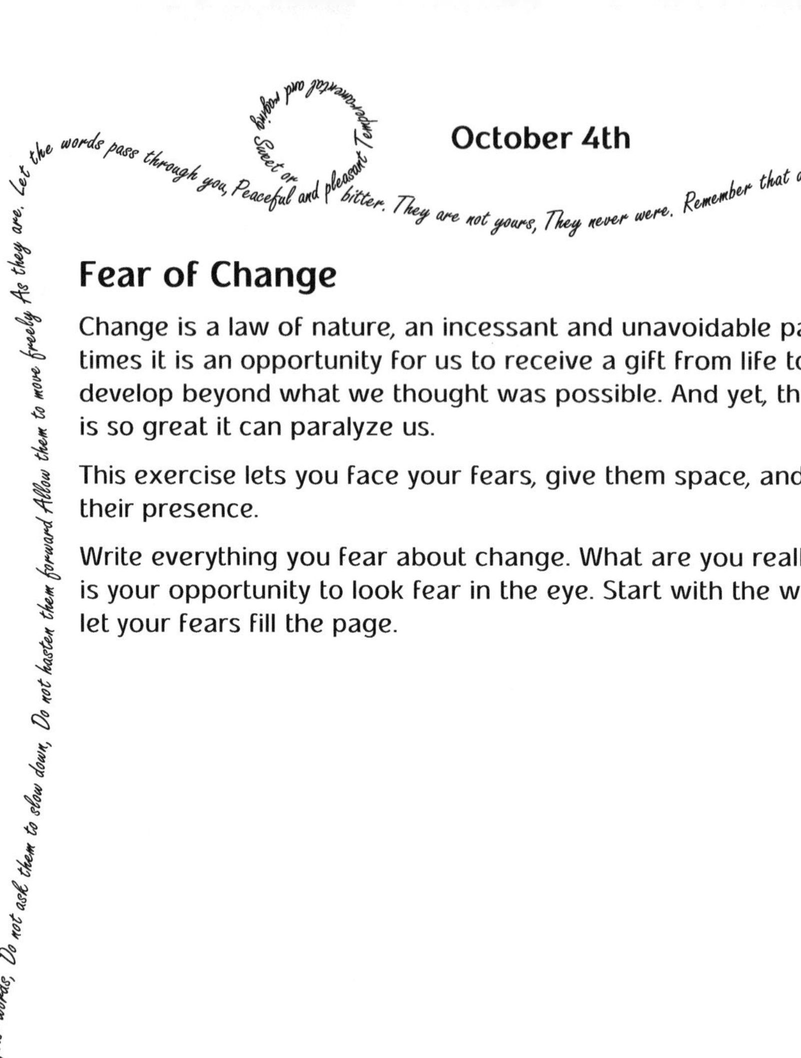
Let the words flow through you, Like the water flowing in the stream Place no dam over your words, Do not ask them to slow down, Do not hasten them forward Allow them to move freely As they are. Let the words pass through you, Peaceful and pleasant Temperamental and raging Sweet or bitter. They are not yours, They never were. Remember that all they want Is to reach their

## October 4th

# Fear of Change

Change is a law of nature, an incessant and unavoidable part of life. Many times it is an opportunity for us to receive a gift from life to grow and develop beyond what we thought was possible. And yet, the fear of change is so great it can paralyze us.

This exercise lets you face your fears, give them space, and acknowledge their presence.

Write everything you fear about change. What are you really afraid of? This is your opportunity to look fear in the eye. Start with the words **I fear...** and let your fears fill the page.

*With the sea. Do not over flow, Do not hang on words. Learn from the river: Its only designation is To carry water*

## A Letter to Fear

Fear is an inseparable part of life's journey, but we can't allow it to be our guide.

Write a letter to your greatest fear. When fear exists, it is present in your life. You can ignore it, but chances are that it will not disappear by itself. Now you have a chance to establish an honest relationship with fear, and to clarify things about your life in its presence (or perhaps its life in your presence?)

Write it a letter that starts with the words **Dear Fear...**

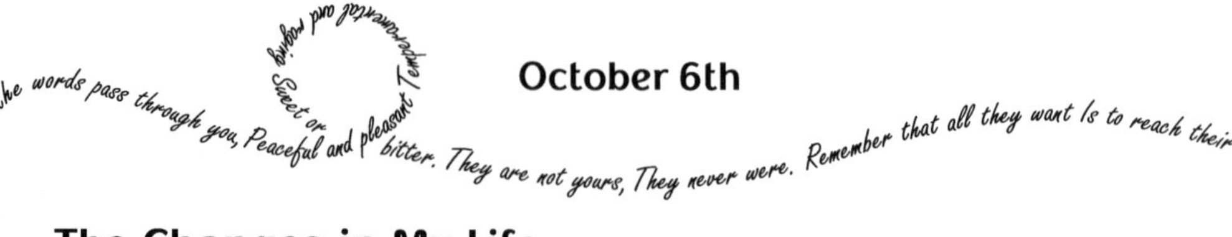
Let the words flow through you, Like the water flowing in the stream Place no dam over your words, Do not ask them to slow down, Do not hasten them forward Allow them to move freely As they are. Let the words pass through you, Peaceful and pleasant Temperamental and raging Sweet or bitter. They are not yours, They never were. Remember that all they want Is to reach their

## October 6th

# The Changes in My Life

Write about the changes you have created in your life that you are proud of. Describe every change you dared to make, every breakthrough, and every path you successfully paved, despite the difficulty, the fear, or the uncertainty. Don't leave anything out.

At the end of the exercise, look at the list in front of you, and write what qualities and values were required to make these changes. These qualities are yours, and they will help you create every new change you hope to have in your life.

## October 7th

*With the sea. Do not over flow, Do not hang on words. Learn from the river: Its only designation is To carry water*

# I Would Never Dare

What are the changes you would never dare make in your life? Write them down, and as you write, allow them to flow freely from within. Describe all the things you would never dare to create, say, do, wear, and anything else you can think of.

Start with the words **I would never dare...** and fill the page.

Afterwards, return to your list, and at the end of each category, write **Is this the truth?** and answer the question.

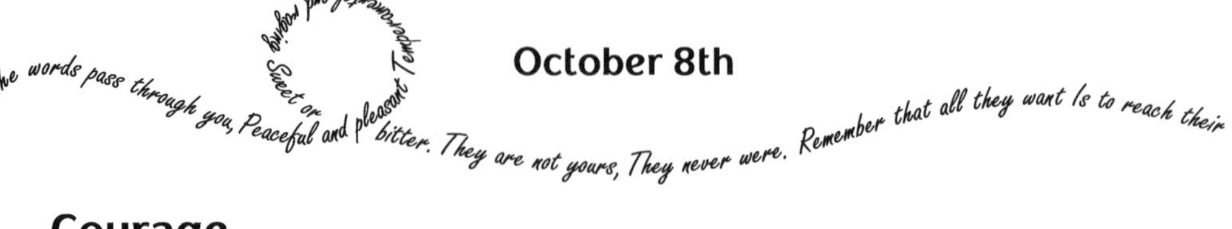
Let the words flow through you, Like the water flowing in the stream Place no dam over your words, Do not ask them to slow down, Do not hasten them forward Allow them to move freely As they are. Let the words pass through you, Peaceful and pleasant Temperamental and raging Sweet or bitter. They are not yours, They never were. Remember that all they want Is to reach their

## October 8th

# Courage

Courage means overcoming fear, rather than ignoring it.

Think of something that frightened you very much and you courageously overcame it. Well done!

Now describe what it was. Speak about the fear, about the moment of overcoming it, and the feelings that followed. Try to engrave that sensation in your body, so it will again give you the courage to choose the right course of action, to choose change, to choose you. Elaborate on the details of your courage as you write about it.

## October 9th

# Non-dominant Hand Writing

This exercise is inspired by a technique that was invented by **Lucia Capacchione***. The non-dominant hand writing technique is a chance to practice how not to respond automatically to our world. On a deeper level, this is an opportunity to make room inside us for a different part of ourselves, to express our weaker or weakened sides, those we give less space to in our daily lives. Make room for these elements here and now. Write a whole page with your non-dominant hand.

Start with the words **The things that I want...** and write everything that comes to mind.

**Recovery of Your Inner Child*, Touchstone, 1991.

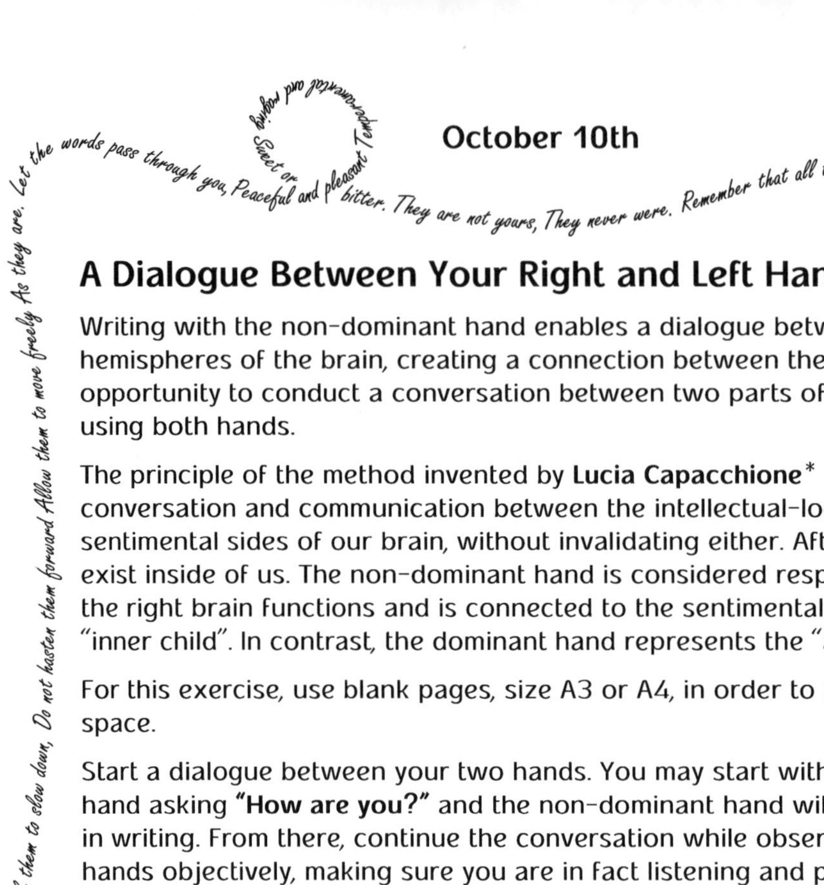
Let the words flow through you, Like the water flowing in the stream Place no dam over your words, Do not ask them to slow down, Do not hasten them forward Allow them to move freely As they are. Let the words pass through you, Peaceful and pleasant Temperamental and raging Sweet or bitter. They are not yours, They never were. Remember that all they want Is to reach their

**October 10th**

## A Dialogue Between Your Right and Left Hands

Writing with the non-dominant hand enables a dialogue between the two hemispheres of the brain, creating a connection between them. It is an opportunity to conduct a conversation between two parts of ourselves, using both hands.

The principle of the method invented by **Lucia Capacchione*** enables conversation and communication between the intellectual-logical and the sentimental sides of our brain, without invalidating either. After all, both exist inside of us. The non-dominant hand is considered responsible for the right brain functions and is connected to the sentimental body, the "inner child". In contrast, the dominant hand represents the "adult".

For this exercise, use blank pages, size A3 or A4, in order to allow for more space.

Start a dialogue between your two hands. You may start with the dominant hand asking **"How are you?"** and the non-dominant hand will respond in writing. From there, continue the conversation while observing your hands objectively, making sure you are in fact listening and providing full expression to each hand and each part inside of you.

At the end of the conversation, with your dominant hand, write the essence of the experience here.

* *Recovery of Your Inner Child*, Touchstone, 1991.

## October 11th

# Reading is an Open Door to a Magical World

This is the birthday of French author **François Mauriac,** born in 1885.

"Reading is an open door to a magical world," he wrote. "If you would tell me the heart of a man, tell me not what he reads, but what he rereads."

This exercise is inspired by Mauriac. Is reading a door for you as well? What would you choose to reread?

Write about one door that has opened up before you, thanks to reading a book or a story that was significant for you.

Let the words flow through you, Like the water flowing in the stream Place no dam over your words, Do not ask them to slow down, Do not hasten them forward Allow them to move freely As they are.

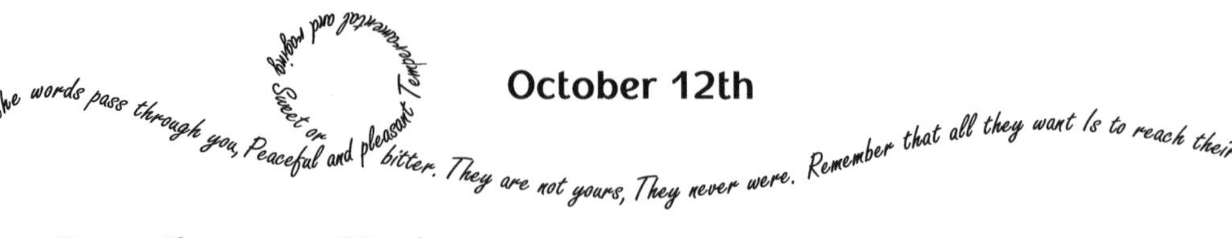
Let the words pass through you, Peaceful and pleasant Temperamental and raging Sweet or bitter. They are not yours, They never were. Remember that all they want Is to reach their

October 12th

## Parading my Choices

We make countless choices at any given moment in our lives. Most are small and mundane, while others are significant and crucial. Do you feel that you actually choose in each and every moment?

Write the parade of choices in your life, significant moments of choices you have made and you still make, despite difficulties and fears that stand in your way. Write about what you chose in the past, and what you continue to choose every morning. This is an opportunity to observe your choices and your priorities in life.

Start with the words **I choose...**

## October 13th

*With the sea. Do not over flow, Do not hang on words. Learn from the river: Its only designation is To carry water*

# Writing Against the Tide

Many times in life we "go with the flow," giving in to circumstances, patterns and habits. "That's the way it goes," we tell ourselves, although that is not necessarily so. Therefore, from time to time, we should stop moving in the flow of life and observe it from the sidelines. That way we can assess if we are going in the right - the best - direction for us. Perhaps strong currents are carrying us away without control?

This exercise invites you to correspond with the expression "swimming against the tide." Write where in your life you were required to "go with the flow", or where you would have wanted to make an effort and swim against the current. Don't hesitate! Write against the tide. Now.

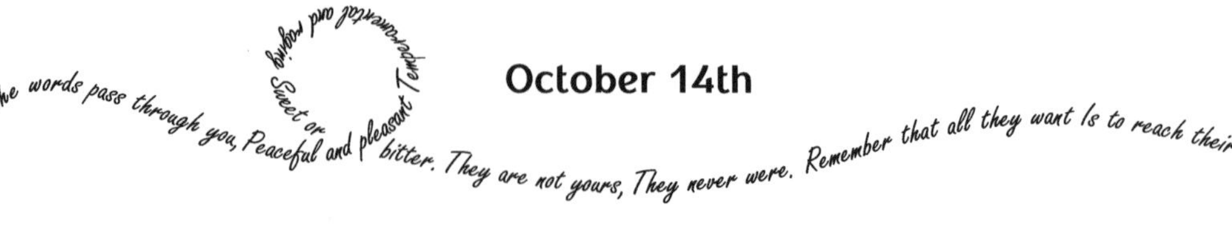
Let the words pass through you, Peaceful and pleasant Temperamental and raging Sweet or bitter. They are not yours, They never were. Remember that all they want Is to reach their
Let the words flow through you, Like the water flowing in the stream Place no dam over your words, Do not ask them to slow down, Do not hasten them forward Allow them to move freely As they are.

October 14th

## A Laboratory of Changes

Think about the next 24 hours in your life as an opportunity to practice "change" on all levels. Allow yourself to go to sleep or wake up at a different time than you usually do, choose to take a different route than the one you normally take, sit somewhere different, speak to or meet new people, tell someone something you have never dared to say, eat food you have never tried before, and so on - whatever or whenever change can be introduced in your routine.

Create an imaginary day just like that one, a laboratory of changes so to speak. Write all the changes you expect to experience that day. Describe it from beginning to end, and relate through your writing to whatever feelings come up as you imagine the day.

*With the sea. Do not over flow, Do not hang on words. Learn from the river: Its only designation is To carry water*

## Physical Changes

Write a list of all the physical changes you would be happy to see in your body, your home and your environment.

The purpose here is to focus on visible changes - a haircut, a new couch, a new color. Allow yourself to go wild! **It's only a list**.

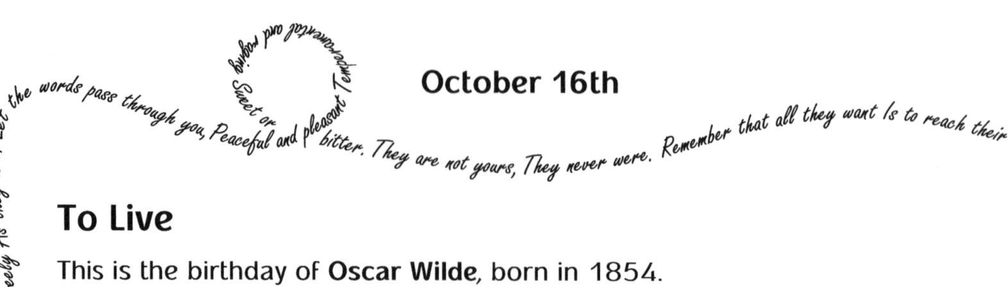
Let the words flow through you, Like the water flowing in the stream Place no dam over your words, Do not ask them to slow down, Do not hasten them forward Allow them to move freely As they are. Let the words pass through you, Peaceful and pleasant Temperamental and raging Sweet or bitter. They are not yours, They never were. Remember that all they want Is to reach their



## To Live

This is the birthday of **Oscar Wilde**, born in 1854.

"To live is the rarest thing in the world. Most people exist, that is all," he wrote.

This is an exercise inspired by Wilde: write life as a rare work of art. Do you live your life as an artist? Do you create your days as you wish to live them?

Write what it means for you to live your life at the best, most ideal level.

Start with the words **To live is...**

*With the sea. Do not over flow, Do not hang on words. Learn from the river: Its only designation is To carry water*

## Oops! Did I Make a Mistake?

Our life is fraught with mistakes, but actually there is no such thing as a "mistake" if we have learned and grown because of it. Nevertheless, we often walk around feeling we've made a "mistake" or "missed out", or we think "what a shame".

Write a list of all the mistakes you have made in your life. Do not hold back. Allow yourself to admit that something you said or did was a mistake.

Then choose the worst mistake from your list, and as you write, explore what you learned from it, what changed within you because of it, and what person you have become as a result.

If you fail to find something good in it, use your imagination. Create something good that might have come from your worst mistake.

Let the words flow through you, Like the water flowing in the stream Place no dam over your words, Do not ask them to slow down, Do not hasten them forward Allow them to move freely As they are. Let the

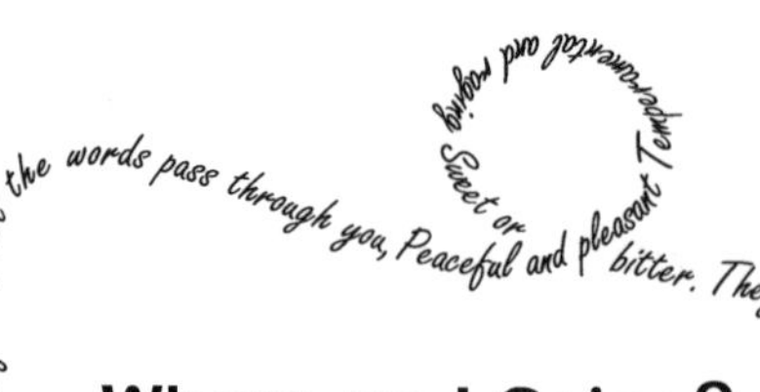
words pass through you, Peaceful and pleasant Temperamental and raging Sweet or

bitter. They are not yours, They never were. Remember that all they want Is to reach their

## October 18th

# Where am I Going?

Close your eyes for a few moments, breathe deeply, and become one with your inner self. When you are quiet and calm, ask yourself the following questions: Where am I going? What is my direction? What road am I paving for myself?

Do not attempt to find answers. Hold on to the questions and allow the answers to appear on their own. Do not keep any answer in particular. When an answer appears, return to the question - perhaps a new answer will surface.

When you feel ready, write a text that describes where you are going. Start with the words **I am going...** Let the answers surprise you.

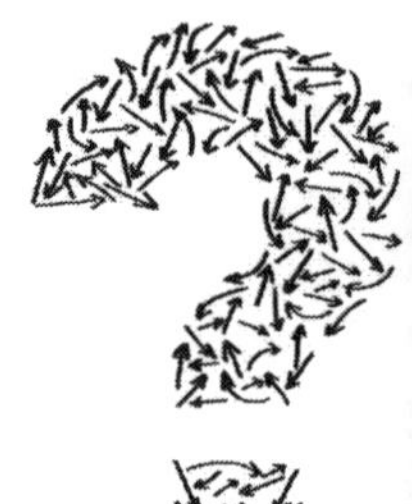

## October 19th

# Writing my Childhood

This is the birthday of author and poet **Nurit Zarchi**, born in 1941.

“When I write, I think about my childhood,” Zarchi once said. “Everything happens during childhood. This is where all the keys lie. The question is, what form do we give our childhood?”

What childhood did you experience? Would you be able to write about your childhood differently than you usually do, and give it new shape? Perhaps you could rewrite it as a tale of triumph and courage?

Today you have a chance to do that. Briefly write about your childhood, and create a meaningful story that fills one page.

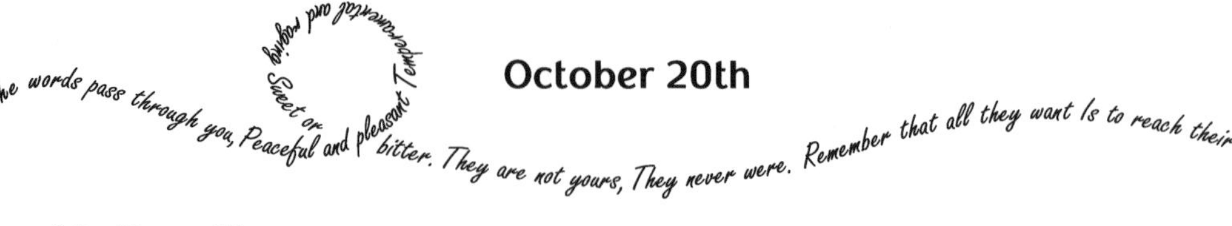
Let the words pass through you, Peaceful and pleasant Temperamental and raging Sweet or bitter. They are not yours, They never were. Remember that all they want Is to reach their

Let the words flow through you, Like the water flowing in the stream Place no dam over your words, Do not ask them to slow down, Do not hasten them forward Allow them to move freely As they are. Let the

## Mother Tongue

Today is the birthday of poet **Agi Mishol**, born in 1946.

This exercise is inspired by her poem "Mother Tongue". In it she recounts the story of her birth to her biological mother and how poetry became her new mother.

We have all come into this world through our biological mothers, yet as years go by, we may find mothering in different places, in art and in people. What new "mother tongue" have you discovered over the course of your life? What has become your mother – a place that supports you, a place that has become home for you?

"Later you shrivelled into a thumb
that became an eraser
atop a pencil
that I sucked on until I turned it
around and began to write
poetry
that returned to me
as mother."

"Mother Tongue." *Less Like A Dove*, Translated by Joana Chen, Shearsman Books, 2016.

# October 21st

## Saying No

What do you say **no** to in your life?

Write a list of all the things you say "no" to in your life today. Don't hold back. Allow yourself to widen and deepen that list in every aspect of your life. Dare to say **no**.

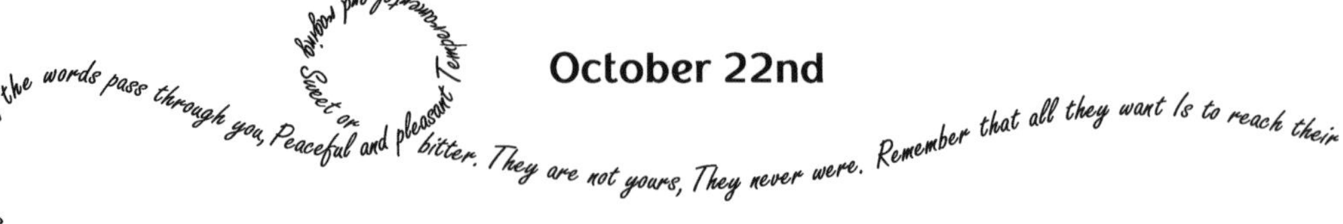
Let the words flow through you, Like the water flowing in the stream Place no dam over your words, Do not ask them to slow down, Do not hasten them forward Allow them to move freely As they are. Let the words pass through you, Peaceful and pleasant Temperamental and raging Sweet or bitter. They are not yours, They never were. Remember that all they want Is to reach their

## October 22nd

# Saying Yes

What do you say **yes** to in your life?

Write all the things that you want and are happy to say a big "yes" to in your life. Start with the words **I say yes...** Open yourself up to as many new possibilities as you can imagine and shout from your soul: **Yes, yes, yes**!

With the sea. Do not over flow, Do not hang on words. Learn from the river: Its only designation is To carry water

## Writing Change

Think of a challenging event you went through recently, something you experienced that evoked discomfort, difficulty, frustration or pain. Close your eyes and remember as many details of the incident you can.

Now rewrite the event, and modify it however you like; you have no obligation to write what actually happened. Create **any change** you want. Imagine you are an author with the freedom to write anything that comes to mind.

You may start your writing with a quote from what actually happened, and continue from there with complete fiction. Again, don't hold yourself back. Write anything you desire!

When you are done, write one line about how you feel now. **What has changed in you?**

"You cannot step into the same river twice." **Heraclitus**

## October 24th

# The First Time

Write about your first times. Describe in writing everything you did for the first time: something you created, a mountain you climbed, a place you reached. Remember the first time you bungee jumped, kissed, loved, gave birth, wrote, fell. Start with the words **The first time...** and let the feelings that the first time evokes fill you as you write.

*Let the words flow through you, Like the water flowing in the stream Place no dam over your words, Do not ask them to slow down, Do not hasten them forward Allow them to move freely As they are. Let the words pass through you, Peaceful and pleasant Temperamental and raging Sweet or bitter. They are not yours, They never were. Remember that all they want Is to reach their*

## October 25th



# Permission

Turn the word **permission** over in your mind, and let it roll down your pen onto the page. What does this word evoke in you? Do you feel that you have permission? What do you have permission for?

Start with the words **I have permission** ... and write freely. Let the writing take you to new realms where there are no restrictions or limits. Everything is permitted here.

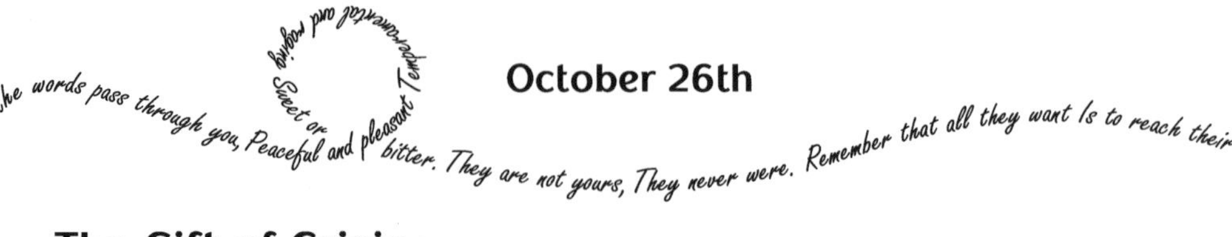
Let the words flow through you, Like the water flowing in the stream Place no dam over your words, Do not ask them to slow down, Do not hasten them forward Allow them to move freely As they are. Let the words pass through you, Peaceful and pleasant Temperamental and raging Sweet or bitter. They are not yours, They never were. Remember that all they want Is to reach their

**October 26th**

## The Gift of Crisis

Think about one of the crises you have experienced in your life, or a painful, difficult period from the past. Describe the crisis in one or two sentences, and then list all the gifts you received from it, despite the hardship and suffering you experienced. What did you learn? What opportunities did the crisis make possible? Perhaps you discovered inner strength? Met new people? Make a list and visualize how you can regard that crisis as beneficial, a period of growth.

If you can view all the crises in your life this way, you may find you have a reservoir of gifts that you received from those moments. All those gifts and qualities have formed the person you are today.

# October 27th

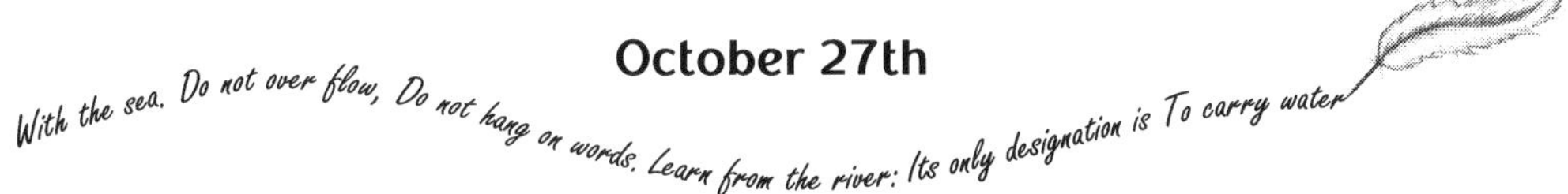
With the sea. Do not over flow, Do not hang on words. Learn from the river: Its only designation is To carry water

## Dying is an Art

This is the birthday of poet and author **Sylvia Plath**, born in 1932.

"Dying is an art, like everything else," she wrote in her poem "Lady Lazarus".

This exercise is inspired by Plath. Go outdoors and sit down with your journal in a beautiful spot. Look around you at the trees, the stones, the flowers, the animals. Try to identify everything that holds death and everything that holds life. Start documenting. Nature contains all things. Discover the nature arrayed in front of you, in its cyclicity of life and death.

**Write the art of death. Write the art of life.**

"Rage, rage against the dying of the light."
**Dylan Thomas**, author and poet, born this day in 1914.

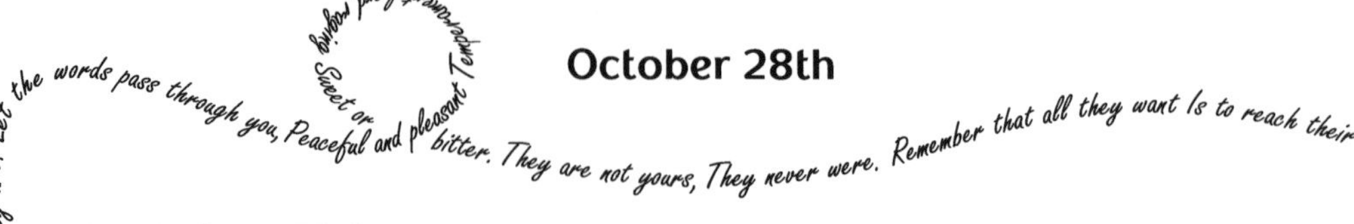
Let the words flow through you, Like the water flowing in the stream Place no dam over your words, Do not ask them to slow down, Do not hasten them forward Allow them to move freely As they are. Let the words pass through you, Peaceful and pleasant Temperamental and raging Sweet or bitter. They are not yours, They never were. Remember that all they want Is to reach their

## October 28th

# Just One Thing

What is the one thing you do that, if you were to stop doing it, your quality of life would improve significantly? Write about that thing and its presence in your life right now.

Dare to meet it head-on.

With the sea. Do not over flow, Do not hang on words. Learn from the river: Its only designation is To carry water

## The Text I Would Never Write

Write the text you would never write. You wouldn't dare to write. It can be the most banal, distorted, fragmented, tasteless, cloying of texts. It can be furious, sharp, aggressive, sexual - anything you choose.

Take this opportunity to write in a way you are not used to writing, to experience something unfamiliar.

# October 30th

## All You Need Is...

Do you usually share your needs with others, telling them what you really need? What do you need right now in your life? Physically, emotionally, mentally, spiritually?

Give yourself permission to write about all these needs and acknowledge them, without censuring yourself. Fill the page with all the things you need. Start with the words **I need...**

Now read your list and write what you do to satisfy your needs.

"The moment of change is the only poem." **Adrienne Rich**
"Images for Godard", *The Will to Change*, W. W. Norton & Company, 1971.

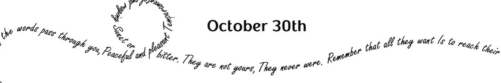

## The Gate to Heaven

This is the birthday of poet **John Keats**, born in 1795.

This exercise is inspired by his poem "Endymion", in which he confesses that for his love he is willing to let go of creation and glory, even his life, because to him, love is the gate to heaven.

What is the gate to heaven for you? Is there something in your life that you would let go of everything for? Maybe even die for? Would you be willing to do anything for that value or person?

"He who has a why to live for can bear almost any how." **Friedrich Nietzsche**

# November

## Writing to Reflect

Let the words flow through you, Like the water flowing in the stream Place no dam over your words, Do not ask them to slow down, Do not hasten them forward Allow them to move freely As they are. Let the words pass through you, Peaceful and pleasant Tempermental and raging Sweet or bitter. They are not yours, They never were. Remember that all they want Is to reach their

## November 1st

*With the sea. Do not over flow, Do not hang on words. Learn from the river: Its only designation is To carry water*

# I Know

Write a text that starts with the words **I know...**

What do you really know, deep inside? Remind yourself through writing. This exercise is about agreeing to meet intimate, simple, deep knowledge. Recognize and own your wisdom and your knowledge.

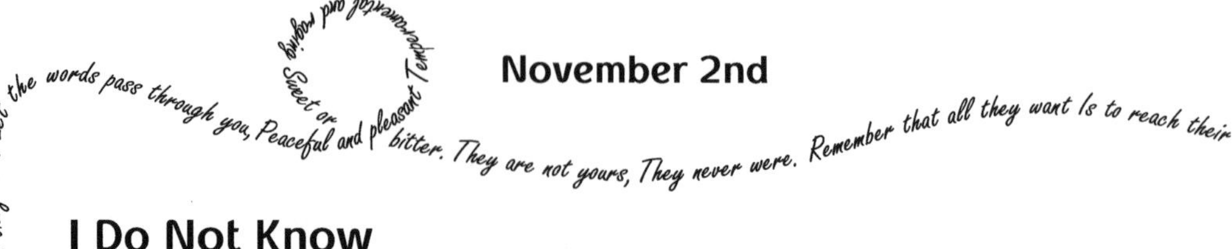
Let the words flow through you, Like the water flowing in the stream Place no dam over your words, Do not ask them to slow down, Do not hasten them forward Allow them to move freely As they are. Let the words pass through you, Peaceful and pleasant Temperamental and raging Sweet or bitter. They are not yours, They never were. Remember that all they want Is to reach their

**November 2nd**

# I Do Not Know

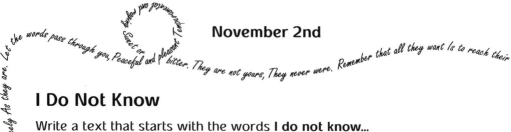

Write a text that starts with the words **I do not know...**

What don't you know? What do you actually allow yourself not to know? This exercise is about emptying out the knowledge of everything that you think you know. Recognize and own your lack of knowledge.

# November 3rd

*With the sea. Do not over flow, Do not hang on words. Learn from the river: Its only designation is To carry water*

## What is Happiness?

Happiness is something half the world dreams about and the other half pursues. It is a slippery notion that certainly deserves our reflection and exploration.

What is happiness to you? When do you experience happiness? Is it about moments or is it an ongoing sensation? What brings happiness into your life? Write everything you know about happiness in general and your happiness in particular.

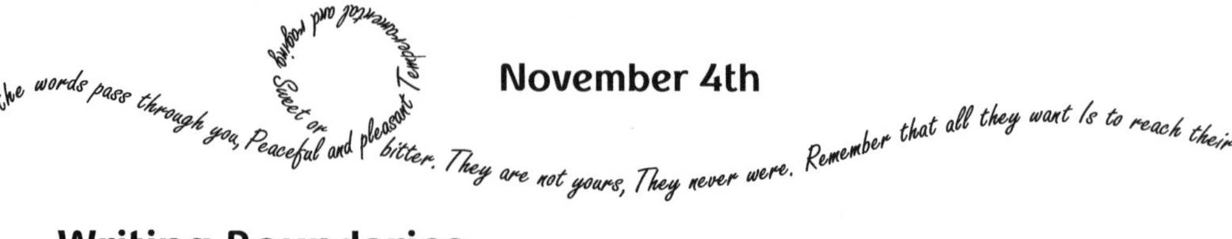
Let the words flow through you, Like the water flowing in the stream Place no dam over your words, Do not ask them to slow down, Do not hasten them forward Allow them to move freely As they are. Let the words pass through you, Peaceful and pleasant Temperamental and raging Sweet or bitter. They are not yours, They never were. Remember that all they want Is to reach their

## November 4th

# Writing Boundaries

What are boundaries for you? When do you break through boundaries? When do you feel that your boundaries are being crossed? What feelings arise when your boundaries are broken or blurred?

Write about your boundaries to get to know them a little better and strengthen them for yourself.

Where do you set clear boundaries, and where do you ignore or blur them?

*With the sea. Do not over flow, Do not hang on words. Learn from the river: Its only designation is To carry water*

## Writing Your Reflection

Look in the mirror. Look closely into your eyes for a few moments. Now write about the reflection in front of you. Who is the person looking at you from the mirror? Describe everything that is visible, and then write about what is beyond the visible. Meet yourself.

Start with the words **When I look in the mirror...**

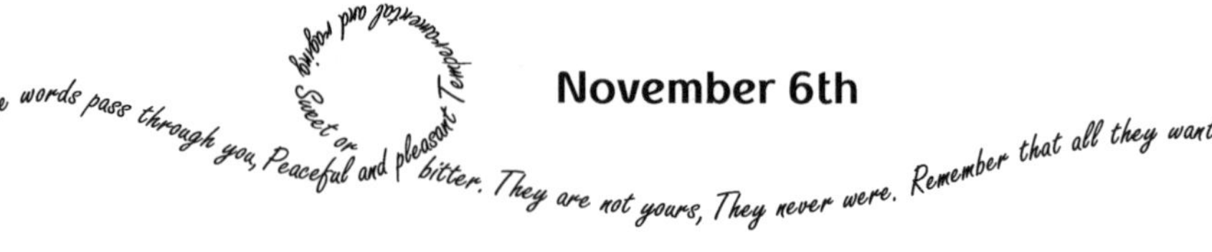
Let the words flow through you, Like the water flowing in the stream Place no dam over your words, Do not ask them to slow down, Do not hasten them forward Allow them to move freely As they are. Let the words pass through you, Peaceful and pleasant Temperamental and raging Sweet or bitter. They are not yours, They never were. Remember that all they want Is to reach their

**November 6th**

## An Island of Silence

Write about your silence. The silence inside you. What are the words emanating from the silence?

Perhaps you are restless at this moment and in fact are not used to being in silence.

This is an opportunity for you to connect to a moment of silence in your life, even if it is only an imagined moment. Remember such a moment and write about it. Find yourself an island of silence inside the words, even if those words are turbulent. Allow silence to speak to you through writing.

## Being Human

This is the birthday of French author **Albert Camus**, born in 1913.

"There always comes a time when one must choose between contemplation and action," he wrote in "The Myth of Sisyphus". This is how Camus defined being "human".

This exercise is inspired by Camus. What does being human mean to you? When do you really feel human? How do you behave that makes you a human being? Write a text that starts with the words **Being human...**

Let the words flow through you, Like the water flowing in the stream Place no dam over your words, Do not ask them to slow down, Do not hasten them forward Allow them to move freely As they are.

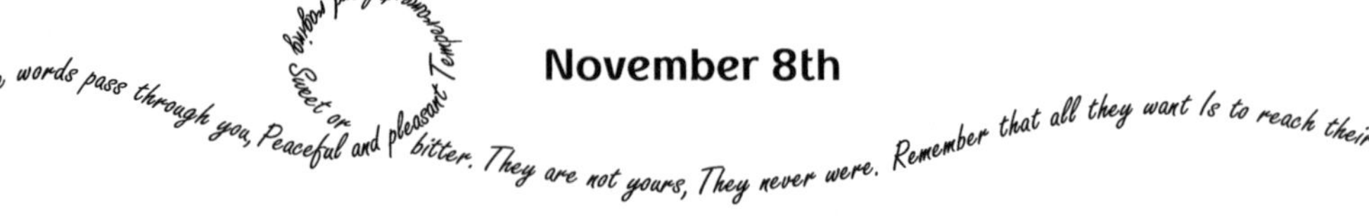
Let the words pass through you, Peaceful and pleasant Temperamental and raging Sweet or bitter. They are not yours, They never were. Remember that all they want Is to reach their

## November 8th

# A Message to the World

If you could write a message to the world right now that is only one page long, a message that would reach every human being on the face of the earth, what would you write?

# November 9th

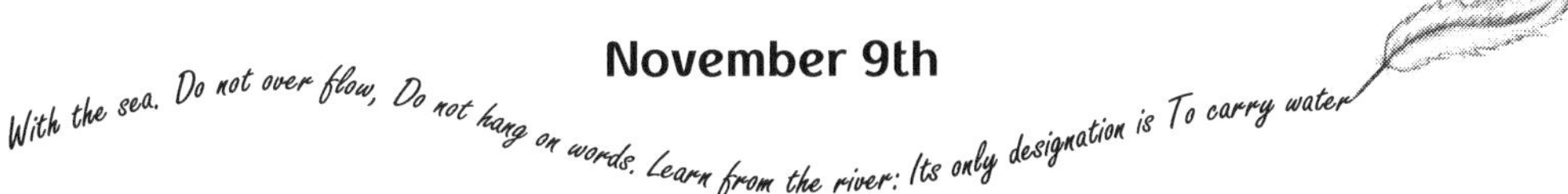
With the sea. Do not over flow, Do not hang on words. Learn from the river: Its only designation is To carry water

## Dear Therapist

This is the birthday of American poet **Anne Sexton**, born in 1928.

In her poem "Said the Poet to the Analyst", Sexton explains to her therapist how she wants him to treat her: "My business is words. ... / Your business is watching my words."

This exercise is inspired by Sexton's poem. Write a letter or a poem to your therapist. What would you like to ask /say to/ explain or clarify for them? If you do not have a therapist, write the letter to someone you love and value, but wish understood you better.

"Things are more chaotic, and if I can write a poem, I come into order again, and the world is again a little more sensible, and real."

*Anne Sexton: Telling the Tale*, edited by Steven E. Colburn, University of Michigan Press, 1988.

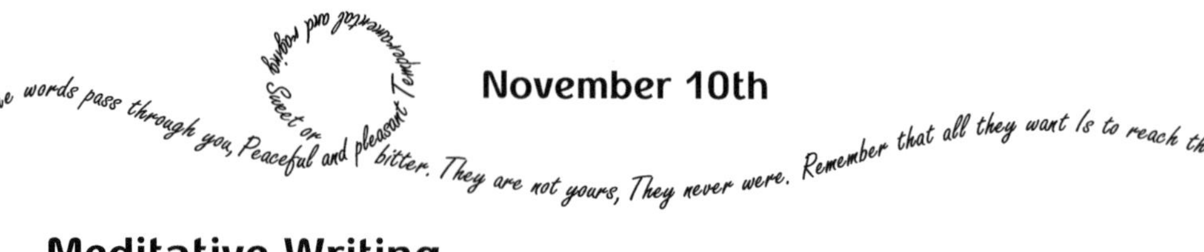
Let the words flow through you, Like the water flowing in the stream Place no dam over your words, Do not ask them to slow down, Do not hasten them forward Allow them to move freely As they are. Let the words pass through you, Peaceful and pleasant Temperamental and raging Sweet or bitter. They are not yours, They never were. Remember that all they want Is to reach their

## November 10th

# Meditative Writing

In this exercise you are asked to write the presence of this moment.

Write a text that describes where you are now, at this unique point in time, the present.

As you write, remain in the present, and describe yourself and your experience **right now**, physically (the place, the surroundings, the sensations), emotionally (what feelings are awakened in you at this moment) and mentally (what thoughts come and go).

This **meditative writing exercise** means you observe and acknowledge where you are. Your writing should flow, with your pen following this moment. Each time the moment has been recorded, let it go and remain present, write in the new moment.

"Past and future veil God from our sight; burn up both of them with fire." **Rumi**
*The Essential Rumi*, edited and translated by Coleman Barks, HarperOne, 2004.

## November 11th

With the sea. Do not over flow, Do not hang on words. Learn from the river: Its only designation is To carry water

# What Are You Living for?

This is the birthday of Russian author **F.M. Dostoevsky**, born in 1821.

"The mystery of human existence lies not in just staying alive, but in finding something to live for," he wrote in *The Brothers Karamazov*.

This exercise is inspired by Dostoevsky. Reflect on your life for a moment. What are you living for? Have you found what it is in your life that makes you happy to wake up every morning? Look into your heart and write to discover the truth of what gives meaning to your life.

Let the words flow through you, Like the water flowing in the stream Place no dam over your words, Do not ask them to slow down, Do not hasten them forward Allow them to move freely As they are. Let the words pass through you, Peaceful and pleasant Temperamental and raging Sweet or bitter. They are not yours, They never were. Remember that all they want Is to reach their

## November 12th

# Listen to Me

This is the birthday of author **Michael Ende**, born in 1929.

This exercise is inspired by **Momo**, Ende's magnificent fictional child, who is blessed with the gift of attentive listening.

Listening is a rare commodity these days. Most of us prefer to talk than listen. What kind of listening would you wish for yourself? Write a text about listening to yourself, or to someone you wish would listen to you. You can write to several potential listeners. Write about the kind of listening that you need. Start with the words **Listen to me...**

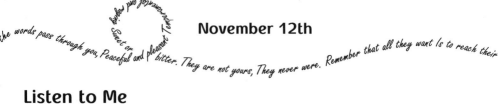

"When you talk, you are only repeating what you already know. But if you listen, you may learn something new." **Dalai Lama XIV**

*With the sea. Do not over flow, Do not hang on words. Learn from the river: Its only designation is To carry water*

## Writing Music

Put on any background music that you love, without lyrics. Now write the music, turning its sounds and vibrations into words. Fill in the words missing from the melody. Turn the notes into words and fill the page.

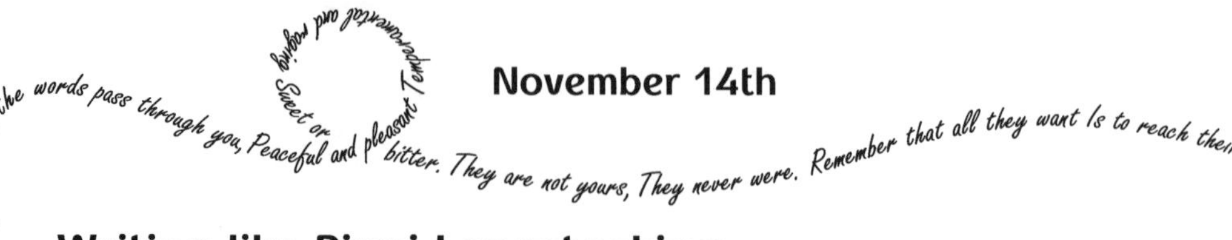
Let the words pass through you, Peaceful and pleasant Temperamental and raging Sweet or bitter. They are not yours, They never were. Remember that all they want Is to reach their
Let the words flow through you, Like the water flowing in the stream Place no dam over your words, Do not ask them to slow down, Do not hasten them forward Allow them to move freely As they are.

November 14th

## Writing like Pippi Longstocking

This is the birthday of Swedish author **Astrid Lindgren**, born in 1907. Lindgren created Pippi Longstocking.

Pippi Longstocking is one of my favorite literary characters. She is brave. She is an anarchist seeking justice. She is hopelessly optimistic – anything is possible as far as she's concerned. There is no limit to her creativity. In order to make her life more fascinating than it actually is, she constantly makes up stories, weaving imaginary tales from her inventive mind.

Come and write like Pippi Longstocking; tell stories about yourself and your life that never happened and never could, experiences that you supposedly had, people that you allegedly met, and wondrous places you have visited in your imagination. Go ahead and make believe – and most of all, have fun with your writing!

## November 15th

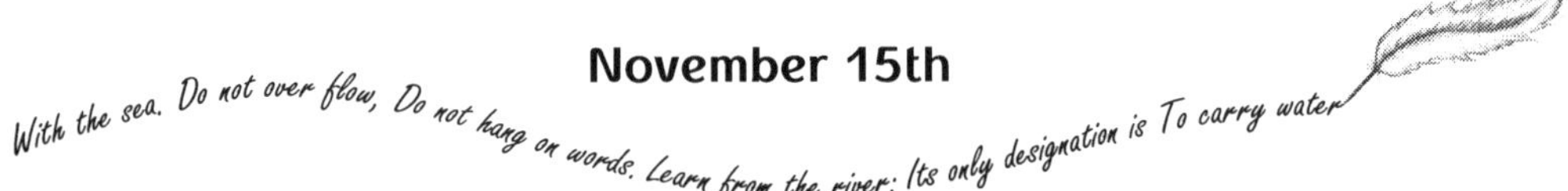
With the sea. Do not over flow, Do not hang on words. Learn from the river: Its only designation is To carry water

# Awakening

Turn the word **awakening** over in your mind and let it roll down your pen onto the page.

What does the word awaken within you? Do you feel awake and alert in your life? What would you be happy to wake up to in your life? Remember a time in your life when you experienced complete wakefulness.

Write an invitation for your awakening. Start with the words **I am waking up**... and continue intuitively. Let writing awake you from within

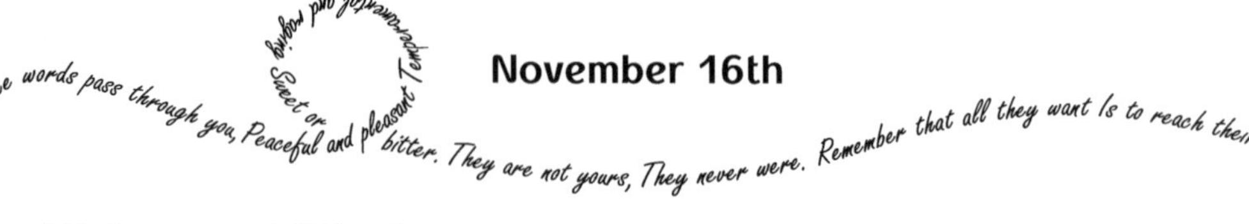
Let the words flow through you, Like the water flowing in the stream Place no dam over your words, Do not ask them to slow down, Do not hasten them forward Allow them to move freely As they are. Let the words pass through you, Peaceful and pleasant Temperamental and raging Sweet or bitter. They are not yours, They never were. Remember that all they want Is to reach their

## November 16th

# Vision and Blindness

This is the birthday of author **José de Sousa Saramagos**, born in 1922.

This exercise is inspired by his novel *Blindness*. Imagine a world where everyone around you is blind, and you are the only one who can see what is really happening. Write what you see to the blind world. Start with the words **I see...**

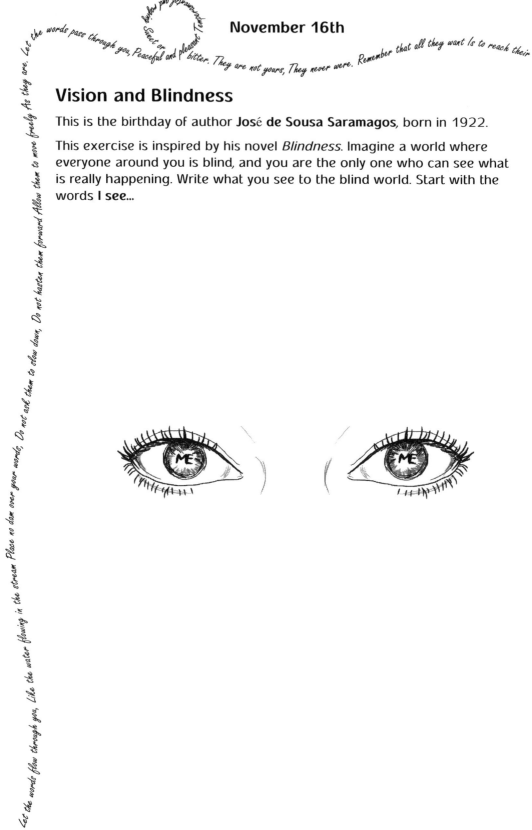

ME

ME

## November 17th

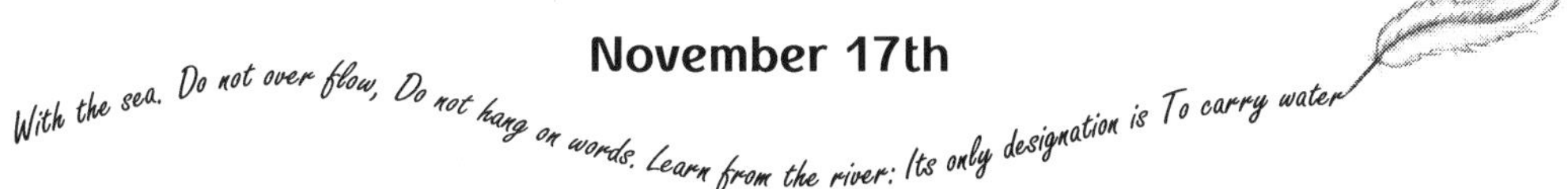
With the sea. Do not over flow, Do not hang on words. Learn from the river: Its only designation is To carry water

# After They All Leave

This is the birthday of poet **Dhalia Ravikovitch**, born in 1936.

In her poem "Surely you remember" she wrote, "After they all leave, I remain alone with the poems."*

This exercise is inspired by Ravikovitch. Write what happens inside you after everyone leaves. What sensations, feelings, musings or thoughts come to you when you are alone?

* *Hovering at a Low Altitude: The Collected Poetry of Dahlia Ravikovitch*, translated by Chana Bloch and Chana Kronfeld, W.W. Norton, 2009.

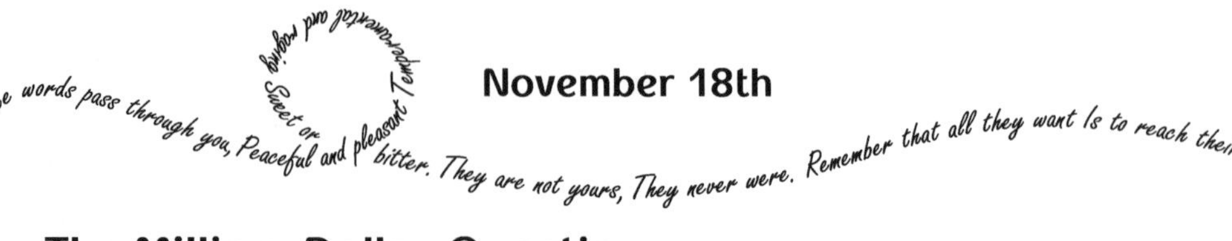
Let the words flow through you, Like the water flowing in the stream Place no dam over your words, Do not ask them to slow down, Do not hasten them forward Allow them to move freely As they are. Let the words pass through you, Peaceful and pleasant Temperamental and raging Sweet or bitter. They are not yours, They never were. Remember that all they want Is to reach their

**November 18th**

## The Million-Dollar Question

We are all used to giving advice, saying what we think and offering solutions. Many times, however, it is better to ask a question - there are so many potentially life-changing questions that need asking!

Have you ever been asked such a question?

If so, write how it has touched you or affected your life. Start your writing with that question; describe the story behind it and everything that grew out of it.

If you don't remember being asked such a question, write the question that would honestly make you happy if someone were to ask you.

## November 19th

*With the sea. Do not over flow, Do not hang on words. Learn from the river: Its only designation is To carry water*

# A Conversation with Time

It disappears quickly. It runs away. You always say what a pity it is that you don't have enough of it, that you would like to have much much more. It's worth a lot of money, you've been told. And you steal it for yourself at every opportunity.

When you are having fun, it flies. When you are bored, you want to kill it. When did you last clear some time for yourself to have a conversation with Time? Were you ever able to find out why it is always slipping away, and where it goes?

This exercise is an opportunity for a private chat with Time. Close your eyes and imagine how it looks. Free your imagination - invite Time into your home for a relaxed conversation over a cup of coffee, and really get to know it.

Record that conversation here, and when you are finished, allow Time to whisper a message in your ear - one that will stay with you forever.

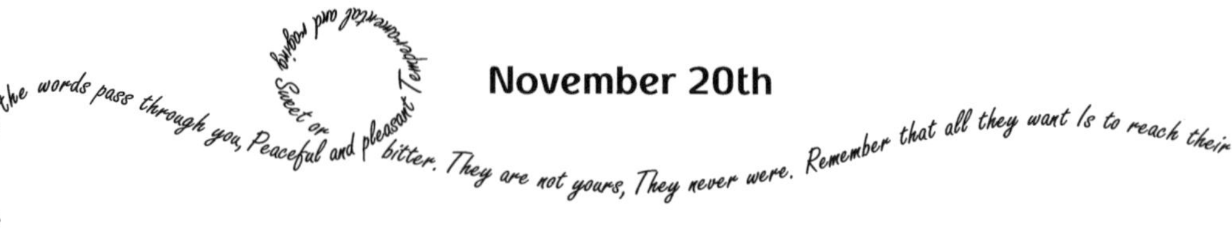
Let the words flow through you, Like the water flowing in the stream Place no dam over your words, Do not ask them to slow down, Do not hasten them forward Allow them to move freely As they are. Let the words pass through you, Peaceful and pleasant Temperamental and raging Sweet or bitter. They are not yours, They never were. Remember that all they want Is to reach their

**November 20th**

## The Words of a Kind Person

Remember a person who was kind to you, someone who always spoke to you as if you were important, complimented your work, encouraged you to discover yourself, saw the best in you and gave you strength.

Write yourself a letter from this person, a letter that reminds you who you are; what your strengths and unique qualities are. Imagine this person is dictating directly into your ear exactly what you need to hear right now. Don't hesitate – write everything down. Accept with love all the presents this person gives you through their words.

*With the sea. Do not over flow, Do not hang on words. Learn from the river: Its only designation is To carry water*

## A Questionnaire for Someone Close

Think of a person who is close to you, someone you feel as if there are many things you do not know about them, but would love to know. Write this person a letter with all your questions. Allow yourself to ask everything you want to know. Even if you never receive an answer to any of your questions, the act of writing them down means something.

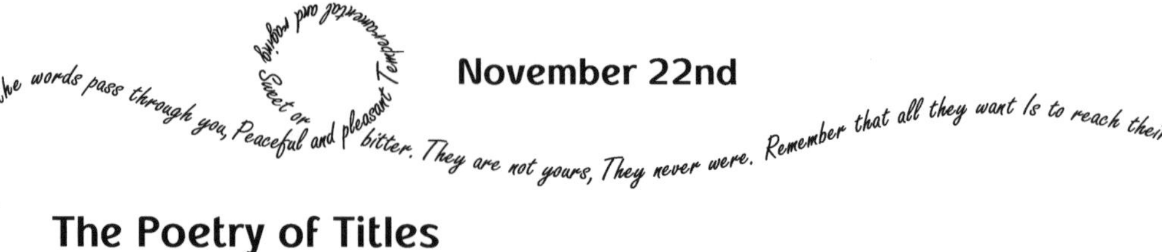
Let the words flow through you, Like the water flowing in the stream Place no dam over your words, Do not ask them to slow down, Do not hasten them forward Allow them to move freely As they are. Let the words pass through you, Peaceful and pleasant Temperamental and raging Sweet or bitter. They are not yours, They never were. Remember that all they want Is to reach their

## November 22nd

# The Poetry of Titles

Walk around the house and copy book titles into your journal that beckon to you - write 10 to 15 titles.

When you have completed your collection, sit comfortably and write a poem – or any text – that contains the titles of those books. Great thought has been put into each book and every title. Look at how much beauty is created from integrating all the titles of the books you've chosen – those that may have allowed you to enter new worlds.

*With the sea. Do not over flow, Do not hang on words. Learn from the river: Its only designation is To carry water*

## Certainty and Doubt

Write a text comprised of nothing but certainties. List ten things you know to be accurate and true, and end every sentence with an exclamation mark.

Once you have done this, cast doubt on all these certainties. Write the same text again, but turn the exclamation marks into question marks. Next to each question, add a line or two that explains why the original idea is not as definite as you have been accustomed to thinking.

When you are finished, write how you are feeling.

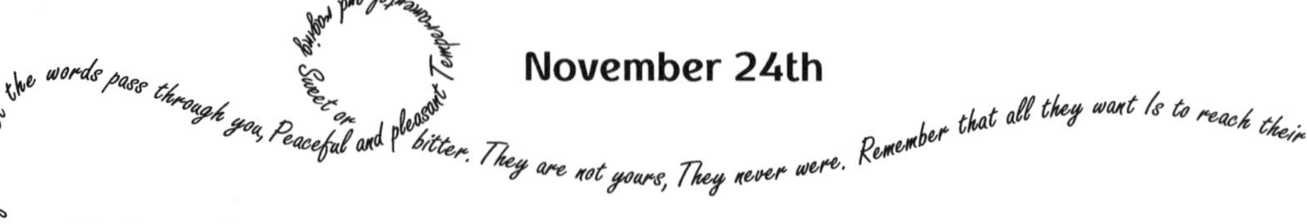
Let the words flow through you, Like the water flowing in the stream Place no dam over your words, Do not ask them to slow down, Do not hasten them forward Allow them to move freely As they are. Let the words pass through you, Peaceful and pleasant Temperamental and raging Sweet or bitter. They are not yours, They never were. Remember that all they want Is to reach their

### November 24th

## Belonging

Explore your sense of belonging through writing. Do you feel that you are part of something larger, part of a group? Where do you feel that you belong, and where do you feel like a "stranger"? To whom or what do you belong?

Start your writing with the words **I belong...**

## November 25th

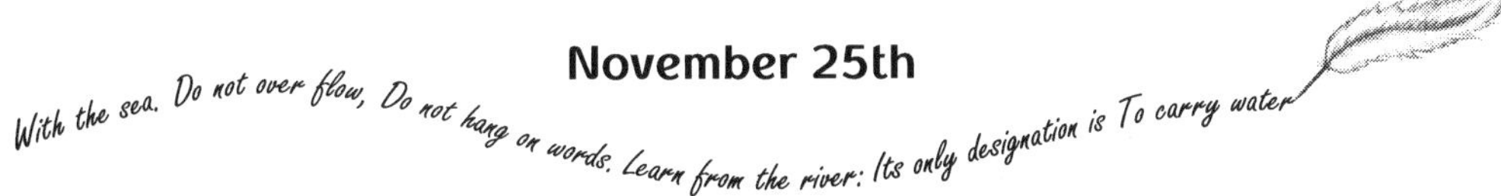
With the sea. Do not over flow, Do not hang on words. Learn from the river: Its only designation is To carry water

# Poetry in the Café

Take your journal and something to write with and go sit in your favorite coffee shop. Now, listen with your full attention, and start transcribing the words and sentences you hear around you, as well as descriptions of people, moments and thoughts that arise. Write everything that grabs your attention. Do that for at least 10 minutes.

Afterwards, turn some of the words and sentences that you have written into a poem. Enjoy playing with the mundane words from the coffee shop and turning them into poetry.

I learned to write
in the Dark
on long drives at nights
in cafe's
at the local pub
I learned in the Dark
To love

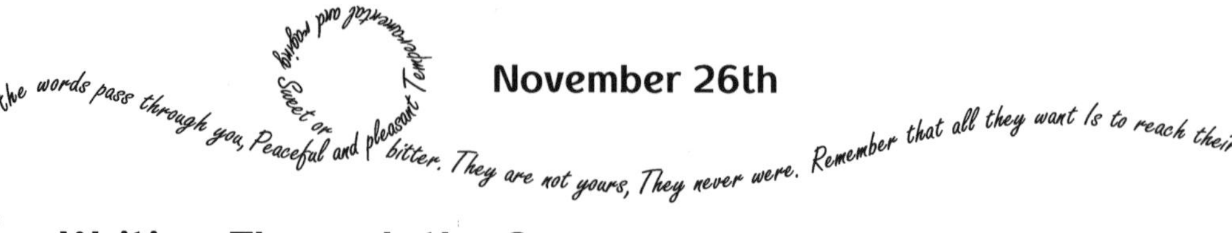
Let the words pass through you, Peaceful and pleasant Temperamental and raging Sweet or bitter. They are not yours, They never were. Remember that all they want Is to reach their

## November 26th

# Writing Through the Senses

Choose a significant event that has happened to you recently and write about it from the perspective of one of your senses: sight, hearing, smell, taste or touch. Or perhaps the sixth sense?

This is an opportunity to focus your attention on one sense only. Concentrate on the event and write about it as if only one of your senses was present. Allow that sense to express itself.

*With the sea. Do not over flow, Do not hang on words. Learn from the river: Its only designation is To carry water*

## I am Hungry

What are you hungry for? Write all the things that this question awakens inside.

Start with the words **I am hungry...** and let them take you on an internal exploration of the true hunger in your life.

Allow yourself to meet your hunger and satisfy it in words.

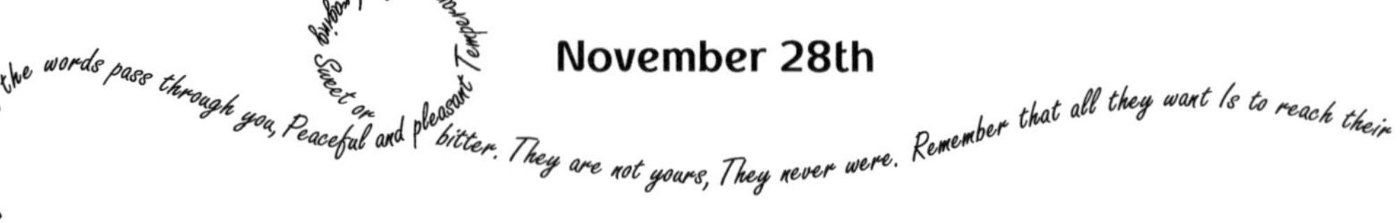
Let the words flow through you, Like the water flowing in the stream Place no dam over your words, Do not ask them to slow down, Do not hasten them forward Allow them to move freely As they are. Let the words pass through you, Peaceful and pleasant Temperamental and raging Sweet or bitter. They are not yours, They never were. Remember that all they want Is to reach their

**November 28th**

## Writing Fear

What is the one thing you most fear to write about? Write it here.

Put it on paper, together with the fear it creates in you.

## November 29th

*With the sea. Do not over flow, Do not hang on words. Learn from the river: Its only designation is To carry water*

# I Want

Explore your desires and give them expression. What do you want most right now?

Write it here. Start with the words **I want**... and let them guide you in your writing.

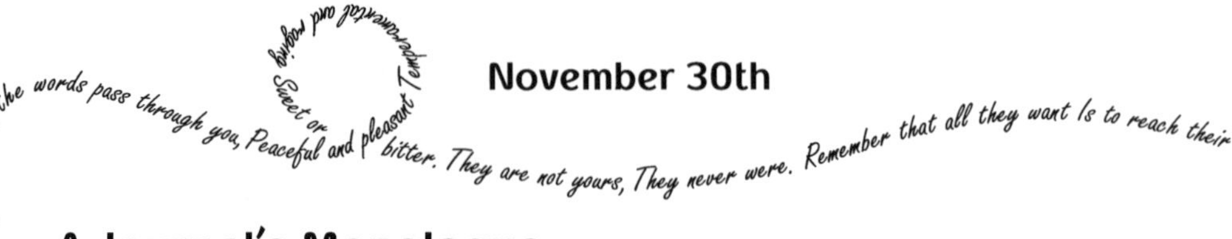
Let the words flow through you, Like the water flowing in the stream Place no dam over your words, Do not ask them to slow down, Do not hasten them forward Allow them to move freely As they are. Let the words pass through you, Peaceful and pleasant Temperamental and raging Sweet or bitter. They are not yours, They never were. Remember that all they want Is to reach their

## November 30th

# A Journal's Monologue

Stop for a moment and sense the journal you are writing. Comprehend the life it is keeping safe for you.

In this exercise, you want your journal to speak to you. Let it write through you in the first person. Just listen and transcribe its words. Feel how the words are created within the journal and emerge to be reproduced on its pages. What is the journal asking of you? What does it have to say to you now? Write its words.

With the sea. Do not over flow, Do not hang on words. Learn from the river: Its only designation is To carry water

# Winter

## WRITING FROM THE HEART

## Writing in Winter

In the winter, nature converges inward. Growth occurs in darkness, underground, within the seed sown in the fall.

In this season, we have an opportunity to eradicate the weeds that have grown in the soil, ask liberating questions, dare to touch forgotten places, revive suppressed dreams, stories and desires. Unlike spring and summer, which are seasons of light, winter invites us to work with shadows and in unlit places, and give less significance to the visible and the familiar.

Winter has a symbolic connection to the role of death in life. It is a time of endings and goodbyes; then, at the peak of the season, out of great darkness, a small light appears. This light grows stronger as the days begin to lengthen, until spring arrives and all that lay in the frozen earth emerges into the light.

In ancient times, as the days of the cold season shortened, man sought help in fighting darkness. For that purpose, throughout human history, symbols and holidays were set and celebrated each year, at the peak of winter.

In Judaism, at Hanukah – the Festival of Lights – one candle is lit every night incrementally for the eight days of the holiday until the Menorah (eight-branched candelabra) is fully lit. In Christianity, the Christmas fir tree decorated with sparkling lights represents resistance to harsh winter conditions. In Hinduism, Diwali, the five-day holiday of light, celebrates the triumph of light over darkness. Even primitive cultures used bonfires to engender, in the heart of darkness, the rebirth of light.

This is the time we are called upon to accept darkness, and to see it as part of life. This is our opportunity to go inward, in order to find the light within ourselves and illuminate the darkness from the center of our being.

**This portal invites you to light the candle inside of you.**
**In this season, you are invited to write in order to say goodbye, to dream and to share your stories.**

# December

## Writing to Say Goodbye

Let the words flow through you, Like the water flowing in the stream Place no dam over your words, Do not ask them to slow down, Do not hasten them forward Allow them to move freely As they are. Let the words pass through you, Peaceful and pleasant Temperamental and raging Sweet or bitter. They are not yours, They never were. Remember that all they want Is to reach their

With the sea. Do not over flow, Do not hang on words. Learn from the river: Its only designation is To carry water

## The Last Time

Imagine this is the last time you read/write/eat/meet a beloved person. In our day-to-day life, we rarely think of "the last time". However, despite the fact that endings are unpleasant, it may be a good idea to consider this possibility every now and then, to gain a new perspective.

Write a text describing the last time you do or experience one of the things you love in your life. Can you do this?

Start with the words **If it were the last time that I...**

What does it make you feel? Do? Be? Change?

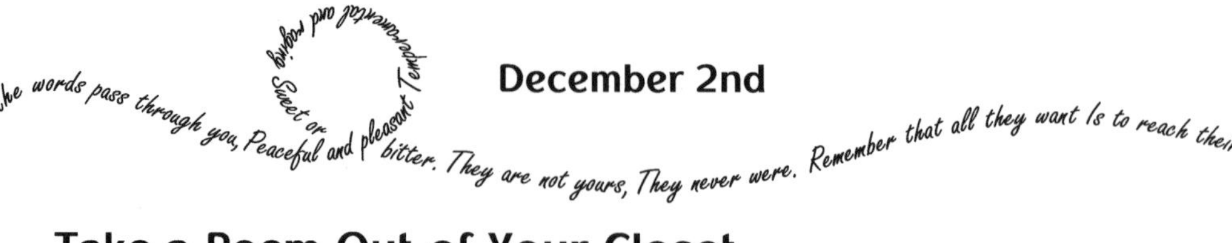
Let the words flow through you, Like the water flowing in the stream Place no dam over your words, Do not ask them to slow down, Do not hasten them forward Allow them to move freely As they are. Let the words pass through you, Peaceful and pleasant Temperamental and raging Sweet or bitter. They are not yours, They never were. Remember that all they want Is to reach their

## December 2nd

# Take a Poem Out of Your Closet

Think about the many hidden spots in your home, the stuffed drawers and closets where there are all kind of things it is time to part with – piles of papers, notebooks, binders, old clothes, shoes that you will never wear, inkless pens, bedsheets that you no longer use.

Go through your whole house in your mind - or, if you like, actually go through your home. Then write a list of all the things you would be happy to clear away.

Now write a poem from this list. Select one listed item to be the title of the poem.

## December 3rd

With the sea. Do not over flow, Do not hang on words. Learn from the river: Its only designation is To carry water

# You are Not Allowed to Write

In this exercise, write the words of all the demons and monsters screaming and shouting inside you "**You are not allowed to write!**" Give those demons a voice. Don't send them away. Become a channel that enables them to fully express themselves.

Allow your demons to detail all the reasons why you shouldn't be writing. No doubt they have many reasons. Fill an entire page with their claims.

Start with the words **You are not allowed to write**...

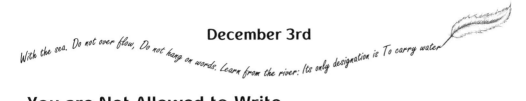

Let the words flow through you, Like the water flowing in the stream Place no dam over your words, Do not ask them to slow down, Do not hasten them forward Allow them to move freely As they are. Let the

bitter. They are not yours, They never were. Remember that all they want Is to reach their

## December 4th

# Must I Write?

This is the birthday of poet **Rainer Maria Rilke**, born in 1875.

In *Letters to a Young Poet** he wrote, "Go into yourself. Search for the reason that bids you write; find out whether it is spreading out its roots in the deepest places of your heart, acknowledge to yourself whether you would have to die if it were denied you to write. This above all – ask yourself in the stillest hour of your night: must I write?"

This exercise is inspired by Rainer Maria Rilke. **Must I write?** Answer this question and explain why.

* Translation by M.D. Herter Norton, W.W. Norton & Company, 1934, pp 18–19.

December 5th

*With the sea. Do not over flow, Do not hang on words. Learn from the river: Its only designation is To carry water*

## Endings are Sometimes

Write about what an ending is for you. What the end of something, a farewell, means to you. Recall something in your life that has ended. What did you experience when it was over?

In addition, write about when things end in your life. Do you end them yourself, or do you wait for them to end and disappear on their own? Try to investigate your behavior patterns at the end of relationships, projects, jobs, or moving home, to name a few.

Start with the words **Endings are...**

Let the words flow through you, Like the water flowing in the stream Place no dam over your words, Do not ask them to slow down, Do not hasten them forward Allow them to move freely As they are.

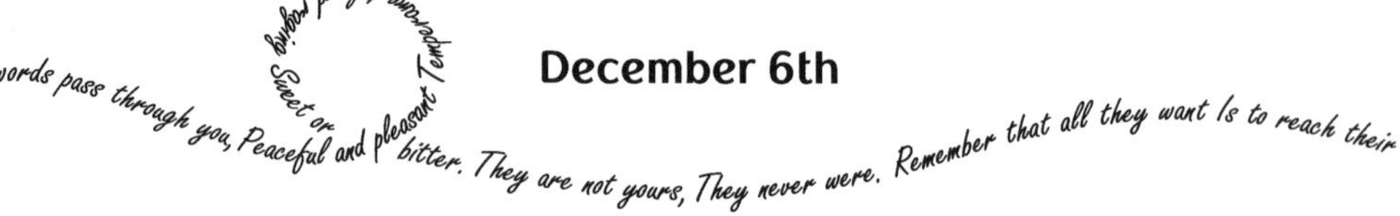
Let the words pass through you, Peaceful and pleasant Temperamental and raging Sweet or bitter. They are not yours, They never were. Remember that all they want Is to reach their

**December 6th**

## Mourning

What did you need to grieve for in your life but didn't mourn?

Write one such thing, and dedicate one writing day to give space to that grief.

If you feel that you need more than one day, take it. Dedicate a defined period of time for grieving, so you feel safe to give pain and sadness the space they need.

Mourning allows you to open important space for something new to take its place.

## December 7th

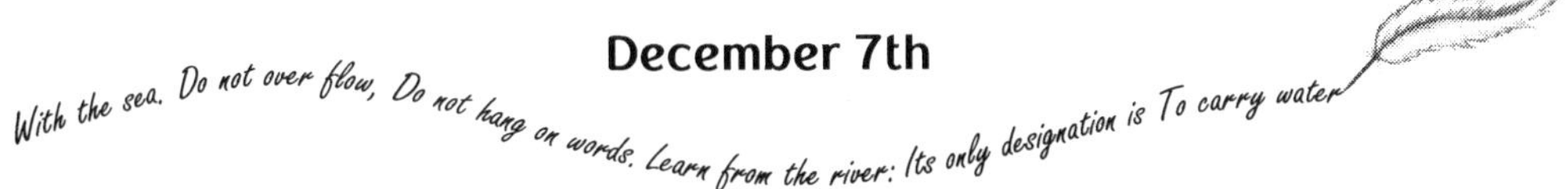
With the sea. Do not over flow, Do not hang on words. Learn from the river: Its only designation is To carry water

# I Do Not Believe

In this exercise, write without pausing about your worst enemy: your lack of faith. Permit yourself to express all your doubts, write everything you do not believe will happen to you, that supposedly you do not deserve.

Write your lack of faith here in order to part with it.

Start with the words **I do not believe...**

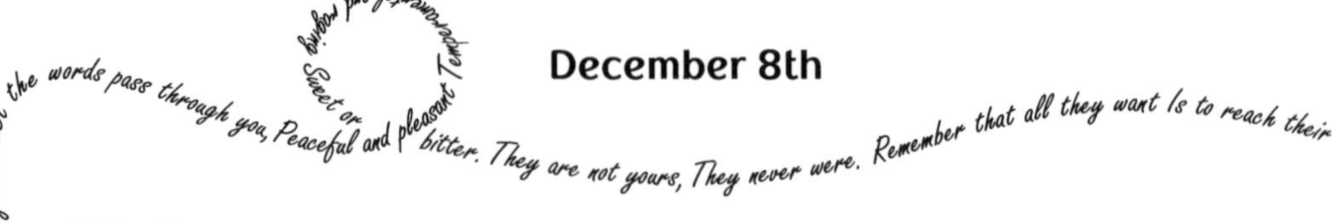
Let the words flow through you, Like the water flowing in the stream Place no dam over your words, Do not ask them to slow down, Do not hasten them forward Allow them to move freely As they are. Let the words pass through you, Peaceful and pleasant Temperamental and raging Sweet or bitter. They are not yours, They never were. Remember that all they want Is to reach their

## December 8th

# I Believe

Faith is one of the potent powers that move the world forward. Were it not for faith, we would never have done anything.

In this exercise give your faith space and magnify it. Write down what and whom you truly believe in. Write to strengthen your belief in yourself and in the world, and include places in need of empowering. Believe!

Start with the words **I believe...**

*With the sea. Do not over flow, Do not hang on words. Learn from the river: Its only designation is To carry water*

## Closure

Do you know the feeling when something has ended, but you are still "there" in spirit, because it is difficult for you to let go? This sensation can appear at the end of a relationship, separation from someone close, moving to a new home, or being fired.

Closure allows us to simply move on and open ourselves up to a new relationship, a new place, a new job, without dragging along pieces of the past.

Write about a circle in your life that is still open and is now time to close. Write why it is still open and what the consequences of that are in your life. Does the fact that it is not closed stop you in any way? Maybe it is delaying the start of a new chapter in your life?

Write what is "stuck" or perhaps still painful, what you wish you had said but did not, and how the final closure of that circle will be better for you.

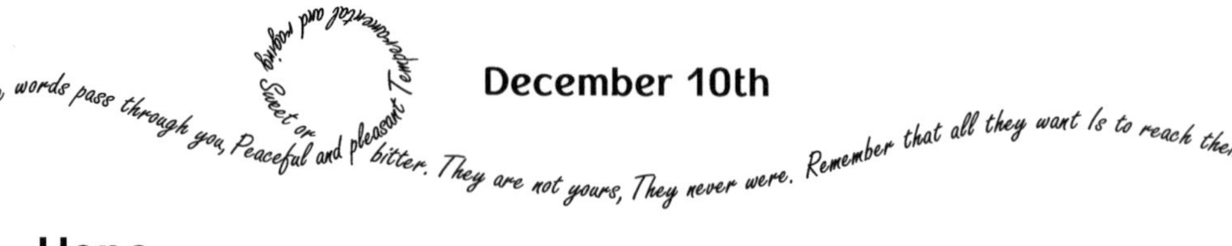
Let the words pass through you, Peaceful and pleasant Temperamental and raging Sweet or bitter. They are not yours, They never were. Remember that all they want Is to reach their

## December 10th

# Hope

This is the birthday of poet Emily Dickinson, born in 1830.

"'Hope' is the thing with feathers – / that perches in the soul – / and sings the tunes without the words – / and never stops- at all-"* wrote Dickinson in her well-known poem.

This is an exercise inspired by Emily Dickinson.

Write your hope. What do you hope for?

* *The Poems of Emily Dickinson*, edited by R. W. Franklin, Harvard University Press, 1999, p 314.

## December 11th

With the sea. Do not over flow, Do not hang on words. Learn from the river: Its only designation is To carry water

# Good Closure

Recall one event in your life that you brought to a successful close, where you feel that it is all behind you, that you did the best you could, and looking back, you feel at peace.

Now write about the process. What led you to reach that closure? What did it require from you? What skills and qualities did you mobilize to deal with the situation– courage, compassion, love? Determination, persistence?

Think of the way you chose to reach closure. You may use the same tools and qualities to bring other open matters and loose ends in your life to a close.

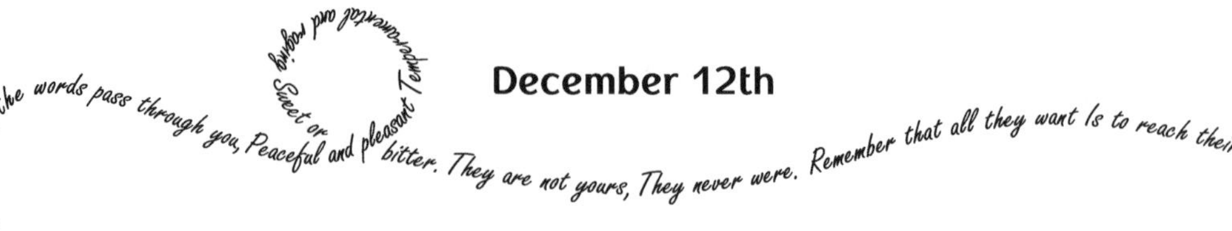
Let the words flow through you, Like the water flowing in the stream Place no dam over your words, Do not ask them to slow down, Do not hasten them forward Allow them to move freely As they are.
Let the words pass through you, Peaceful and pleasant Temperamental and raging Sweet or bitter. They are not yours, They never were. Remember that all they want Is to reach their

## December 12th

# A Final Goodbye to Someone

Think about someone in your life to whom it is time to say goodbye. Perhaps it is someone who is no longer physically in your life or even alive anymore, but you did not have the chance to say goodbye the way you would have liked.

Imagine a meeting with this person and have a conversation with them in writing. Tell him or her everything that you wanted to say or ask and "listen" to their response.

You may be surprised, but you can achieve closure even without the presence of the other. This exercise is designed to help you reach closure on an issue that has been left unresolved, and release the energy that binds you to that person. Write the conversation between the two of you, until you feel relieved and are able to let go.

# December 13th

## Cyclicity

This is the birthday of **Heinrich Heine**, born in 1797.

"Our sweetest hopes rise blooming. /And then again are gone, /They bloom and fade alternate, /And so it goes rolling on"* he wrote.

This exercise is inspired by Heine. Write all the cyclic processes that exist in your life, in every area – physical, intellectual and spiritual. Connect to the nature of your cyclicity and write about what you recognize in yourself. Write all your sunsets and sunrises.

* *Heinrich Heine's Pictures of Travel,* Schaefer & Koradi, 1879, p 233.

**December 14th**

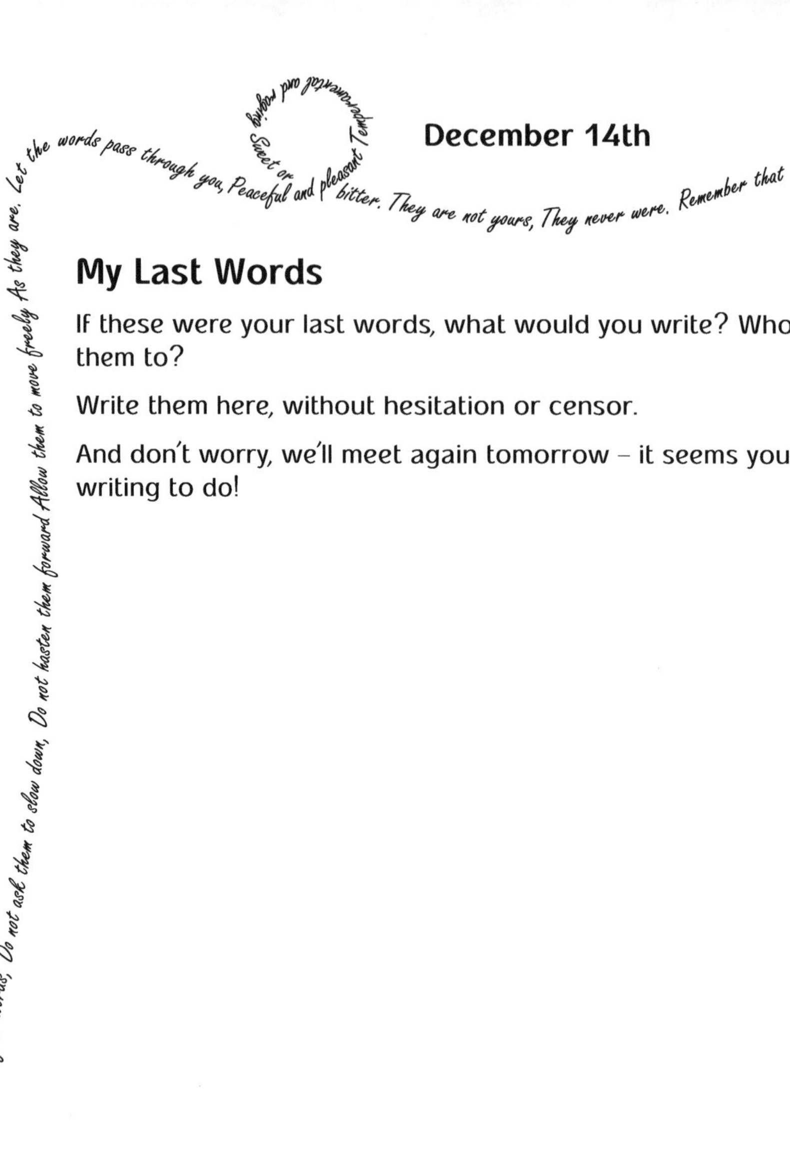
Let the words flow through you, Like the water flowing in the stream Place no dam over your words, Do not ask them to slow down, Do not hasten them forward Allow them to move freely As they are. Let the words pass through you, Peaceful and pleasant Temperamental and raging Sweet or bitter. They are not yours, They never were. Remember that all they want Is to reach their

## My Last Words

If these were your last words, what would you write? Who would you write them to?

Write them here, without hesitation or censor.

And don't worry, we'll meet again tomorrow – it seems you have a lot more writing to do!

*With the sea. Do not over flow, Do not hang on words. Learn from the river: Its only designation is To carry water*

## That Night

Think about a significant night in your life. Now write a text that expresses that night and its meaning.

Start with the words **That night...** and continue from there. What was there about that night that left its mark on you?

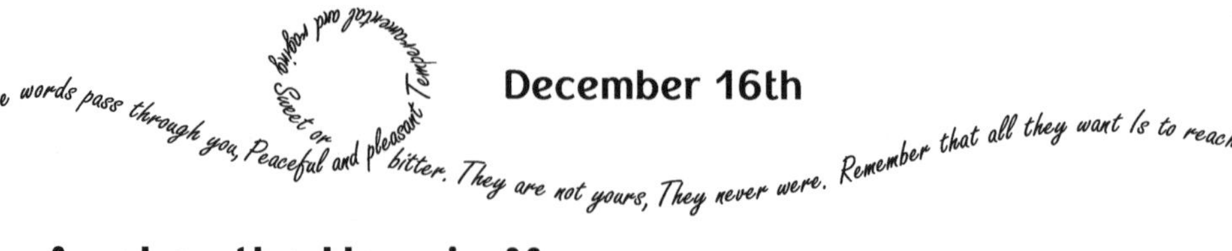
Let the words pass through you, Peaceful and pleasant Temperamental and raging Sweet or bitter. They are not yours, They never were. Remember that all they want Is to reach their

## December 16th

# Awaken the Hero in Me

This is the birthday of author **Jane Austen**, born in 1775.

"But when a young lady is to be a heroine, the perverseness of forty surrounding families cannot prevent her. Something must and will happen to throw a hero in her way," she wrote in *Northanger Abbey*.

This exercise is inspired by Austen. Do you know that you are the hero in the story of your life? Write about the hero who lives within you. Write their characteristics, write about the way they cope with challenges and the way they concede to go on journeys, to observe their life, to learn, to make mistakes, to lose their way and to change.

Let the words flow through you, Like the water flowing in the stream Place no dam over your words, Do not ask them to slow down, Do not hasten them forward Allow them to move freely As they are.

## December 17th

*With the sea. Do not over flow, Do not hang on words. Learn from the river: Its only designation is To carry water*

# Perhaps

Think about the word **perhaps** while writing, and consider what it sparks inside you. Do you understand what it means for you? Does it open new opportunities? Does it represent doubt? What is this word asking of you at this moment? Give it space and write from your core being everything that comes to you when you hear this word.

Let the words flow through you, Like the water flowing in the stream Place no dam over your words, Do not ask them to slow down, Do not hasten them forward Allow them to move freely As they are.

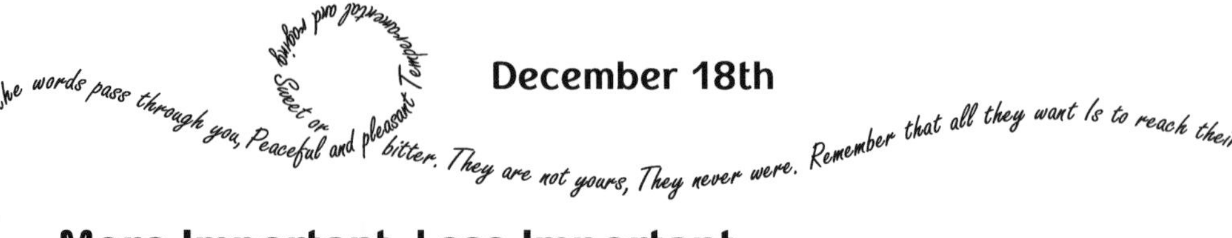
Let the words pass through you, Peaceful and pleasant Temperamental and raging Sweet or bitter. They are not yours, They never were. Remember that all they want Is to reach their

**December 18th**

## More Important, Less Important

Think about the priorities in your life, and write a text that expresses what is significant in your life and the place you give it. What are the things that are important to you? What are the things you want to invest your time and energy in? Write them down.

Now write what is less important. Finally, write down what is not important to you at all.

With the sea. Do not over flow, Do not hang on words. Learn from the river: Its only designation is To carry water

## Words from the Darkness

Imagine the change from light to darkness, that special moment when the sun sets and light disappears. What do you feel as the sun takes its leave and the day grows dark, after it is gone? Do you welcome the darkness?

In this exercise, remain in the dark. Reflect on how you feel being there, and write everything you experience in the darkness.

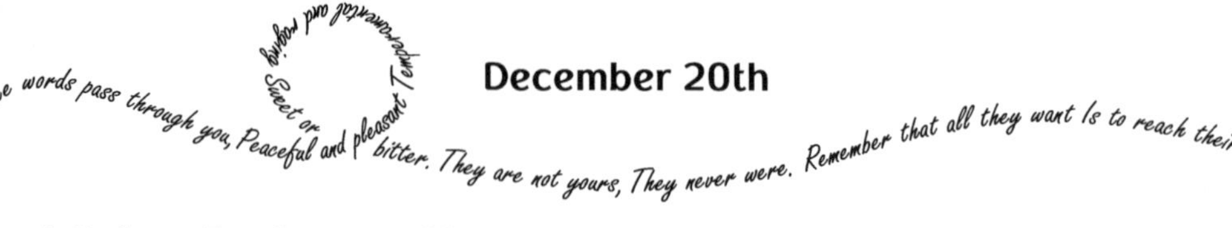
Let the words pass through you, Peaceful and pleasant Temperamental and raging Sweet or bitter. They are not yours, They never were. Remember that all they want Is to reach their

## December 20th

# I Bring Darkness Closer

**Rabbi Nachman of Breslov** a creative, influential and profound leader in Judaism said that without darkness, there would be no light in the world. Light and darkness are two halves of a whole. What is the meaning of darkness in your life? What are the moments that you define as "dark"? List these moments. Allow darkness to emerge through writing. Come closer to it, face it, acknowledge it as a part of life. Write down what it makes you feel and think.

Begin with the words **I bring darkness closer...**

Let the words flow through you, Like the water flowing in the stream Place no dam over your words, Do not ask them to slow down, Do not hasten them forward Allow them to move freely As they are.

## December 21st

*With the sea. Do not over flow, Do not hang on words. Learn from the river: Its only designation is To carry water*

# Turning Darkness into Light

This exercise is inspired by the darkest night of the year. Using your intuition, write nine words that express what "darkness" means to you. Don't think about it; just write everything that comes to mind.

Now write a text that contains all these words, but expresses light. This is your chance to create light out of darkness.

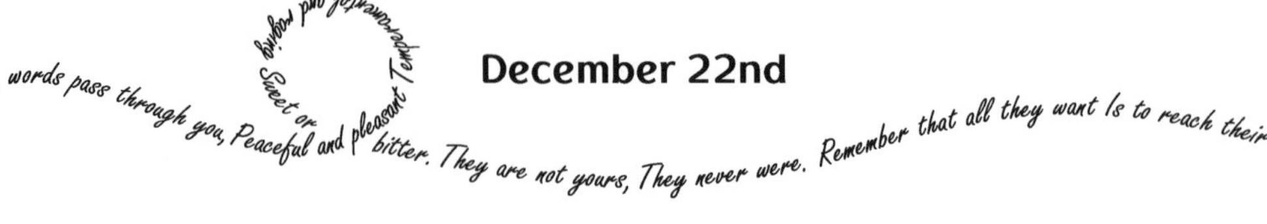
Let the words flow through you, Like the water flowing in the stream Place no dam over your words, Do not ask them to slow down, Do not hasten them forward Allow them to move freely As they are. Let the words pass through you, Peaceful and pleasant Temperamental and raging Sweet or bitter. They are not yours, They never were. Remember that all they want Is to reach their

## December 22nd

# Writing in Light

What is your light? Write about the bright moments in your life and the wonderful rays of light you bring to the world. Write yourself from the light inside you. Do not be afraid. Let the light emerge from deep inside you. Acknowledge it. Acknowledge yourself.

"There will be no triumph of light over darkness as long until we stand for the simple truth, that we must enhance the light, not fight the darkness." **A. D. Gordon** writer and philosopher, born 1856.

*With the sea. Do not over flow, Do not hang on words. Learn from the river: Its only designation is To carry water*

## Lighting a Candle

Darkness is the absence of light. In order to increase the light in our lives, we should be more active every day, every hour. Write about how you bring light into your life and the lives of others. What do you do in order to shine?

"Better to light a candle than curse the darkness." **Ancient Chinese proverb**

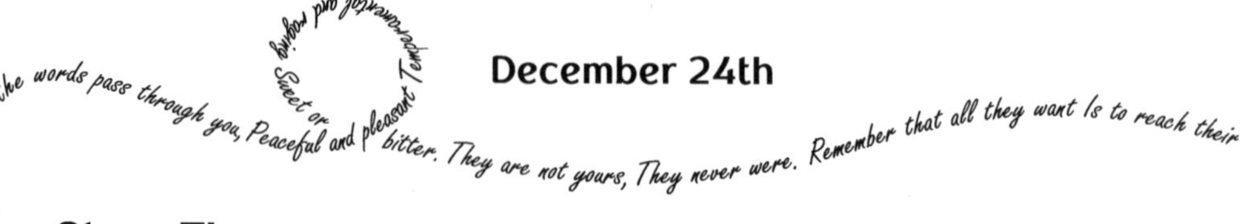
Let the words flow through you, Like the water flowing in the stream Place no dam over your words, Do not ask them to slow down, Do not hasten them forward Allow them to move freely As they are. Let the words pass through you, Peaceful and pleasant Temperamental and raging Sweet or bitter. They are not yours, They never were. Remember that all they want Is to reach their

## December 24th

# Story Therapy

Each of us has a story of courage and heroism, a story we tell to light the way for others, a story that empowers and gives hope in moments of darkness. These stories are therapeutic. They give us strength.

Choose one **therapy story** from your life – something that happened to you or perhaps a story you heard in your childhood and have remembered ever since. Write this story here. Turn on the light with your words.

*With the sea. Do not over flow, Do not hang on words. Learn from the river: Its only designation is To carry water*

## When Things Fell Apart

Recall an event when something in your life fell apart, broke, ended. The moment that you felt you lost the ground under your feet, a moment of "darkness". Describe the feelings you had, the loss you experienced. Remember these moments.

Is it possible that a "dark" incident let "light" into your life? How do you view this event today?

"There is a crack, a crack in everything, / That's how the light gets in." **Leonard Cohen** "Anthem", 1992.

## December 26th

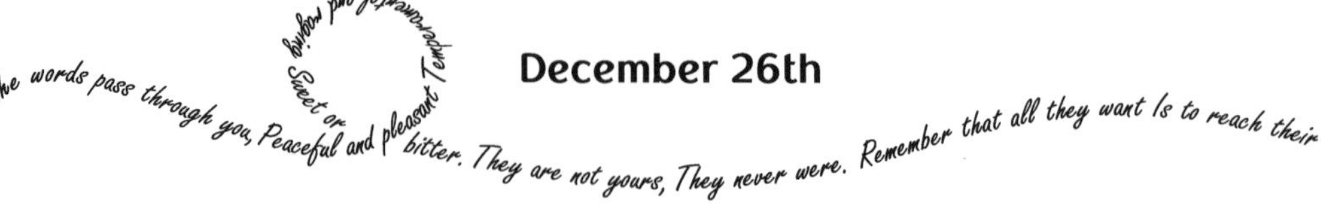
Let the words flow through you, Like the water flowing in the stream Place no dam over your words, Do not ask them to slow down, Do not hasten them forward Allow them to move freely As they are. Let the words pass through you, Peaceful and pleasant Temperamental and raging Sweet or bitter. They are not yours, They never were. Remember that all they want Is to reach their

# A Letter to Death

Imagine that death is an entity that you can actually turn to and have a conversation with . What would you like to say to it? Would you ask something of it?

Write a personal letter to Death, in which you befriend it.

Start with the words **Dear Death...**

# December 27th



## Separation for Regeneration

For three minutes, write a sequence of single words that symbolize separation and ending, words that you associate with endings, discarding and leave-taking.

Then use all these words in order to write a text with the title **A New Beginning.**

The challenge in this exercise is to use all the words that came to you in the context of endings and turn them into a text that expresses vitality and regeneration.

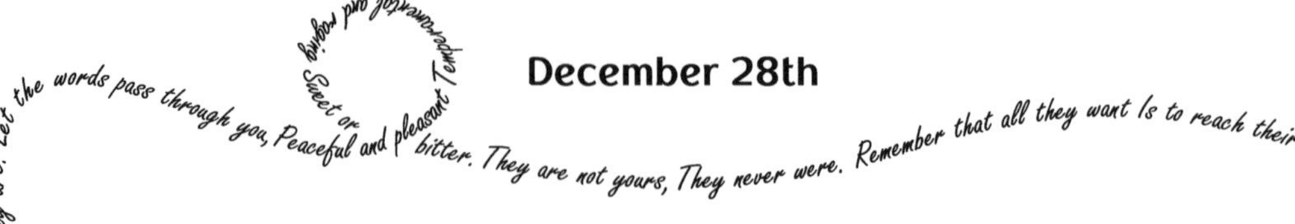
Let the words flow through you, Like the water flowing in the stream Place no dam over your words, Do not ask them to slow down, Do not hasten them forward Allow them to move freely As they are. Let the words pass through you, Peaceful and pleasant Temperamental and raging Sweet or bitter. They are not yours, They never were. Remember that all they want Is to reach their

**December 28th**

## An End as a New Beginning

Take the last sentence from a book, poem or novel that you love. Copy it onto this page and turn that ending into a new beginning. The last sentence of the text you chose will become the first sentence in the new text you write here.

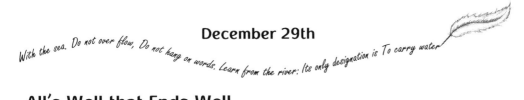

# December 29th

With the sea. Do not over flow, Do not hang on words. Learn from the river: Its only designation is To carry water

## All's Well that Ends Well

It is time to summarize the past year and get ready for the new one. Write down significant themes, important events and discoveries you have encountered over the last year. As you write, reflect on everything you have experienced and all you did in this past year. Look at all the good you have created, and marvel at the wonderful journey you have taken.

Now create in writing your best ending for this year. Write a special, impressive ending that suitably expresses the year that is coming to an end.

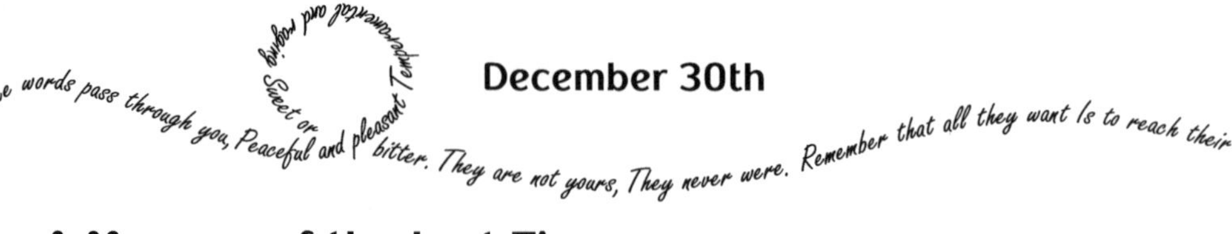
Let the words flow through you, Like the water flowing in the stream Place no dam over your words, Do not ask them to slow down, Do not hasten them forward Allow them to move freely As they are. Let the words pass through you, Peaceful and pleasant Temperamental and raging Sweet or bitter. They are not yours, They never were. Remember that all they want Is to reach their

**December 30th**

## A Memory of the Last Time

Write about your last times; anything you have done, created, or experienced for the last time.

Remember a last kiss, a final hug, a look, a laugh, a dance, or the last time you met a loved one. What memories come to you when you think of all these last times?

Start with the words **The last time...** and let them carry you back in time.

## December 31st

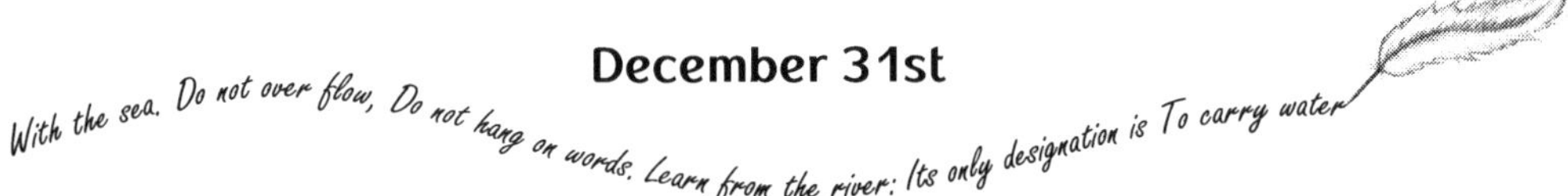
With the sea. Do not over flow, Do not hang on words. Learn from the river: Its only designation is To carry water

# At Year's End

What person are you at the end of this year? What person were you at its beginning?

Write about meaningful events and important ideas you experienced throughout this year that ends today. Then turn them into a text, or a poem, expressing the essence of the process you have undergone throughout the year. Come! Cherish everything you have created, experienced, encountered and completed over the past year.

# January

## Writing to Dream

Let the words flow through you, Like the water flowing in the stream Place no dam over your words, Do not ask them to slow down, Do not hasten them forward Allow them to move freely As they are. Let the words pass through you, Peaceful and pleasant Temperamental and raging Sweet or bitter. They are not yours, They never were. Remember that all they want Is to reach their

## January 1st

*Learn from the river: Its only designation is To carry water With the sea. Do not over flow, Do not hang on words.*

# Happy New Year!

Travel in time to the first day of next year. Where will you be at this moment exactly one year from today?

Use your imagination and remember that from here on, anything is possible. This is your chance to express your aspirations and dreams.

Sail away in your imagination to next year that is "over" and describe it as if you have already lived it. Write about events that you supposedly experienced as memories of what you imagine happened.

When you are done, write a summary of that imaginary coming year, and indicate what was most significant in it for you.

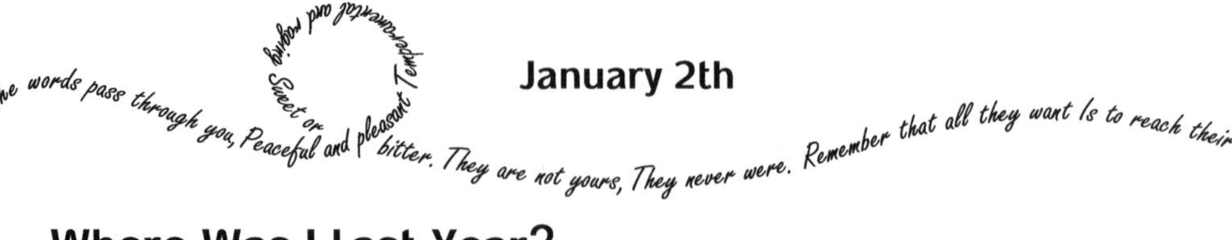
Let the words flow through you, Like the water flowing in the stream Place no dam over your words, Do not ask them to slow down, Do not hasten them forward Allow them to move freely As they are. Let the words pass through you, Peaceful and pleasant Temperamental and raging Sweet or bitter. They are not yours, They never were. Remember that all they want Is to reach their

## January 2th

# Where Was I Last Year?

Write a text that answers the following questions: Who was I last year? Where was I physically, emotionally and mentally? What was I doing at that time? Who was the person living in my body during that year? What guided me on my life's journey?

Use writing to look back at the year that has passed, and the road you have travelled.

Start with the words **Last year...**

With the sea. Do not over flow, Do not hang on words. Learn from the river: Its only designation is To carry water

## A Childhood Dream

Think back to a childhood dream that you have abandoned. Go back to the passion that inspired and excited you as a child, and write about it.

Now write about what happened to your dream over the years, and how writing about it now makes you feel.

January 4th

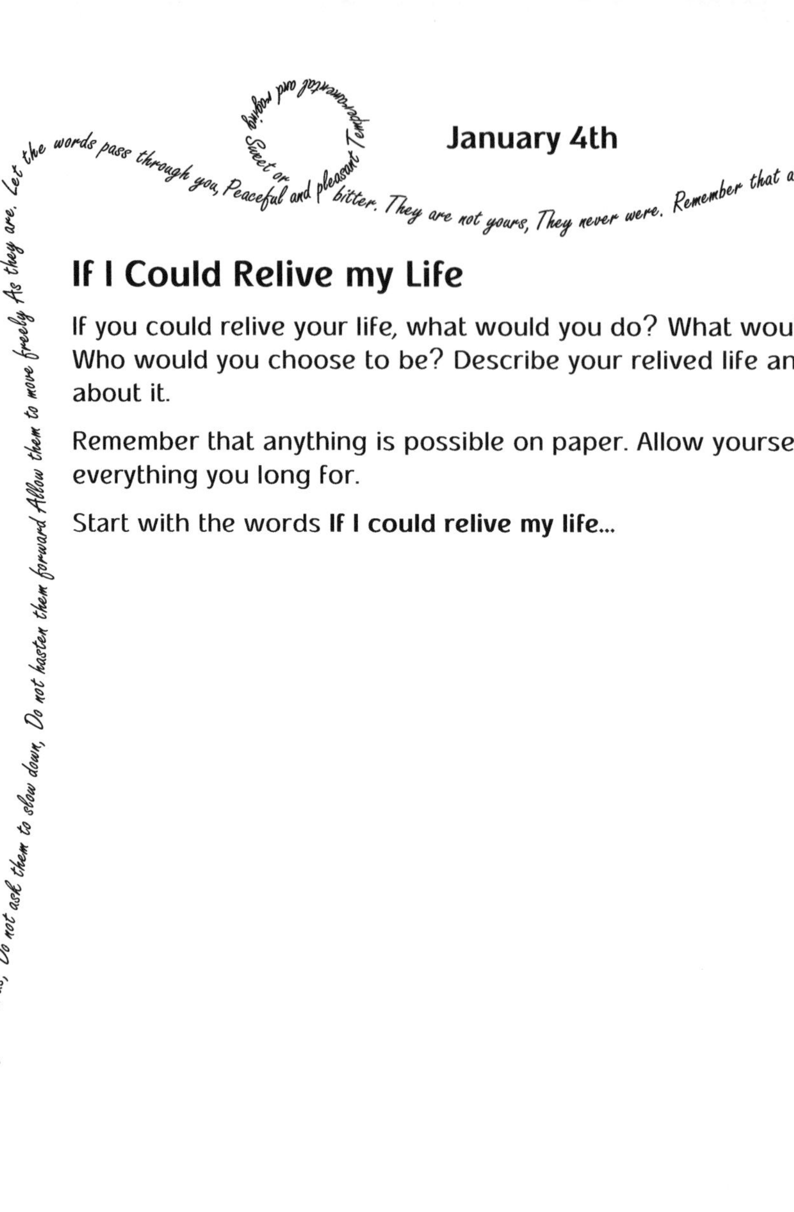
Let the words flow through you, Like the water flowing in the stream Place no dam over your words, Do not ask them to slow down, Do not hasten them forward Allow them to move freely As they are. Let the words pass through you, Peaceful and pleasant Temperamental and raging Sweet or bitter. They are not yours, They never were. Remember that all they want Is to reach their

## If I Could Relive my Life

If you could relive your life, what would you do? What would you create? Who would you choose to be? Describe your relived life and everything about it.

Remember that anything is possible on paper. Allow yourself to express everything you long for.

Start with the words **If I could relive my life...**

## January 5th

*With the sea. Do not over flow, Do not hang on words. Learn from the river: Its only designation is To carry water*

# Three Months to Live

If you were told you had only three months left to live, how would you like to live them? What would you want to leave behind? Is there someone you want to meet? Something you want to create? Write about everything that you wish to happen during the last three months of your life.

Write without fear of death. Write without fear of life.

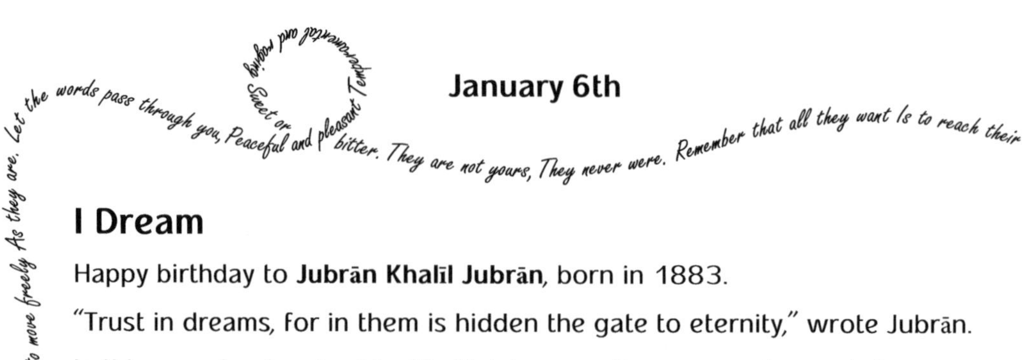
Let the words flow through you, Like the water flowing in the stream Place no dam over your words, Do not ask them to slow down, Do not hasten them forward Allow them to move freely As they are. Let the words pass through you, Peaceful and pleasant Temperamental and raging Sweet or bitter. They are not yours, They never were. Remember that all they want Is to reach their

**January 6th**

# I Dream

Happy birthday to **Jubrān Khalīl Jubrān**, born in 1883.

"Trust in dreams, for in them is hidden the gate to eternity," wrote Jubrān.

In this exercise, inspired by Khalil Jubran, write your most secret dreams. Start with the words **I dream**... and fill the page with all of your dreams and heart's desires.

## January 7th

*With the sea. Do not over flow, Do not hang on words. Learn from the river: Its only designation is To carry water*

# Inventing Words

Do you ever feel that the language available to you is lacking certain words? Take inspiration from Shakespeare in this writing exercise. In the process of writing his plays, Shakespeare invented over 1,700 new words in English.

The option of inventing words is open to you too, even if you don't think a single word is missing. Invent five to seven words and write what they represent for you. Then integrate these words to write a poem or story.

Allow yourself to play! You can return to this page and add new words any time you need one.

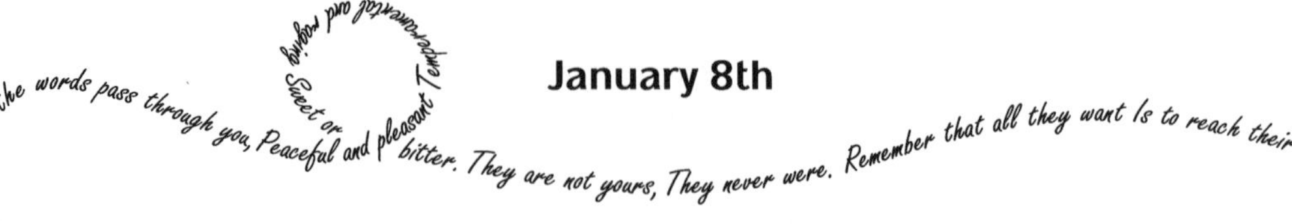
words pass through you, Peaceful and pleasant Temperamental and raging Sweet or bitter. They are not yours, They never were. Remember that all they want Is to reach their

Let the words flow through you, Like the water flowing in the stream Place no dam over your words, Do not ask them to slow down, Do not hasten them forward Allow them to move freely As they are. Let the

**January 8th**

## I Came Into the World

Write down the reason or reasons for which you came to this world. What do you think you were born and destined to do on Earth? Open yourself to curiosity and consider why you are here and why now.

Start with the words **I came into the world**... and let them lead you.

"That's what I consider true generosity: You give your all, and yet you always feel as if it costs you nothing."*

Philosopher and poet **Simone de Beauvoir**, born today in 1908.

* *All Men Are Mortal*, Virgo Press, 1946.

## January 9th

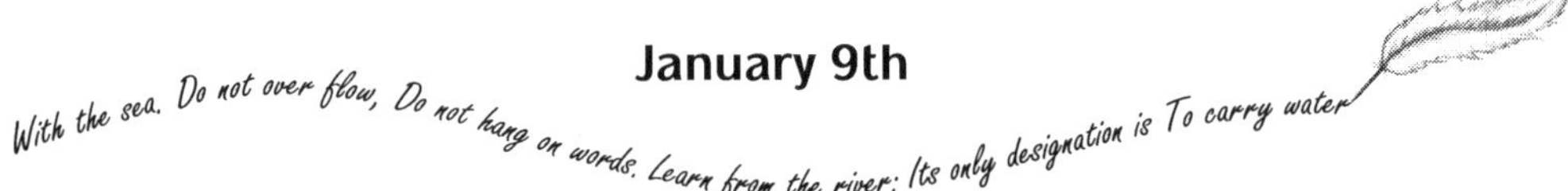
With the sea. Do not over flow, Do not hang on words. Learn from the river: Its only designation is To carry water

# What Do You Need to Make Your Dreams Come True?

Do you think your childhood home gave you everything you needed to fulfill your potential and destination in life? If you had had the perfect childhood, who would you have become? What would you have wanted to be given in order to fulfill yourself and your dreams?

Write a list of the things you needed as a child but may have not received. If you feel that you did receive exactly what you needed, write about the significant things you received that made you the person you are today.

Now hang this list somewhere you will see it often, and give yourself what you need today.

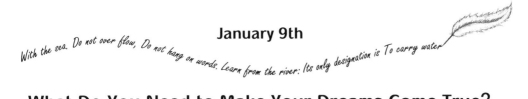

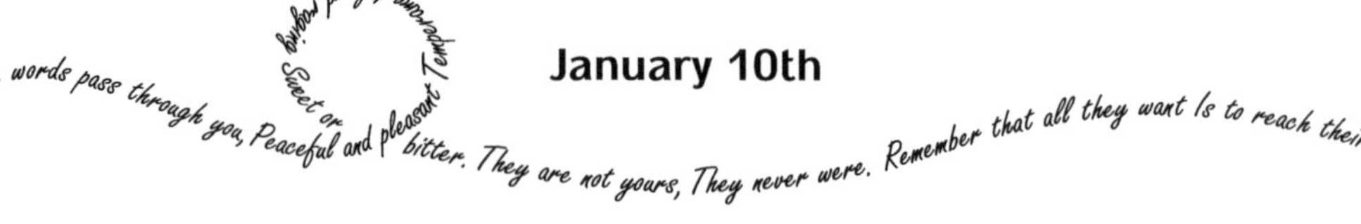
Let the words flow through you, Like the water flowing in the stream Place no dam over your words, Do not ask them to slow down, Do not hasten them forward Allow them to move freely As they are. Let the words pass through you, Peaceful and pleasant Temperamental and raging Sweet or bitter. They are not yours, They never were. Remember that all they want Is to reach their

**January 10th**

## Memories of the Future

Write your memories of the future. Time travel into the future and "copy" a page from the journal you find there inside an imaginary drawer. You can travel to any year you choose– ten or twenty years from now. What do you discover there?

Start with the words **I remember...**

## January 11th

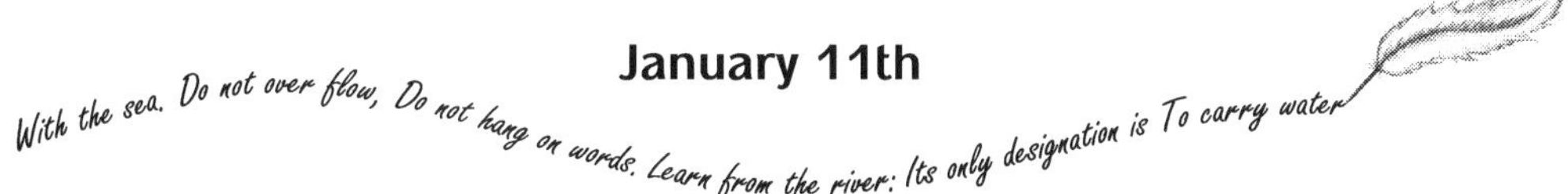
With the sea. Do not over flow, Do not hang on words. Learn from the river: Its only designation is To carry water

# When I Grow Up

What do you want to be when you grow up? Ask yourself with the fresh and curious eyes of a child. Answer the question again and again, until you have completely filled this page. This question is always relevant, no matter how old we are. Don't be afraid of finding new answers, or old ones you abandoned long ago. Don't think about what is or is not possible. Allow yourself to dream.

Start with the words **When I grow up...**

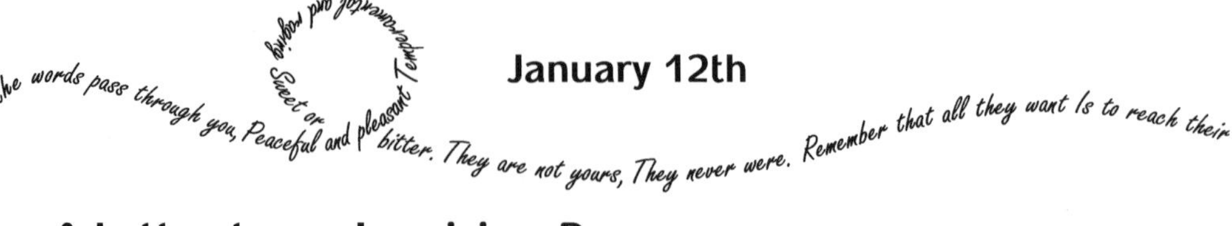

Let the words pass through you, Peaceful and pleasant Tempermental and raging Sweet or bitter. They are not yours, They never were. Remember that all they want Is to reach their

## January 12th

# A Letter to an Inspiring Person

Think of a person who inspires you, a man or a woman you look up to, and want to be like in some way. It can be a relative, someone who is no longer alive, or even a person you have never met.

What is it about this person that impresses you most? Write them a letter of appreciation telling them why they inspire you.

Let the words flow through you, Like the water flowing in the stream Place no dam over your words, Do not ask them to slow down, Do not hasten them forward Allow them to move freely As they are. Let the

*With the sea. Do not over flow, Do not hang on words. Learn from the river: Its only designation is To carry water*

## What if I Make my Dream Come True?

What does making a dream come true mean to you? Are you afraid to achieve your dream? What will happen in your life if you fulfill your heart's deepest desire? Write about that.

Quickly write a series of sentences intuitively, starting with the words **If I make my dream come true...**

## The Dream Maker

Write the monologue of a fulfilled and gratified person, someone who has attained all their dreams. Write without inhibition, without delaying, without excuses. Write as someone who recognizes their qualities, their worth and the gifts they bring to the world – someone who lives life to the fullest.

Become that person and write in their words, without embellishment. Experience how it feels to be such a person.

Start with the words **My dreams have come true...**

## January 15th



# God, Give me a Small Line of Verse

This is the birthday of Esther "Etty" Hillesum, born in 1914.

Etty Hillesum composed a personal journal* that inspiringly describes her inner life during World War II and the Holocaust.

"Give me a small line of verse from time to time, oh God," she wrote in her journal.

In this exercise inspired by Hillesum, consider: what would you like to ask your God? Allow yourself to ask for everything!

Write a text that begins with the words **God, give me...**

* *Etty Hillesum: An Interrupted Life, The Diaries, 1941–1943* and *Letters from Westerbork*, Picador, 1996.

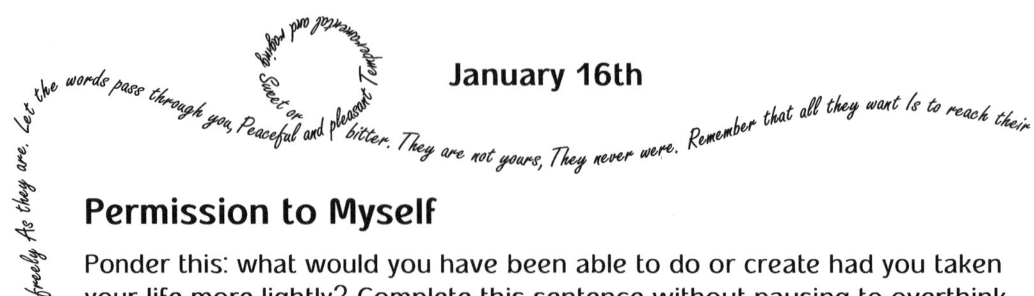
Let the words pass through you, Peaceful and pleasant Temperamental and raging Sweet or bitter. They are not yours, They never were. Remember that all they want Is to reach their
Let the words flow through you, Like the water flowing in the stream Place no dam over your words, Do not ask them to slow down, Do not hasten them forward Allow them to move freely As they are.

## January 16th

# Permission to Myself

Ponder this: what would you have been able to do or create had you taken your life more lightly? Complete this sentence without pausing to overthink it – **If I'd taken life more lightly, I would have given myself permission to...**

Consider what you have written and contemplate the possibility of introducing more lightness into your life.

## January 17th

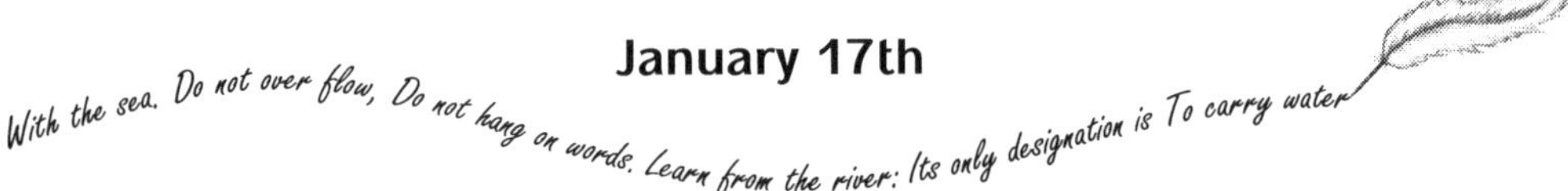
With the sea. Do not over flow, Do not hang on words. Learn from the river: Its only designation is To carry water

## Dream Catcher

Write about a dream you dreamed last night or the night before. If you can't remember your latest dreams, write about a memorable dream you had in the past, or someone else's dream that impressed you.

Write everything that you can remember from the dream: the experience, symbols, sensations, metaphors.

Your writing can be like a dream itself, without any order or logic, without limits of time or space, without a structured plot.

Be specific and describe the dream in detail. You can add to the description whatever else comes to mind - there is no limit to your imagination.

Once you are finished, turn the language of your dream into poetry. Write a poem with everything that came to you in the dream.

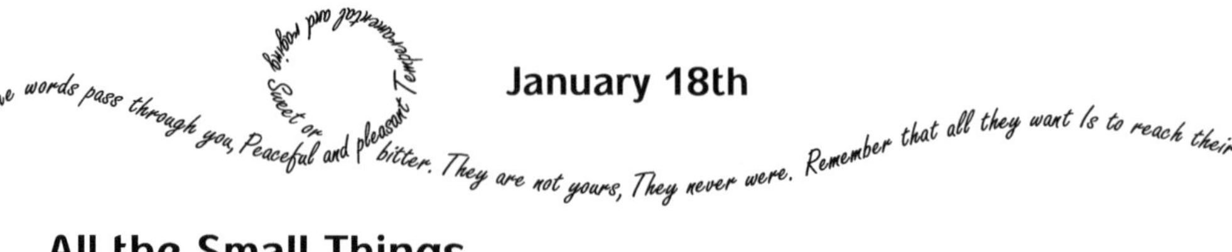
Let the words flow through you, Like the water flowing in the stream Place no dam over your words, Do not ask them to slow down, Do not hasten them forward Allow them to move freely As they are.
Let the words pass through you, Peaceful and pleasant Temperamental and raging Sweet or bitter. They are not yours, They never were. Remember that all they want Is to reach their

**January 18th**

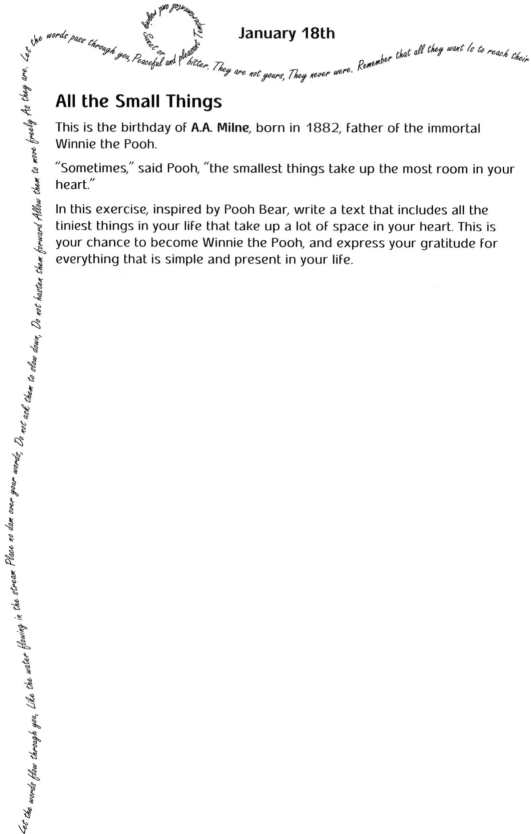

## All the Small Things

This is the birthday of **A.A. Milne**, born in 1882, father of the immortal Winnie the Pooh.

"Sometimes," said Pooh, "the smallest things take up the most room in your heart."

In this exercise, inspired by Pooh Bear, write a text that includes all the tiniest things in your life that take up a lot of space in your heart. This is your chance to become Winnie the Pooh, and express your gratitude for everything that is simple and present in your life.

# January 19th



## Self Portrait

Select a photograph of yourself that you love, or one that you feel expresses who you are. (It can be a photograph from your childhood.) Look at this photo and write a text that is a self-portrait, outlining your character.

Begin by observing your eyes, and then go on to look at the whole image. Delve into yourself. Write words that rise from within and describe the image before you. Start with specifics, such as features and colors, and gradually allow yourself to discover new depths. Write the associations and sensations that the photograph awakens in you. Look with fresh eyes at who you were when the photo was taken. **Who do you really see in the photograph?**

Let the words flow through you, Like the water flowing in the stream Place no dam over your words, Do not ask them to slow down, Do not hasten them forward Allow them to move freely As they are.

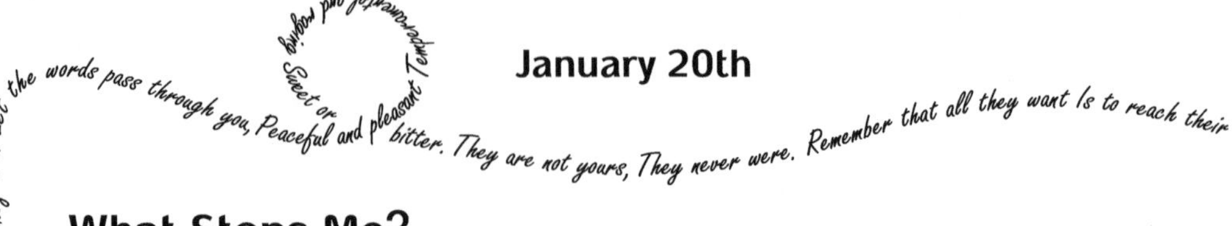
Let the words pass through you, Peaceful and pleasant Temperamental and raging Sweet or bitter. They are not yours, They never were. Remember that all they want Is to reach their

January 20th

## What Stops Me?

Write everything that stops you. Detail all the inhibitions and reservations you feel in respect to different parts of your life and the people in it. Write intuitively everything that comes to you from within.

Ask yourself over and over again: **What stops me**?

*With the sea. Do not over flow, Do not hang on words. Learn from the river: Its only designation is To carry water*

## What is My Real Name?

Does your first name express who you are? In the Aboriginal culture, it is customary for people to change their names throughout their lives. The names they give themselves express their character and uniqueness, or the gift they bring to the world. Their first name expresses who they are simply and accurately.

Close your eyes and connect to your real name, which resides deep inside you – a name that represents you, your qualities, your virtues and values. When the name comes to you, write it down and describe what it represents in your life.

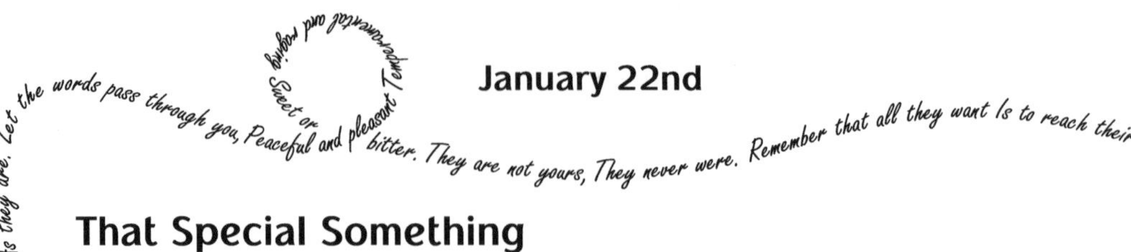
Let the words flow through you, Like the water flowing in the stream Place no dam over your words, Do not ask them to slow down, Do not hasten them forward Allow them to move freely As they are.
Let the words pass through you, Peaceful and pleasant Temperamental and raging Sweet or bitter. They are not yours, They never were. Remember that all they want Is to reach their

## January 22nd

# That Special Something

Write a list of all the meaningful compliments you have ever received and encouragement you remember ever being given. It may be overwhelming, but don't hold back. Write it all and accept it all.

Do you recognize aspects that repeat themselves? Do you sense that the people looking at you from outside see something that you find difficult to see in yourself? Accept the "you" described in these words.

Now write yourself a text or a poem composed of all the compliments you have ever received. Start the text with the compliment you love most. You are special! Own it.

## The Perfect Day

Imagine how a perfect day in your life would look – the best day ever.

Sail away in your imagination, without obstacles or inhibitions, to any time and place you choose, where you can do anything your heart desires.

What would that day be like?

When you finish writing, choose one small thing from your perfect day and make it part of your life today!

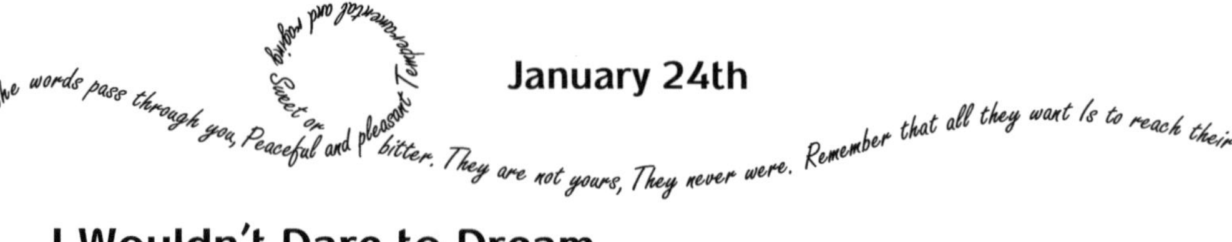
Let the words flow through you, Like the water flowing in the stream Place no dam over your words, Do not ask them to slow down, Do not hasten them forward Allow them to move freely As they are. Let the words pass through you, Peaceful and pleasant Temperamental and raging Sweet or bitter. They are not yours, They never were. Remember that all they want Is to reach their

January 24th

# I Wouldn't Dare to Dream

Write all the things you wouldn't dare dream about in life. Do not hesitate!

Write the longest possible list and describe every sensation that comes to you as you write.

Start with the words **I would never dare dream about...**

## A Room of my Own

This is the birthday of author and poet **Virginia Woolf**, born in 1882.

Thanks to her clear profound writing, a door opened for women all over the world into a room of their own.

This is an exercise inspired by her book *A Room of One's Own*. Write your entry into "a room of your own" and describe it in your own words. Write what it looks like, where it is located, what is in it, what it is made of, and what view is revealed outside its windows.

Start with the words **My room...**

"So long as you write what you wish to write, that is all that matters..." **Virginia Woolf**
*A Room of One's Own*, Hogarth Press, 1929, p.105.

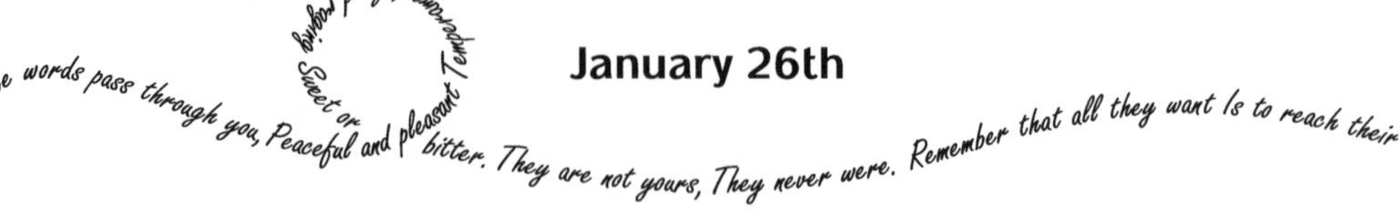
Let the words flow through you, Like the water flowing in the stream Place no dam over your words, Do not ask them to slow down, Do not hasten them forward Allow them to move freely As they are. Let the words pass through you, Peaceful and pleasant Temperamental and raging Sweet or bitter. They are not yours, They never were. Remember that all they want Is to reach their

**January 26th**

## Yesterday's Dreams

Do you remember a moment in your life where you fulfilled a dream against all odds? Think back to that moment and write about it. What does it feel like when you realize a dream? What qualities in you are required now to make an old dream come true?

# January 27th

## Down the Rabbit Hole

This is the birthday of **Lewis Carroll**, the creator of *Alice in Wonderland*, who was born in 1832.

This exercise, inspired by his famous book, is called "Down the Rabbit Hole."

Every day, we have many opportunities to go down the rabbit hole.

How much are we truly prepared to stray from the path we are taking, to make mistakes, to taste and experience, to grow and shrink? How much are we prepared to give up our old, familiar reality for the experience of a new adventure?

Are we willing to walk on a road that we have never walked before? To meet our "Wonderland"?

Go outside with pen and paper, and start walking, observing, as you go, everything that is happening, until something grabs your attention. It can be a feeling, an animal, a voice from afar, a magnificent sight, a fragrance...

From this moment on, just as Alice pursued the White Rabbit, start following whatever has caught your attention. Follow it in writing, without knowing where you are going or how you will get back.

Devote yourself to this pursuit, be curious, leave your comfort zone, don't hold back – and write it.

Let the words flow through you, Like the water flowing in the stream Place no dam over your words, Do not ask them to slow down, Do not hasten them forward Allow them to move freely As they are.

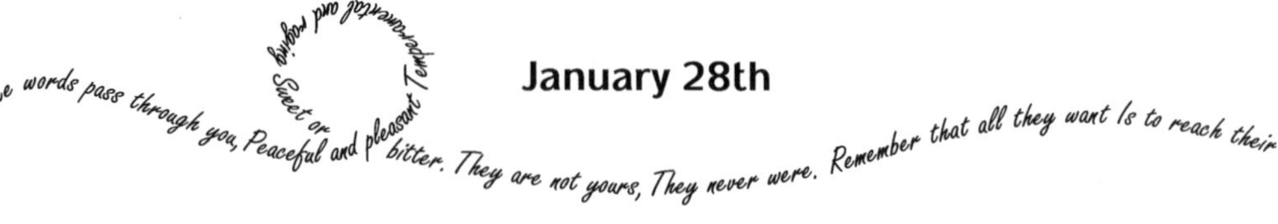
Let the words pass through you, Peaceful and pleasant Temperamental and raging Sweet or bitter. They are not yours, They never were. Remember that all they want Is to reach their

**January 28th**

## Who am I?

This is an exercise inspired by the Caterpillar in *Alice in Wonderland*. Write a text that answers the question **Who am I?**

Write everything that comes to you from within when you hear that question, but always **not** knowing who you are. Write freely without stopping or trying to control the answers. Discover through your writing who you are now, at this very minute.

Let go of everything you know about yourself, and put aside who you were, even a moment ago. Be curious and make room for new answers to the immortal question **Who am I, really?**

"Be yourself; everyone else is already taken." **Oscar Wilde**

With the sea. Do not over flow, Do not hang on words. Learn from the river: Its only designation is To carry water

## I am Not

Write a text that starts with the words **I am not**...

Acknowledge everything that you are not, at this moment in time.

You do not love. You do not want. You are unlike one or another person. This is an opportunity for you to write your "not" and give it space. When you have finished, observe how everything that you are not makes you feel.

Can you investigate the possibility of creating a connection or building a bridge from your soul to everything you are not? How do you feel about that?

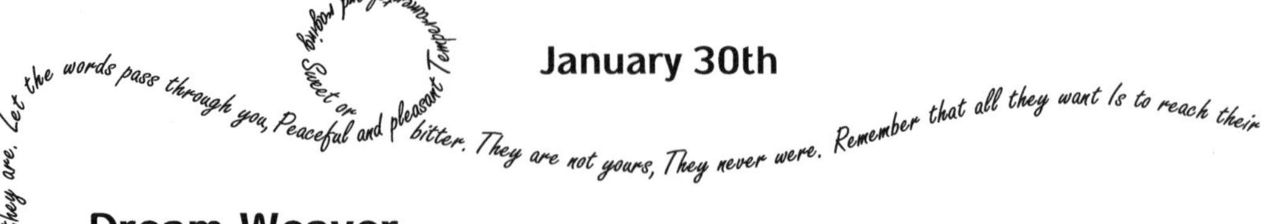
Let the words flow through you, Like the water flowing in the stream Place no dam over your words, Do not ask them to slow down, Do not hasten them forward Allow them to move freely As they are. Let the words pass through you, Peaceful and pleasant Temperamental and raging Sweet or bitter. They are not yours, They never were. Remember that all they want Is to reach their

**January 30th**

## Dream Weaver

If you were a dream weaver who could weave any dream of any shape or color, how would you weave your dreams? The entire world? Go wild on paper, as if it were a gigantic canvas. Weave, draw or write your dreams. All materials and colors known to man are at your disposal.

## God's Words

God speaks in poetry.

When you are writing, God's hand occasionally touches you.

God speaks to you through those words, through your writing.

What is He whispering in your ear? Write His words.

Write the words you would be happy to hear and would fill your heart with hope and joy.

# February

## Writing to Tell

Let the words flow through you, Like the water flowing in the stream Place no dam over your words, Do not ask them to slow down, Do not hasten them forward Allow them to move freely As they are. Let the words pass through you, Peaceful and pleasant Temperamental and raging Sweet or bitter. They are not yours, They never were. Remember that all they want Is to reach their

## What is My Story?

Every person is a walking archive of stories. Everyone has a large reserve of stories that they take with them wherever they go. Write a text that starts with the words **My story is...**

Return to that opening phrase again and again, and discover another of your stories, living and breathing within you.

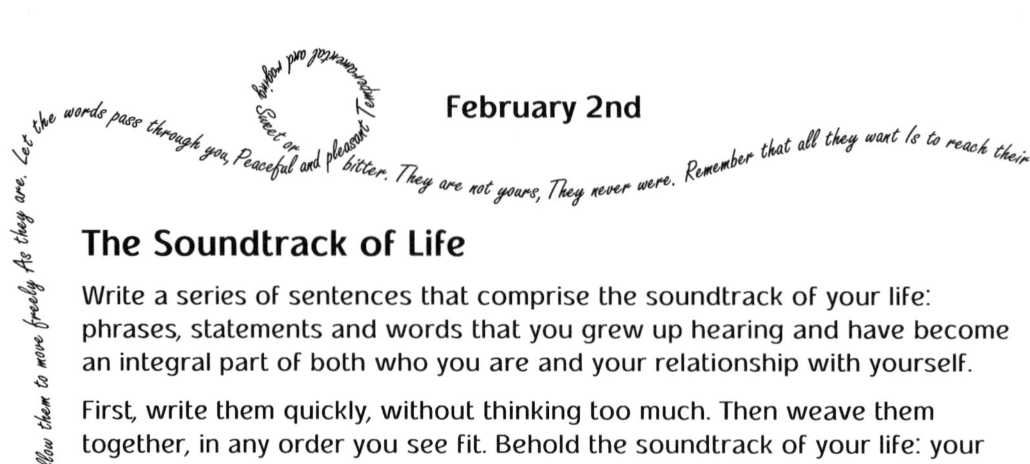


## February 2nd

# The Soundtrack of Life

Write a series of sentences that comprise the soundtrack of your life: phrases, statements and words that you grew up hearing and have become an integral part of both who you are and your relationship with yourself.

First, write them quickly, without thinking too much. Then weave them together, in any order you see fit. Behold the soundtrack of your life: your opinions, your stories, your beliefs.

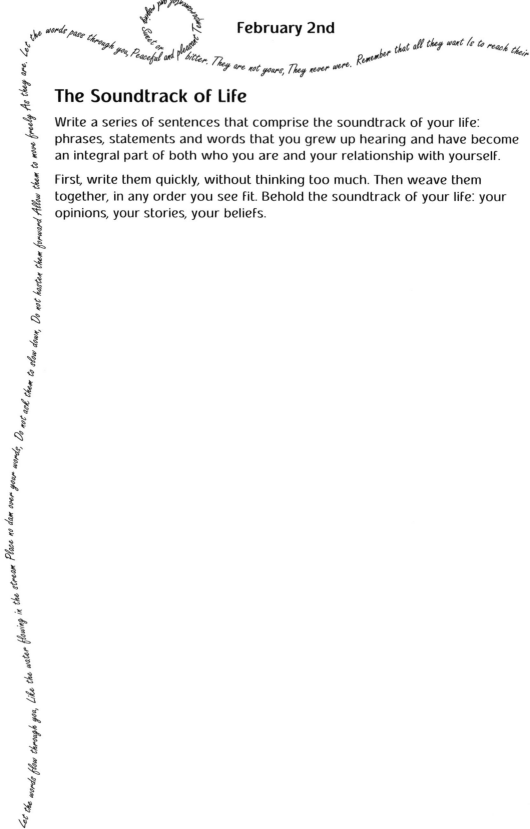

## February 3rd

With the sea. Do not over flow, Do not hang on words. Learn from the river: Its only designation is To carry water

# Why Do I Write?

Happy birthday to author **Paul Auster**, born in 1947.

This is an exercise inspired by his book of autobiographical essays *Why Write?**

Why do you write actually? Why would you write at all? Do you love writing? Are you happy to write?

Share the reasons you write, and describe what writing gives you.

* Burning Deck Books, 1996.

"To leave the world a little better than you found it. That's the best a man can ever do."
**Paul Auster**. *Timbuktu: A Novel*, Henry Holt & Company, 2010, p.59.

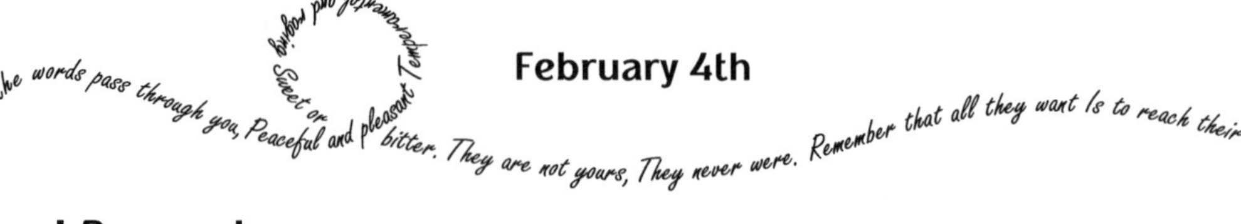
Let the words flow through you, Like the water flowing in the stream Place no dam over your words, Do not ask them to slow down, Do not hasten them forward Allow them to move freely As they are. Let the words pass through you, Peaceful and pleasant Temperamental and raging Sweet or bitter. They are not yours, They never were. Remember that all they want Is to reach their

## February 4th

# I Remember

Write a text that starts with the words **I remember**. Write any memory that comes to you right now, from yesterday, last year or your childhood. Small memories or big, important or insignificant. Simply devote yourself to the memories and everything that cries out to be expressed on paper at this moment.

Let the words **I remember** take you for a short trip down memory lane.

## When I Decided not to Forget

Write a text that starts with the words **When I decided not to forget...**

Every time you complete a section, or don't know what else to write, repeat these words.

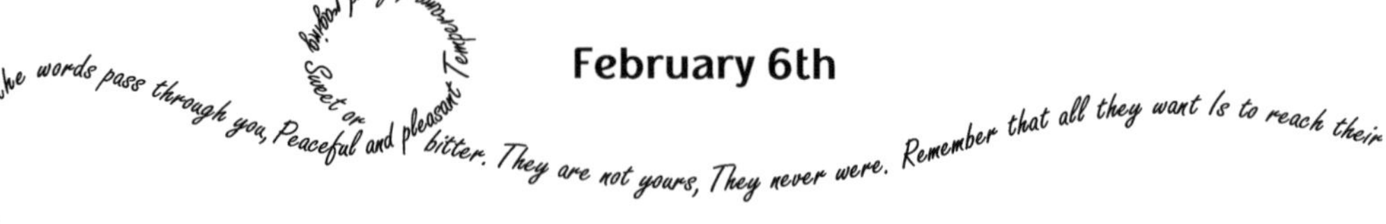
Let the words flow through you, Like the water flowing in the stream Place no dam over your words, Do not ask them to slow down, Do not hasten them forward Allow them to move freely As they are. Let the words pass through you, Peaceful and pleasant Temperamental and raging Sweet or bitter. They are not yours, They never were. Remember that all they want Is to reach their

## February 6th

# I Met a Smart Person Who Told Me

Write a story that begins with these words. Be intuitive and write without pausing. Do not attempt to **understand** what this person told you. Simply write everything that comes to your mind.

# February 7th

## Good Days, Bad Days

This is the birthday of author **Charles Dickens**, born in 1812.

"It was the best of times; it was the worst of times." This sentence opens his novel, *A Tale of Two Cities.*

This is an exercise inspired by Dickens. Was there a time that was simultaneously both bad and good for you? Write your own text starting with Dickens' line.

Let the words flow through you, Like the water flowing in the stream Place no dam over your words, Do not ask them to slow down, Do not hasten them forward Allow them to move freely As they are.

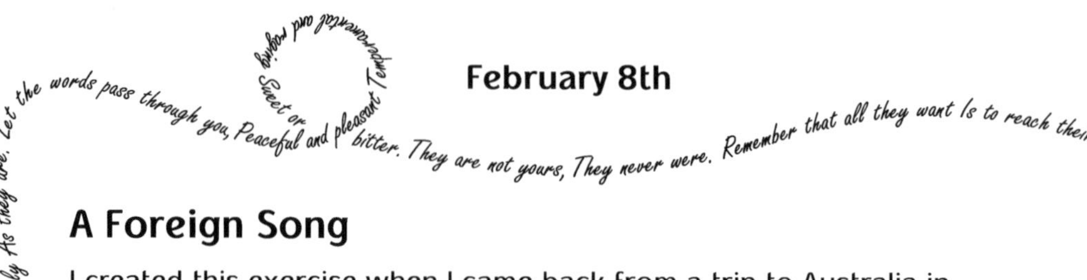
Let the words pass through you, Peaceful and pleasant Temperamental and raging Sweet or bitter. They are not yours, They never were. Remember that all they want Is to reach their

## February 8th

# A Foreign Song

I created this exercise when I came back from a trip to Australia in possession of wonderful Aboriginal music. As I did not understand the language at all, I invented "translations" to the songs I was listening to. Later, I fell in love with the idea and began searching the Internet for songs in foreign languages, such as Maori, Chinese, Japanese, and then writing my own lyrics to their music.

I invite you to have the pleasure of doing the same. Choose a song in a foreign language. As you listen to it, begin transcribing it in real time. Imagine that you know the language well; connect to the music, and become a channel through which the words are freely transformed from the foreign language into English. It is a unique experience.

When you have finished, close your eyes and make up a title for the song.

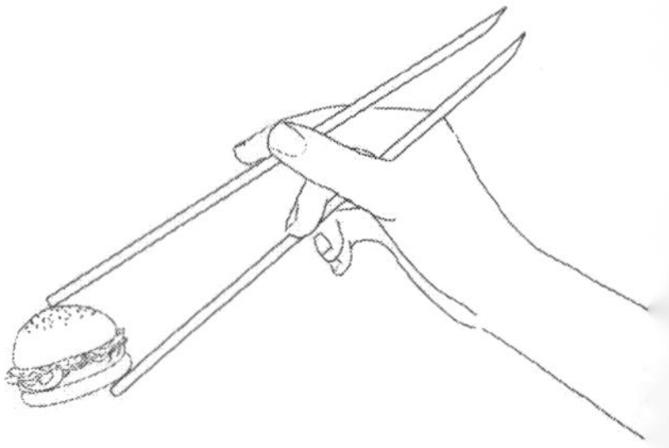

# February 9th

## Autobiography

Choose the person you would like to write the story of your life. Someone who knows you very well, who looks at you with kindness and appreciates the path you are taking in life.

Now imagine this person handing you a one-page summary of the story of your life, written from his or her point of view.

Now, write down what was inscribed on the imaginary page presented to you.

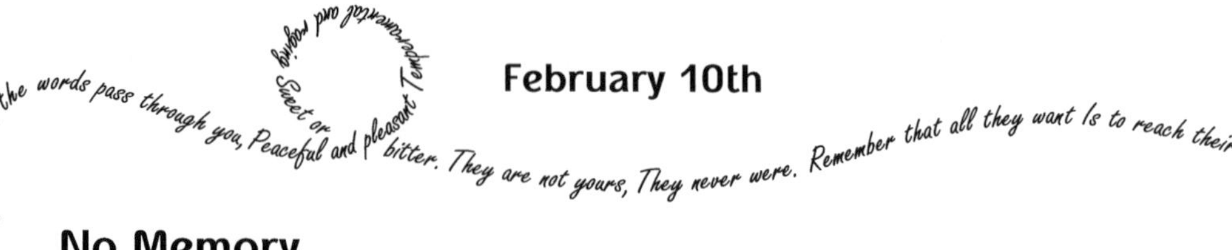
Let the words pass through you, Peaceful and pleasant Temperamental and raging Sweet or bitter. They are not yours, They never were. Remember that all they want Is to reach their
Let the words flow through you, Like the water flowing in the stream Place no dam over your words, Do not ask them to slow down, Do not hasten them forward Allow them to move freely As they are. Let the

## February 10th

# No Memory

Write a text that begins with the words **I do not remember**, and record things that you truly cannot remember, events that you do not remember happening and/or events that have never happened. Write the words **I can't remember** over and over again, and complete the sentences.

Then, choose one of the things you don't remember and describe it in detail, **as if you really do remember it.** Write it as an event out of your memory and give it new life. You can invent anything – imagine smells, sounds and sights. You can describe facial features, detail sentences spoken. Whatever you want.

## February 11th

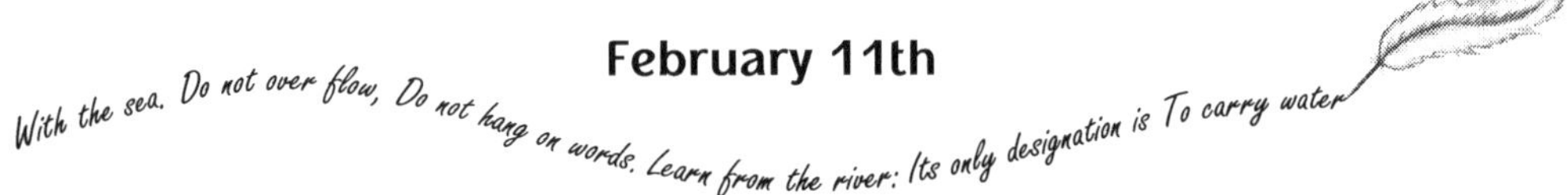
With the sea. Do not over flow, Do not hang on words. Learn from the river: Its only designation is To carry water

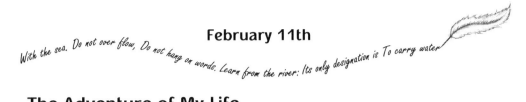

# The Adventure of My Life

Write the word **adventure**. Do you connect to it? How does it make you feel?

Do you experience your life as an adventure? How adventurous do you allow yourself to be? Were you adventurous in the past? Would you like to live in an adventure?

Explore everything this word arouses in you and write it down.

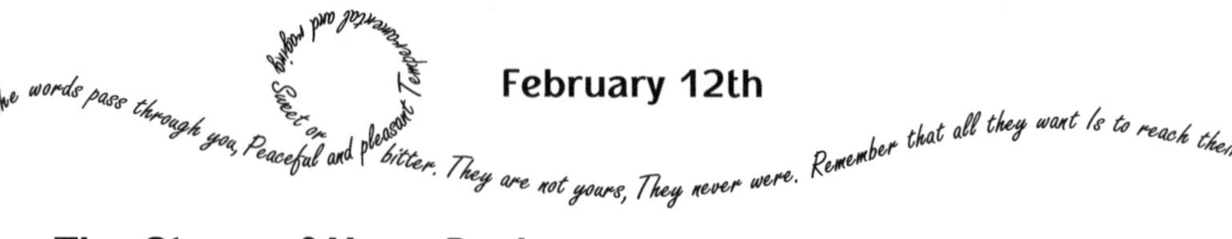
Let the words flow through you, Like the water flowing in the stream Place no dam over your words, Do not ask them to slow down, Do not hasten them forward Allow them to move freely As they are. Let the words pass through you, Peaceful and pleasant Temperamental and raging Sweet or bitter. They are not yours, They never were. Remember that all they want Is to reach their

## February 12th

# The Story of Your Body

Close your eyes for a few moments and scan your body from top to bottom. Linger in the areas where you feel uncomfortable, or where a certain part of your body signals you that it needs attention. During these moments of rest, breathe into that part of your body and "expand" it within you. Feel its texture, its color and its shape. Focus all your attention on it. It has its own language, words, history and maybe even a story to tell you.

When you feel ready, take a pen and let your body speak to you through your words. Write its monologue. Let it tell you why it is hurting, what it needs and what it is missing. Listen to it.

At the end, close your eyes and remain attentive. Is there anything you would like to tell your body?

With the sea. Do not over flow, Do not hang on words. Learn from the river: Its only designation is To carry water

## I Want to Tell You

Write a text that starts with the words **I want to tell you...**

Address your writing to a person you wish to tell something to, from the heart.

What would you want to tell? Who would you be happy to tell it to?

You can really say it here and now.

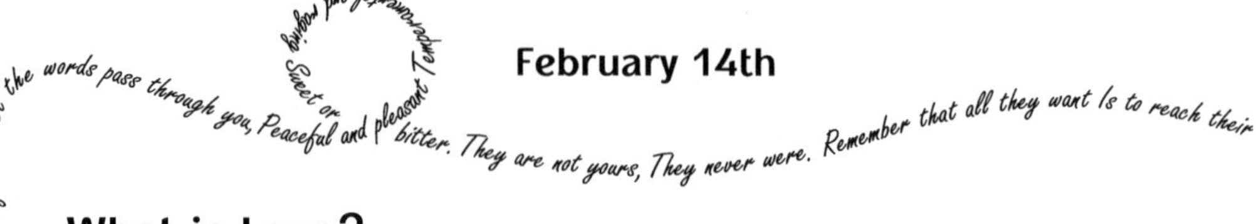
Let the words flow through you, Like the water flowing in the stream Place no dam over your words, Do not ask them to slow down, Do not hasten them forward Allow them to move freely As they are. Let the words pass through you, Peaceful and pleasant Temperamental and raging Sweet or bitter. They are not yours, They never were. Remember that all they want Is to reach their

**February 14th**

## What is Love?

This is an exercise for Valentine's Day. Philosophers, poets and authors write about love endlessly, and yet it is impossible not to continue writing about it. In honor of this day, write a text that describes the experience of love for you. What is love? What does it ask of you? What does it give you?

*With the sea. Do not over flow, Do not hang on words. Learn from the river: Its only designation is To carry water*

## The Story of My Life

Write a short, one-page version of the story of your life.

This is an opportunity to express the story of your life clearly and concisely. Begin. Experiment. Write.

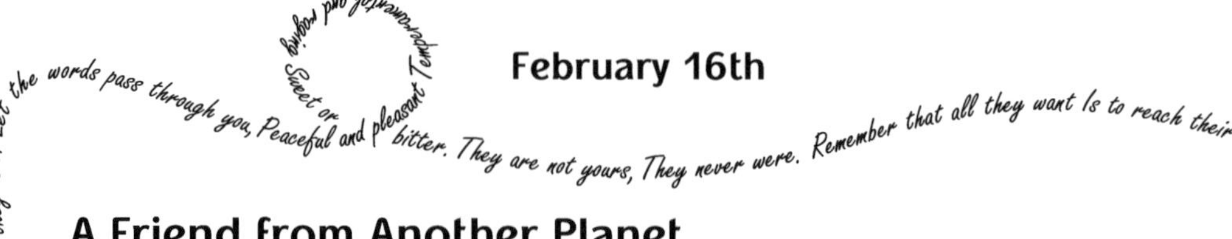
Let the words flow through you, Like the water flowing in the stream Place no dam over your words, Do not ask them to slow down, Do not hasten them forward Allow them to move freely As they are. Let the words pass through you, Peaceful and pleasant Temperamental and raging Sweet or bitter. They are not yours, They never were. Remember that all they want Is to reach their

**February 16th**

## A Friend from Another Planet

Imagine a curious alien from another planet suddenly lands for a visit in your home. It takes its time to look around your house, at the people living in it, your environment and your way of life. Then it sends a report to its friends describing the life of human beings here on earth.

Write its report. Let yourself observe your life through its alien eyes.

*With the sea. Do not over flow, Do not hang on words. Learn from the river: Its only designation is To carry water*

## A New Perspective

The way we tell the story of our life and our point of view in telling it are very significant. Since we are the authors of our lives, we can tell our story any way we choose. Occasionally it is good to distance ourselves from the story we know, to get a new perspective.

Think of a childhood memory (something simple and not very dramatic) that involved you and other people. First, write it from your point of view, and then write from the point of view of someone else who was present at the time.

Reflect on the similarities and the differences between the stories.

**February 18th**

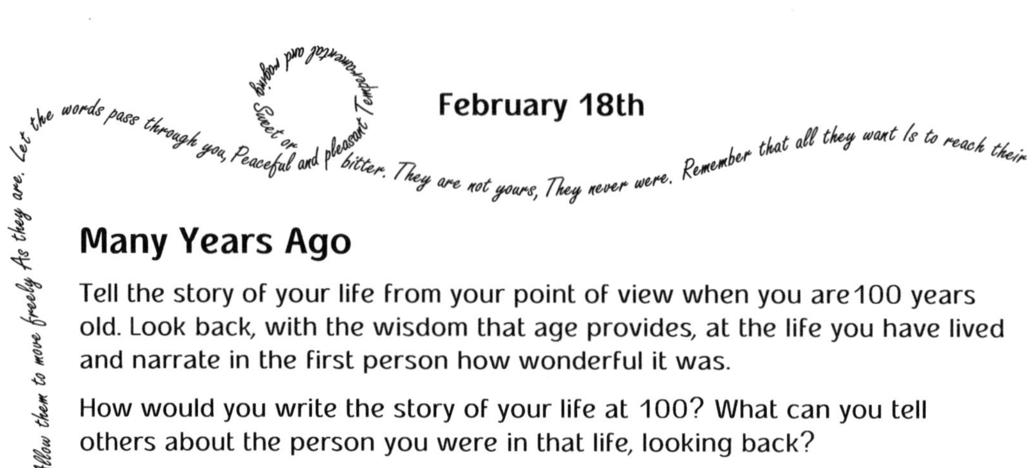
Let the words flow through you, Like the water flowing in the stream Place no dam over your words, Do not ask them to slow down, Do not hasten them forward Allow them to move freely As they are. Let the words pass through you, Peaceful and pleasant Temperamental and raging Sweet or bitter. They are not yours, They never were. Remember that all they want Is to reach their

## Many Years Ago

Tell the story of your life from your point of view when you are 100 years old. Look back, with the wisdom that age provides, at the life you have lived and narrate in the first person how wonderful it was.

How would you write the story of your life at 100? What can you tell others about the person you were in that life, looking back?

With the sea. Do not over flow, Do not hang on words. Learn from the river: Its only designation is To carry water

## Make Every Story Interesting

Think of something about yourself that is not very important, something that you would not put any effort into telling, something absolutely meaningless. Now, write it in the most fascinating or amusing manner you can, in any genre you choose: comedy, thriller, horror, documentary, romance or any other genre that comes to mind.

Turn your boring detail into a captivating and unique story, as if it were the most important detail in the story of your life.

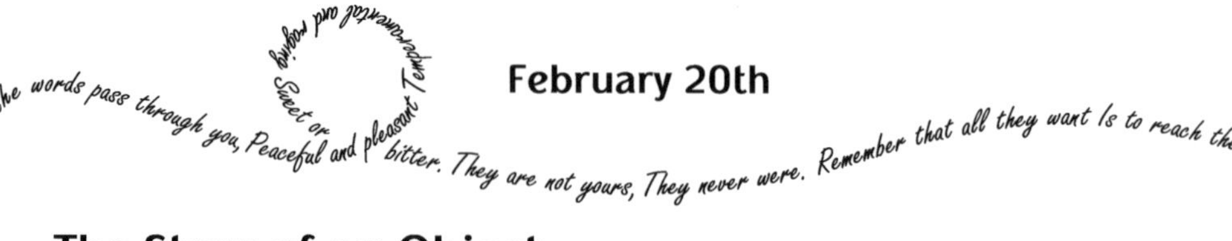
Let the words flow through you, Like the water flowing in the stream Place no dam over your words, Do not ask them to slow down, Do not hasten them forward Allow them to move freely As they are.
Let the words pass through you, Peaceful and pleasant Temperamental and raging Sweet or bitter. They are not yours, They never were. Remember that all they want Is to reach their

**February 20th**

## The Story of an Object

Open a drawer or closet in your home, and take out an object that is significant to you and has been with you for many years. Place it in front of you.

Look at it carefully for a few minutes. Then begin to describe it. Write about its appearance, what it is made of, what it signifies, how it serves you.

Slowly and gradually write its story. Where did it come from? What is its purpose? What is its history? And what memories and sensations does it awaken in you?

When you are done, consider whether there is a connection between the story of the object and the story of your life. Write about it.

*With the sea. Do not over flow, Do not hang on words. Learn from the river: Its only designation is To carry water*

## The Story of Your Name

Write the story of your first name. Who gave it to you and why? What does it mean? Do you feel any connection to it? Or perhaps you have a nickname you love more?

Tell the story of your name as creatively as you can.

If you don't know the origin of your name or who gave it to you, try to find out or simply make up a story about it.

Let the words pass through you, Peaceful and pleasant Temperamental and raging Sweet or bitter. They are not yours, They never were. Remember that all they want Is to reach their

February 22nd

## The Telling Tree

Sit beside a tree somewhere out in a park, or in your own yard. Rest quietly in its shade and be present for a while. Do nothing.

Let the tree tell you a story. Come to the tree as a blank page, clean and open. Let the tree "write" its words on your page. Listen to its ancient wisdom. Learn everything that it has to teach you. Be prepared to devote yourself to it and be the conduit that communicates everything it has to gift you.

# February 23rd

*With the sea. Do not over flow, Do not hang on words. Learn from the river: Its only designation is To carry water*

## Suddenly

Do you remember a significant turning point in your life? Describe it.

Start with the word S**uddenly,** and let it lead you to a turning point.

If you don't remember, use your imagination and write a text that begins with **Suddenly**... Let the story reveal itself.

February 24th

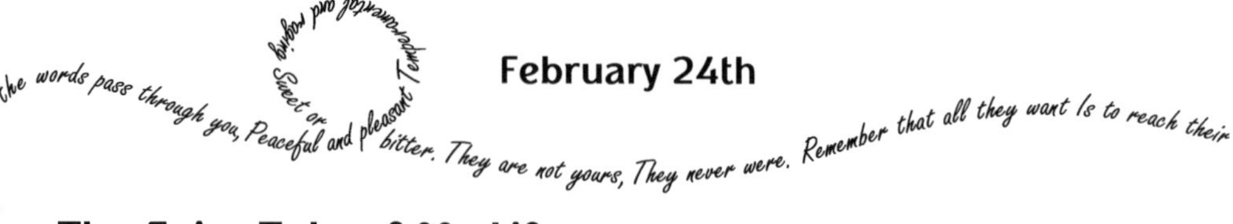
Let the words flow through you, Like the water flowing in the stream Place no dam over your words, Do not ask them to slow down, Do not hasten them forward Allow them to move freely As they are. Let the words pass through you, Peaceful and pleasant Temperamental and raging Sweet or bitter. They are not yours, They never were. Remember that all they want Is to reach their

## The Fairy Tale of My Life

Cinderella, Little Red Riding Hood, or Aladdin? Choose a fairytale character that you felt connected to as a child, adolescent or adult. First, write as many details as you can about the character. Then write their story in the first person, as if they were you, from your point of view and the events of your life. Let yourself mix your life story with theirs.

# February 25th

## A Fairytale Letter

Select a fairytale character who has influenced your life. Now imagine that this character sends you a letter that reveals the essence of their wisdom, together with messages and suggestions, especially for you.

Open the letter and copy it here, word for word.

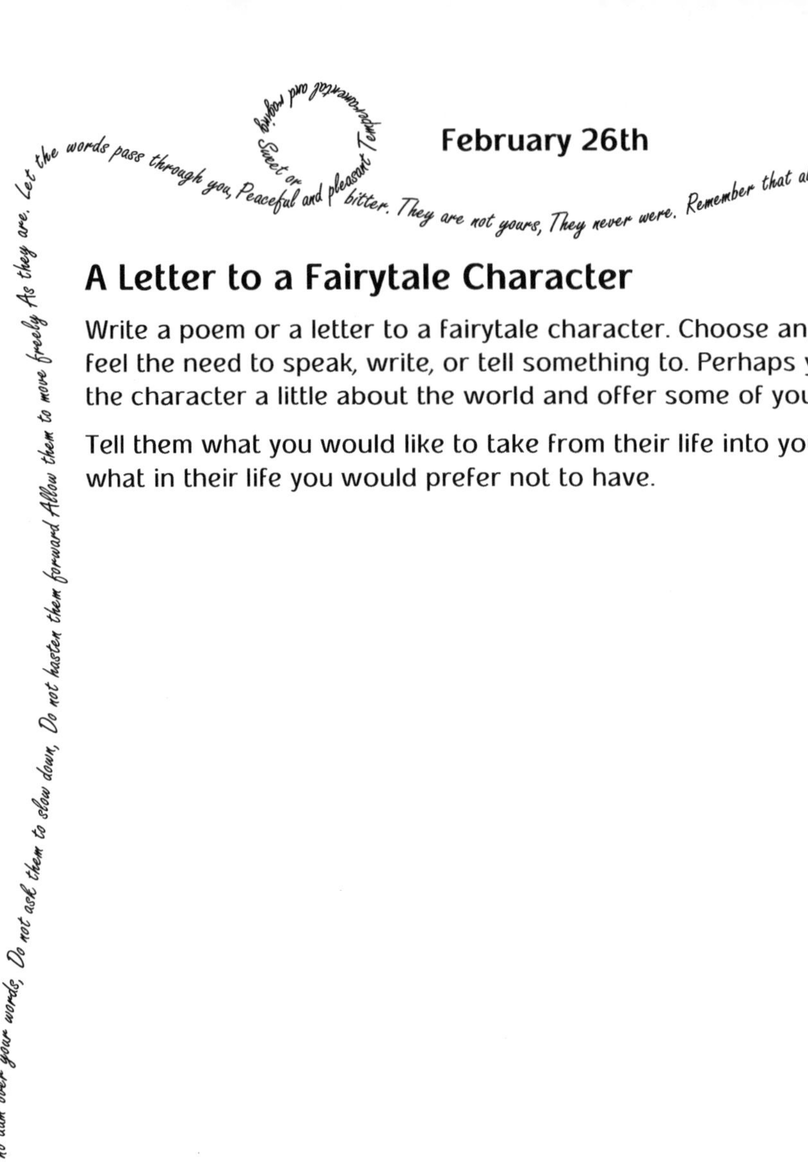
Let the words pass through you, Peaceful and pleasant Temperamental and raging Sweet or bitter. They are not yours, They never were. Remember that all they want Is to reach their
Let the words flow through you, Like the water flowing in the stream Place no dam over your words, Do not ask them to slow down, Do not hasten them forward Allow them to move freely As they are.

## February 26th

# A Letter to a Fairytale Character

Write a poem or a letter to a fairytale character. Choose any character you feel the need to speak, write, or tell something to. Perhaps you want to tell the character a little about the world and offer some of your wisdom.

Tell them what you would like to take from their life into your own, and what in their life you would prefer not to have.

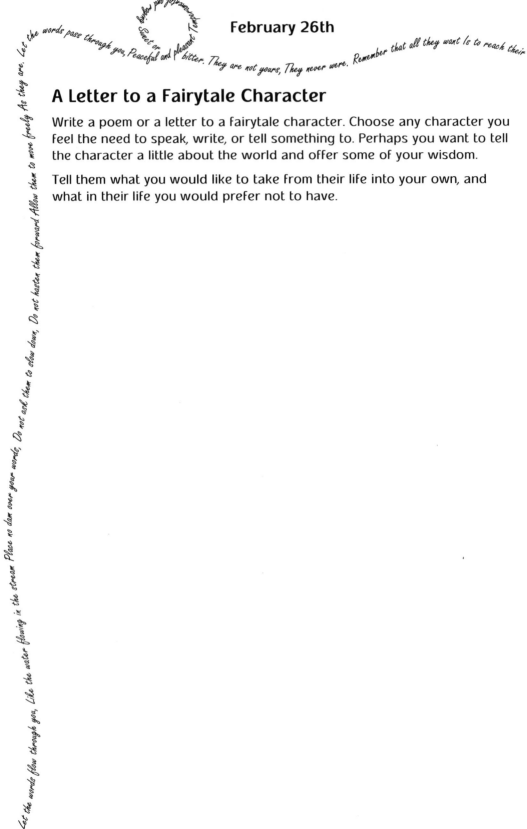

## February 27th

With the sea. Do not over flow, Do not hang on words. Learn from the river: Its only designation is To carry water

# A Hero's Tale

Every one of us has a heroic tale about something we have done, an obstacle we have overcome, a barrier we have crossed, a story that reveals our strengths, and reminds us who we truly are.

In this exercise, choose one tale of courage from your collection of anecdotes and write it down.

If you cannot remember a story of your bravery, invent one.

**February 28th**

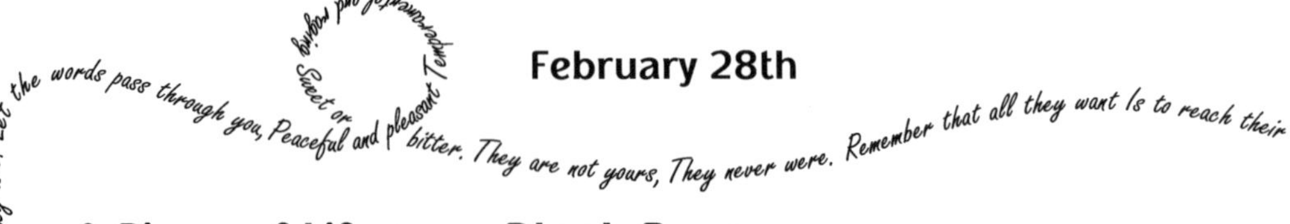
Let the words flow through you, Like the water flowing in the stream Place no dam over your words, Do not ask them to slow down, Do not hasten them forward Allow them to move freely As they are. Let the words pass through you, Peaceful and pleasant Temperamental and raging Sweet or bitter. They are not yours, They never were. Remember that all they want Is to reach their

## A Piece of Life on a Blank Page

Write something you don't usually talk or write about on the blank page below.

Write simply and openly, with no criticism or censorship, directly and authentically. Inscribe a piece of your life on paper.

## February 29th

*With the sea. Do not over flow, Do not hang on words. Learn from the river: Its only designation is To carry water*

## Happily Ever After

Write a story or a poem or any other text that starts or ends with the words above.

Where do these words take you? What does **Happily Ever After** awaken in you?

# Spring

## Writing to Be Free

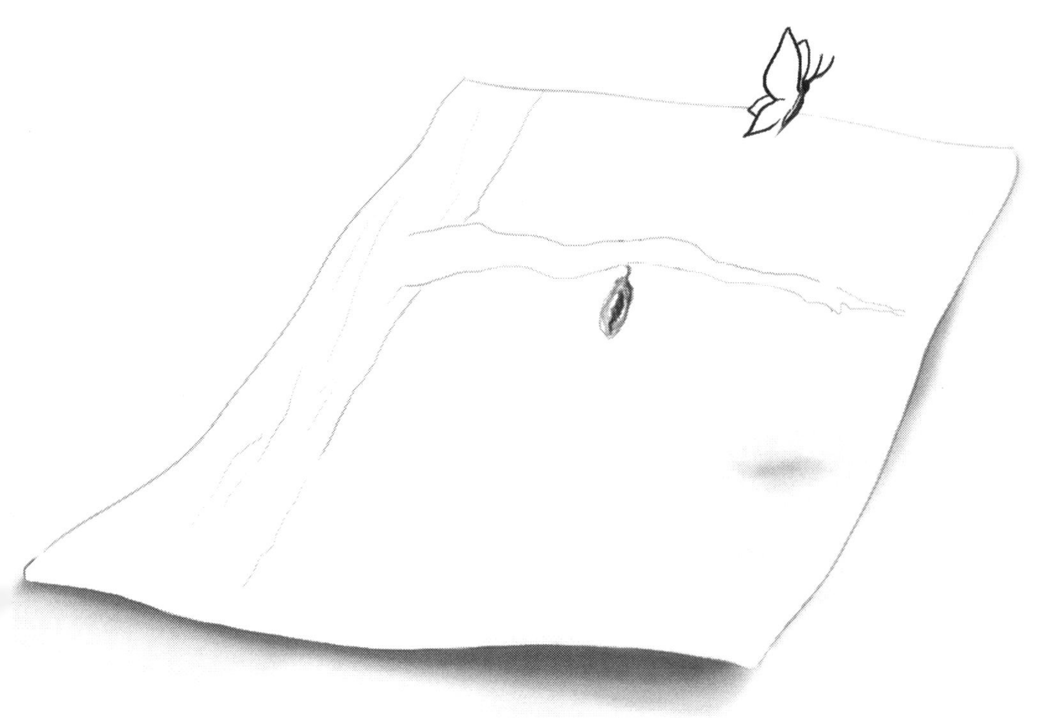

## Writing in Spring

In the spring, buds herald a prelude to full blooming. It is the season of rebirth. At this time, the changes in nature envelop us with the potency of colors, fragrances and sounds. The transformations are so obvious they cannot be ignored.

These changes are an integral part of the laws of nature, and they also take place within us. During this season, the change we sowed in the fall breaks the surface, and after all the internal work of winter, we can suddenly perceive that change in our exterior lives. This is a refreshing season of new alternatives, of deepening our freedom of choice.

As long as we remember that change is natural and unavoidable, we can "work" with it better, navigate within it, and deny the circumstances surrounding us too much control.

These days invite us to participate in an ongoing process of change – change that grows out of recognition, choice, happiness and excitement.

**This portal invites you to write towards freedom.**
**To write in order to cleanse, renew and love.**

# March

## Writing to Cleanse

Let the words flow through you, Like the water flowing in the stream Place no dam over your words, Do not ask them to slow down, Do not hasten them forward Allow them to move freely As they are. Let the words pass through you, Peaceful and pleasant Temperamental and raging Sweet or bitter. They are not yours, They never were. Remember that all they want Is to reach their

doubt
stress
worry
fear
remorse
sad
difficulty
fake
anxiety
mask
shame
regret

## Don't Just Sweep the Floor

Late winter and early spring days invite us to shake off the heaviness of winter and let fresher, lighter energy into our lives. We should use this time to relinquish what no longer serves us – physically, energetically, emotionally or mentally.

Write everything that you wish to "cleanse" from your life these days, inside and out.

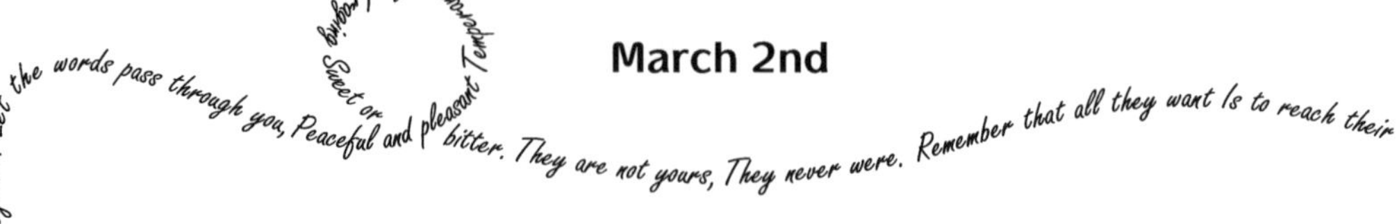
Let the words flow through you, Like the water flowing in the stream Place no dam over your words, Do not ask them to slow down, Do not hasten them forward Allow them to move freely As they are. Let the words pass through you, Peaceful and pleasant Temperamental and raging Sweet or bitter. They are not yours, They never were. Remember that all they want Is to reach their

**March 2nd**

## Emotion Speaks

Choose one significant emotion you wish to clean out of your life right now. This emotion may have appeared for a reason at a certain stage in your life, but it has remained inside you, maintaining its control over you. Perhaps it is time to let it go?

It can be anger, sadness, jealousy, fear or shame. Focus all your attention on the emotion you wish to cleanse yourself of. After choosing it, write from its point of view. Let that emotion speak to you, tell you its history, who it is and when it arrived, **what its purpose was**, and why it is time for it to leave. Listen and write.

## March 3rd

*With the sea. Do not over flow, Do not hang on words. Learn from the river: Its only designation is To carry water*

# A Cleansing Letter

Write a letter to a person who provokes strong emotions in you, a person who triggers anger, jealousy or fear. Write everything you wish to say to this person on a separate piece of paper, and then destroy the letter.

Now, here in the journal, write how you feel after writing and destroying that letter.

March 4th

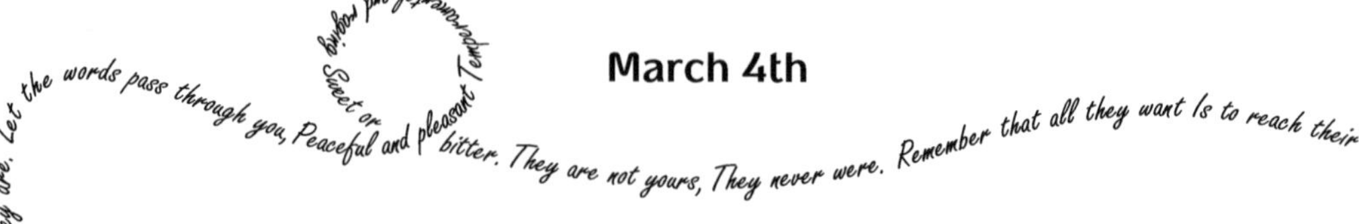
Let the words flow through you, Like the water flowing in the stream Place no dam over your words, Do not ask them to slow down, Do not hasten them forward Allow them to move freely As they are. Let the words pass through you, Peaceful and pleasant Temperamental and raging Sweet or bitter. They are not yours, They never were. Remember that all they want Is to reach their

## A List of Annoying Things

Write all the things that you find annoying, everything that you dislike. Allow yourself to dislike, and even hate. Do not censor yourself and do not underestimate the value of small annoyances. Make room for them. Often these little annoyances control us behind the scenes of our lives. This is a good chance to expose them, look them in the eye, and with that, perhaps even let them go.

## Do Not Write

We usually look for moments to write about, but in this exercise look for moments that you do not want to write about. Moments you would be happy to delete. That you do not want to give space to, share or talk about. Events, feelings or thoughts for which silence suits them beautifully.

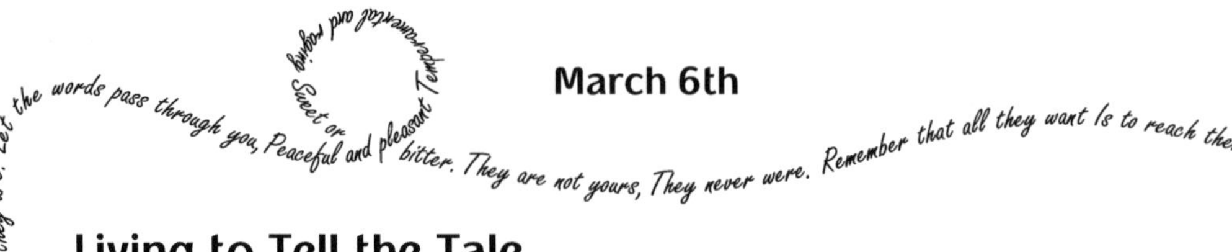
Let the words flow through you, Like the water flowing in the stream Place no dam over your words, Do not ask them to slow down, Do not hasten them forward Allow them to move freely As they are. Let the words pass through you, Peaceful and pleasant Temperamental and raging Sweet or bitter. They are not yours, They never were. Remember that all they want Is to reach their

## March 6th

# Living to Tell the Tale

This is the birthday of novelist **Gabriel García Márquez**, the 1982 Nobel Prize laureate in literature, born in 1927.

"Everything I looked at would provoke inside of me a burning desire to write so I wouldn't die," he writes in his autobiography.

In this exercise, inspired by Márquez, write how you would record your life story, if you were told that your days are numbered. Write a bullet point list of events you have experienced, and you wish to tell the world about before your death, in order to give them life.

"Life is not what one lived, but what one remembers and how one remembers it in order to recount it." **Gabriel García Márquez**.

*Living to Tell the Tale*, trans. Edith Grossman, Knoph, 2003.

## March 7th

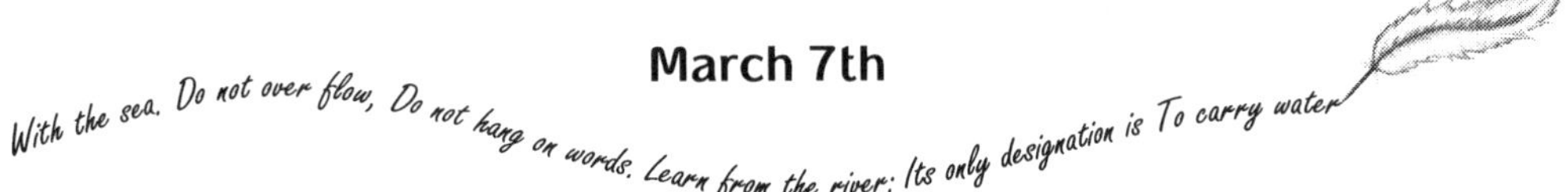
With the sea. Do not over flow, Do not hang on words. Learn from the river: Its only designation is To carry water

# The Diamond Within

Many spiritual doctrines suggest that we should remove the veil of mist hiding the truth from our eyes. In Buddhism they say that every person must remove "the mud and the dust'" from the diamond of which they are made. The Indian mystic guru Osho used a different metaphor, saying we need to "peel the onion layers away."

Write a text that expresses your cleanest place – write about the diamond within you.

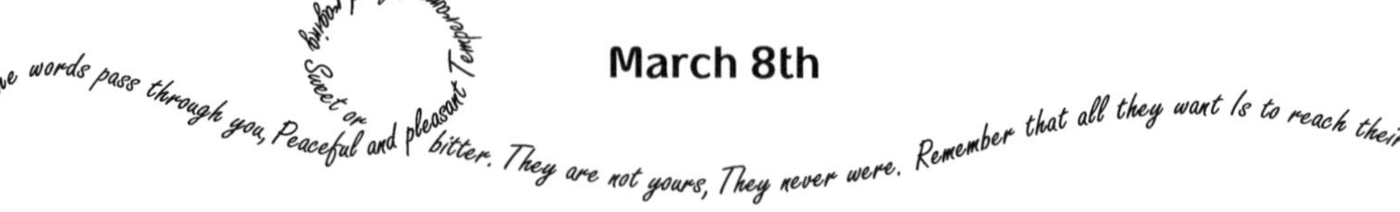
Let the words flow through you, Like the water flowing in the stream Place no dam over your words, Do not ask them to slow down, Do not hasten them forward Allow them to move freely As they are. Let the words pass through you, Peaceful and pleasant Temperamental and raging Sweet or bitter. They are not yours, They never were. Remember that all they want Is to reach their

**March 8th**

## International Women's Day

This is a special exercise in honor of today: meet the first woman.

For generations, women have been carrying the story of the first woman on their backs. Every woman has an "Eve" of her own, a "mother of all living creatures" that lives within her, controlling her life and pulling the strings behind the scenes.

According to book of Genesis, Eve is the first woman and mother. She is the wife of the first man and the mother of Cain, Abel and Seth, and many more children whose names remain unknown. The Bible tells us that she was created in the image of God.

Who is Eve to you? If you were to meet her today, what would you tell her? What would you ask of her?

Write a text addressed to Eve. It can be a poem, a letter, or even a greeting card for International Women's Day, whatever you like.

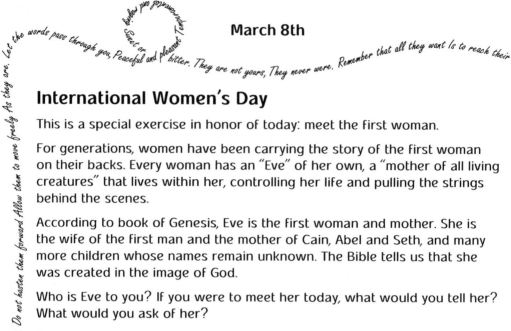

*With the sea. Do not over flow, Do not hang on words. Learn from the river: Its only designation is To carry water*

## The Cleaning Page

Write words, sentences, phrases or concepts on this page that you wish to cleanse from your life forever. Write down everything that you would like to throw away, once and for all.

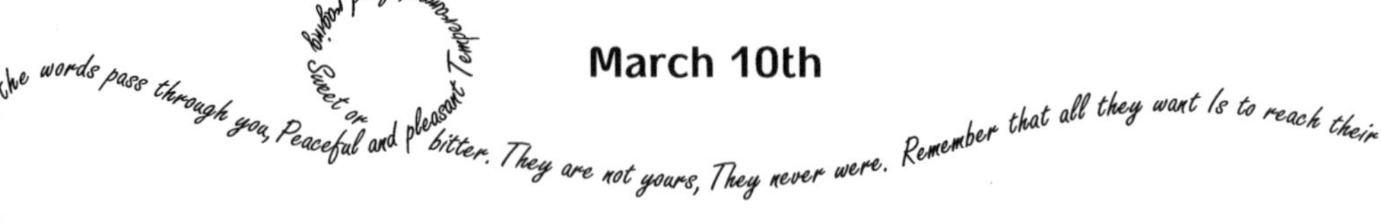
Let the words flow through you, Like the water flowing in the stream Place no dam over your words, Do not ask them to slow down, Do not hasten them forward Allow them to move freely As they are. Let the words pass through you, Peaceful and pleasant Temperamental and raging Sweet or bitter. They are not yours, They never were. Remember that all they want Is to reach their

**March 10th**

## Writing Anger

Write your anger. Write about all the things and people in this world that make you angry. Allow yourself to express your anger from start to finish. Begin with the words **I am angry**... and let the pen take you inward to all the places that infuriate you. You can consider this writing about anger to be an act of release and cleansing. Only when you feel you have written everything and you have nothing more to add, close your eyes, take a few breaths and detect what feelings arise within you now.

## March 11th



# Drinking Tea with Anger

Anger is a strong and significant emotion that should be dealt with and understood. Just like other emotions, it usually has something to show us, inviting us to turn inward, and consider what was really triggered, what boundaries were crossed, within us.

Invite Anger for a calm, quiet chat over a cup of tea. Remember the moment the anger inside you was ignited, and allow that anger to talk to you. It will tell you why it is here, explain how to express it appropriately, and how you can live with it amicably, without fear.

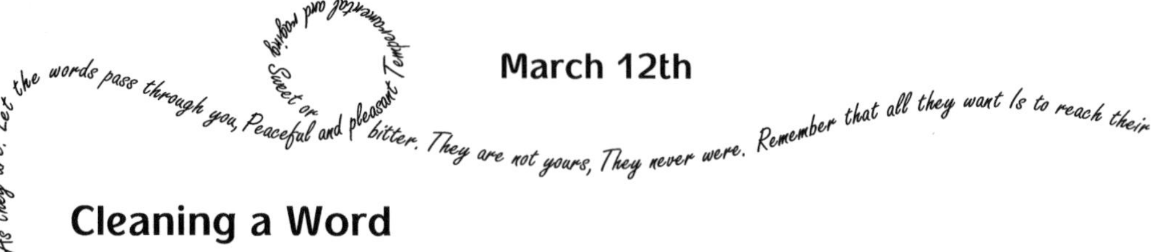
Let the words flow through you, Like the water flowing in the stream Place no dam over your words, Do not ask them to slow down, Do not hasten them forward Allow them to move freely As they are. Let the words pass through you, Peaceful and pleasant Temperamental and raging Sweet or bitter. They are not yours, They never were. Remember that all they want Is to reach their

**March 12th**

## Cleaning a Word

Choose a word that you would be happy to remove from your lexicon forever. One that you hate and try never to use.

Write it in big letters on the page before you. Now use this word in several sentences, and perhaps even write a short story around it. Write it as many times as possible in various connotations. Write it in order to remain with it and to examine what it evokes in you, and why.

Write in order to befriend it. Perhaps then it will agree to leave.

With the sea. Do not over flow, Do not hang on words. Learn from the river: Its only designation is To carry water

## My Mother

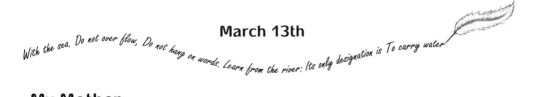

Sometimes, it seems that everything begins and ends with one word: **Mother**. The woman who carried us in her womb for nine months and introduced us to the world.

Write a text that begins with the words **My mother...** and share everything that comes to you from your heart when you think about the woman who brought you into the world.

If you do not want to, or cannot, write about your biological mother, address your writing to Mother Earth or the mother that lives within you.

March 14th

## Mother, Why ...?

Write a text that is entirely made up of questions addressed to your mother. What would you like to ask her? What would you truly want to know about her, about her life, about your relationship?

Allow yourself to ask her in writing everything you ever wanted to know.

## March 15th

# A Parade of Masks

We all walk around wearing any number of masks. Part of the process of growing up is the ability to recognize ourselves behind these masks, in order to come closer to the truth of our real selves.

Write about your daily parade of masks. Starting from the moment you wake up, consider the masks you don in your preparation for the new day – all the ways in which you present yourself to the world.

Describe all the masks you wear as part of the various roles you play in your day-to-day life. Write about the mask you put on for your partner, your children, your friends, your colleagues at work, etc.

What character do you present to the world through the mask you choose? Write nothing but your observations, without any criticism or judgement of the mask.

"Man is least himself when he talks in his own person. Give him a mask, and he will tell you the truth." **Wilde, Oscar**

*The Happy Prince & Other Tales*, Miniature Masterpiece, 2013.

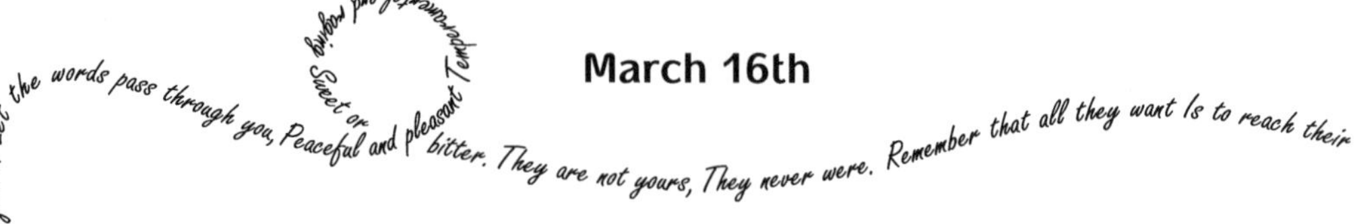
Let the words flow through you, Like the water flowing in the stream Place no dam over your words, Do not ask them to slow down, Do not hasten them forward Allow them to move freely As they are. Let the words pass through you, Peaceful and pleasant Temperamental and raging Sweet or bitter. They are not yours, They never were. Remember that all they want Is to reach their

## March 16th

# The Mask Speaks

From all the masks you wear in your life, select one that you would be happy to take off forever. Perhaps it is a mask that has served you for a very long time, but you don't need it anymore.

Which of your masks is unnecessary? Perhaps it is the "Everything-is-fine" mask? The "I-know-everything" mask? Is it perhaps a victim's mask, or that of an aggressor?

Now write the unwanted mask's words. Let it speak on paper in its own voice and tone. Let the mask explain its origins to you, tell you its history, when and where it was born, and most importantly, what it is trying to cover up.

As you complete your writing, consider whether or not it is time to say goodbye to this particular mask.

*With the sea. Do not over flow, Do not hang on words. Learn from the river: Its only designation is To carry water*

## A World with No Masks

Is a world where people live with no masks possible? Write about what such a utopic world would look like. Who would you meet behind the masks in this world? Who would you be in a world with no masks?

Let the words flow through you, Like the water flowing in the stream Place no dam over your words, Do not ask them to slow down, Do not hasten them forward Allow them to move freely As they are. Let the words pass through you, Peaceful and pleasant Temperamental and raging Sweet or bitter. They are not yours, They never were. Remember that all they want Is to reach their

## March 18th

# Exposed

Turn the word **exposed** over in your mind and let it roll down your pen onto your journal.

What does it awaken in you? Do you feel exposed? Do your words expose or conceal? What does exposure mean to you, and when are you prepared to be exposed?

Now imagine that you take off all your clothes and masks, and allow writing to carry you into realms you have never known before. Expose yourself.

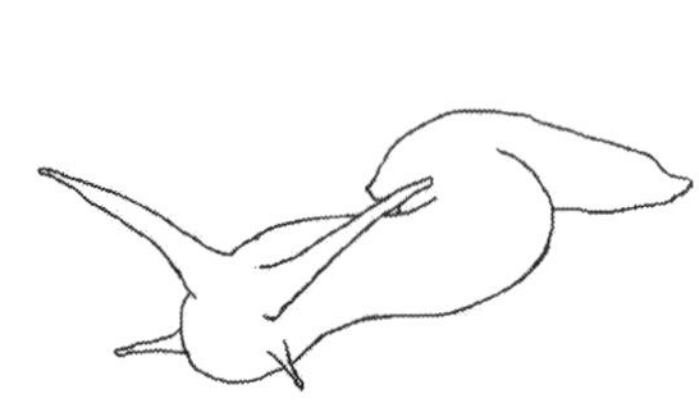

## March 19th



# Farewell to an Object

Choose an object from your home or surroundings to let go of, an item that used to be significant to you in the past, and has completed its role in your life.

A moment before you relinquish it, write a poem or a farewell letter to it. Describe what part of the object will remain with you that has nothing to do with its physical presence. Write what you are freeing within, by letting it go.

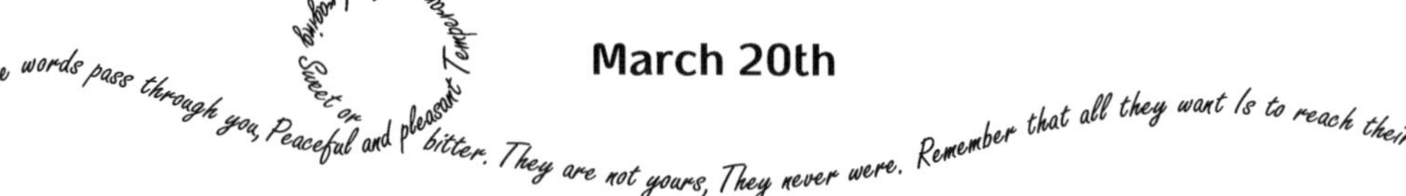
Let the words flow through you, Like the water flowing in the stream Place no dam over your words, Do not ask them to slow down, Do not hasten them forward Allow them to move freely As they are. Let the words pass through you, Peaceful and pleasant Temperamental and raging Sweet or bitter. They are not yours, They never were. Remember that all they want Is to reach their

## March 20th

# Initiation

Today is the birthday of spiritual teacher and author **Elisabeth Haich**, born in 1897.

This is an exercise inspired by her book *Initiation**, which documents, as her memory, instructions for reaching spirituality in Ancient Egypt. Write instructions for your own initiation into spiritual development. Write from a higher place within you, from your inner, mystical guide. What do you require for your initiation? What turns the trivial into the sacred for you?

"You must completely give up your personal viewpoint, your personal inclinations and feelings, learning to love everything and everyone without distinction or discrimination, just as God himself loves everything and everyone!"

* *Initiation*, Aurora Press, 2000, p.149; 174

With the sea. Do not over flow, Do not hang on words. Learn from the river: Its only designation is To carry water

## A Spring Invitation

Today is the equinox, the official beginning of spring. In the ancient world, the spring equinox indicated a new year had begun.

Open your door to spring by writing it an invitation. What does your spring bring with it for you?

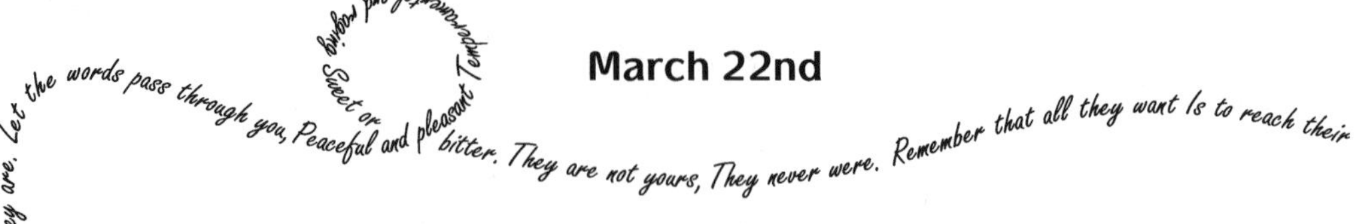
Let the words flow through you, Like the water flowing in the stream Place no dam over your words, Do not ask them to slow down, Do not hasten them forward Allow them to move freely As they are.
Let the words pass through you, Peaceful and pleasant Temperamental and raging Sweet or bitter. They are not yours, They never were. Remember that all they want Is to reach their

March 22nd

## An Ode to Bureaucracy

Write a list of all the things you have to do, take care of, arrange, sort, etc. Write about even the tiniest items that nag you: bureaucratic errands you must run, a phone call you have been intending to make for a long time, a doctor's appointment you have postponed, and so on.

Now, on a separate page, turn your list into a poem, and hang it on your fridge.

## March 23rd



# A Man Approached a Poem

This is the birthday of poet **Israel Eliraz**, born in 1936.

"A man approached a poem and asked permission to enter," he wrote in a poem from his book, *Else*.

This is an exercise inspired by Eliraz. Imagine you have the opportunity to go inside a poem, perhaps into one of its verses. It may be a poem you know and love, or one that has not yet been written.

Now write from inside a verse in the poem. What words do you find there?

You may begin with the words **A man approached a poem...** or **A woman approached a poem...** Allow the text to be born from within as you write.

* Afik, 2014.

Let the words flow through you, Like the water flowing in the stream Place no dam over your words, Do not ask them to slow down, Do not hasten them forward Allow them to move freely As they are.

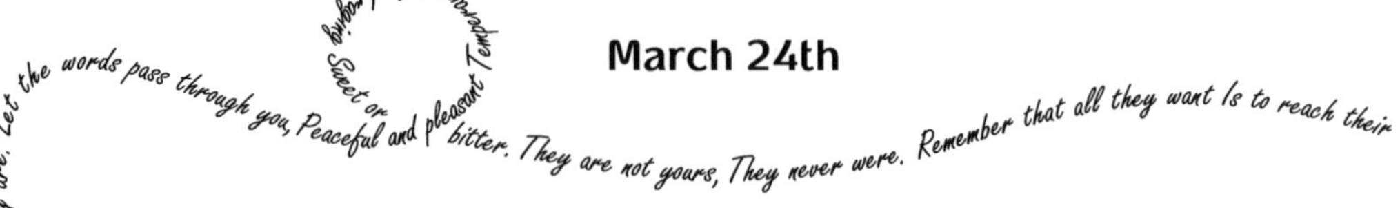
Let the words pass through you, Peaceful and pleasant Temperamental and raging Sweet or bitter. They are not yours, They never were. Remember that all they want Is to reach their

## March 24th

# Never Have I Thought

Write a text that begins with the words above. Let the simplicity of the words carry you inward, to reflect upon the act of writing.

# March 25th

## Boredom

Boredom is a feeling we usually do not notice. It is elusive and deceiving.

Are you often bored – or rarely? What bores you? Who bores you?

Write about things that bore you.

Write them in a way as un-boring as you can.

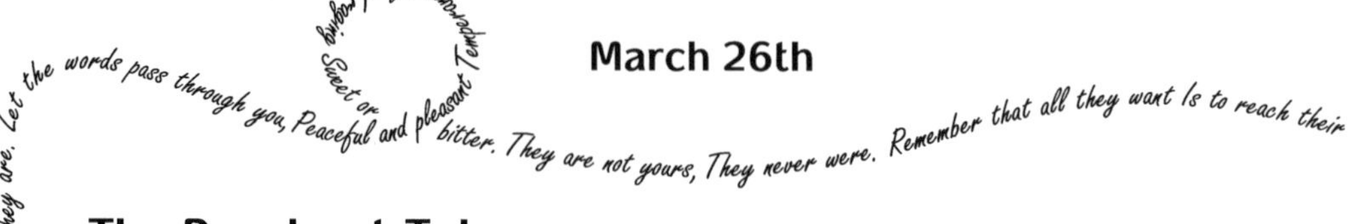
Let the words flow through you, Like the water flowing in the stream Place no dam over your words, Do not ask them to slow down, Do not hasten them forward Allow them to move freely As they are. Let the words pass through you, Peaceful and pleasant Temperamental and raging Sweet or bitter. They are not yours, They never were. Remember that all they want Is to reach their

**March 26th**

## The Road not Taken

Today is the birthday of the poet **Robert Frost**, born in 1874.

This is an exercise inspired by his poem "The Road not Taken". When we choose one road over another, we reject the other road. What is the road you **did not take**, that you chose to abandon? Write a text that describes it.

Can you imagine how your life would look if you had chosen differently?

## March 27th

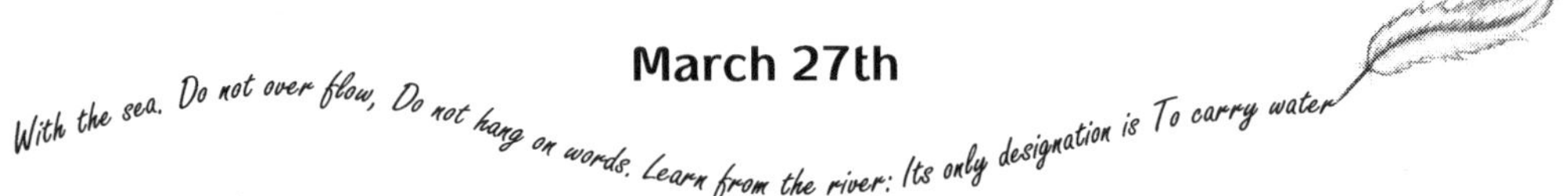
With the sea. Do not over flow, Do not hang on words. Learn from the river: Its only designation is To carry water

# The Road Taken

What does the road you have been paving during your time here on earth look like?

Describe the view along this road in detail; write what you find along the way and about the people by your side.

Are you happy on the road you have chosen? Take a writing tour.

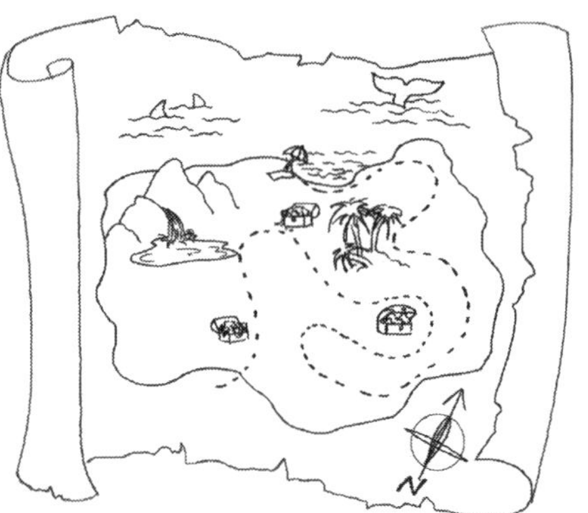
N

Let the words flow through you, Like the water flowing in the stream Place no dam over your words, Do not ask them to slow down, Do not hasten them forward Allow them to move freely As they are.

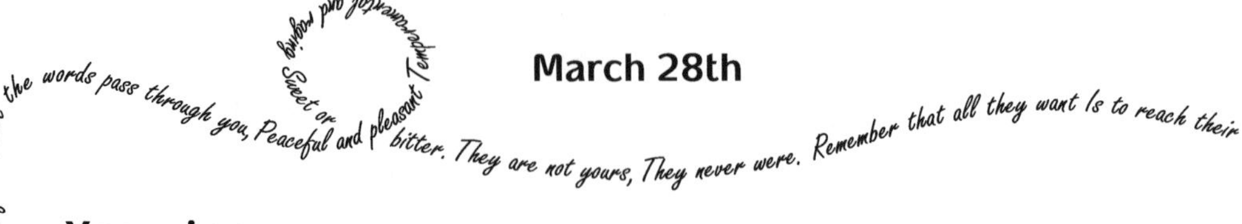
Let the words pass through you, Peaceful and pleasant Temperamental and raging Sweet or bitter. They are not yours, They never were. Remember that all they want Is to reach their

**March 28th**

## Yearning

Turn the word **yearning** over in your mind and let it roll down your pen onto your journal.

What does this word evoke in you? What do you long for? How much do you allow yourself to yearn?

Begin with the words **I yearn...** and write intuitively. Let your writing carry you into the realm of your yearning.

## March 29th

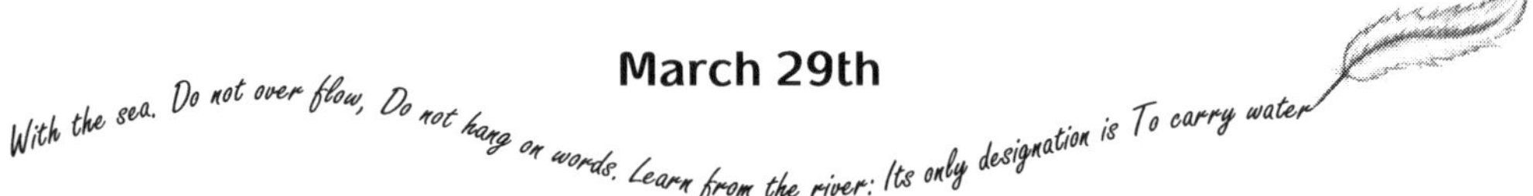
With the sea. Do not over flow, Do not hang on words. Learn from the river: Its only designation is To carry water

# What Will They Say?

We are all familiar with the questions that play in our heads when we want to act, create, choose, be. What will they think of us? What will they say? What will they tell others about us?

In this exercise, I invite you to express everything you worry might happen if they say, think, criticize or judge you. Don't censor yourself. What will they really say? And what will you answer?

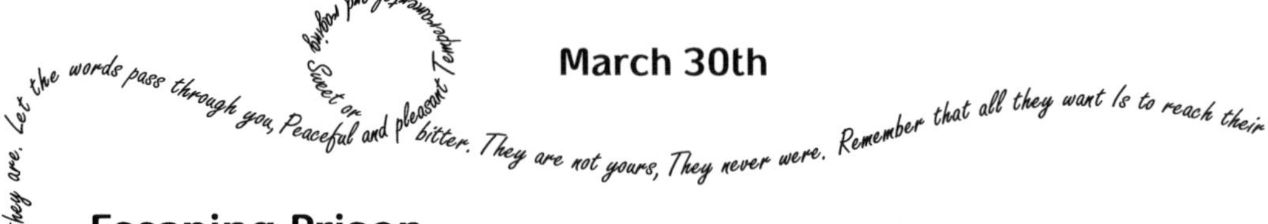
Let the words flow through you, Like the water flowing in the stream Place no dam over your words, Do not ask them to slow down, Do not hasten them forward Allow them to move freely As they are. Let the words pass through you, Peaceful and pleasant Temperamental and raging Sweet or bitter. They are not yours, They never were. Remember that all they want Is to reach their

**March 30th**

## Escaping Prison

What restrains you in your life? What is your "prison", the place in your life that holds you back?

Write about your escape. Begin by writing about what shackles you, and then write how you would like to escape.

## The Whispers of the Heart

After cleaning, within or without, something brightens, becomes clearer. We can see better, hear more.

In this exercise, you are invited to close your eyes and listen to the whisper of your heart.

Be silent for a few moments and listen to the beating of your heart. Breathe deeply into your chest, gently massage it and feel the presence of your heart. And then, simply let it speak. Listen and write its words.

Be open to everything that it has to tell you. This is your chance to ask your heart questions and be answered.

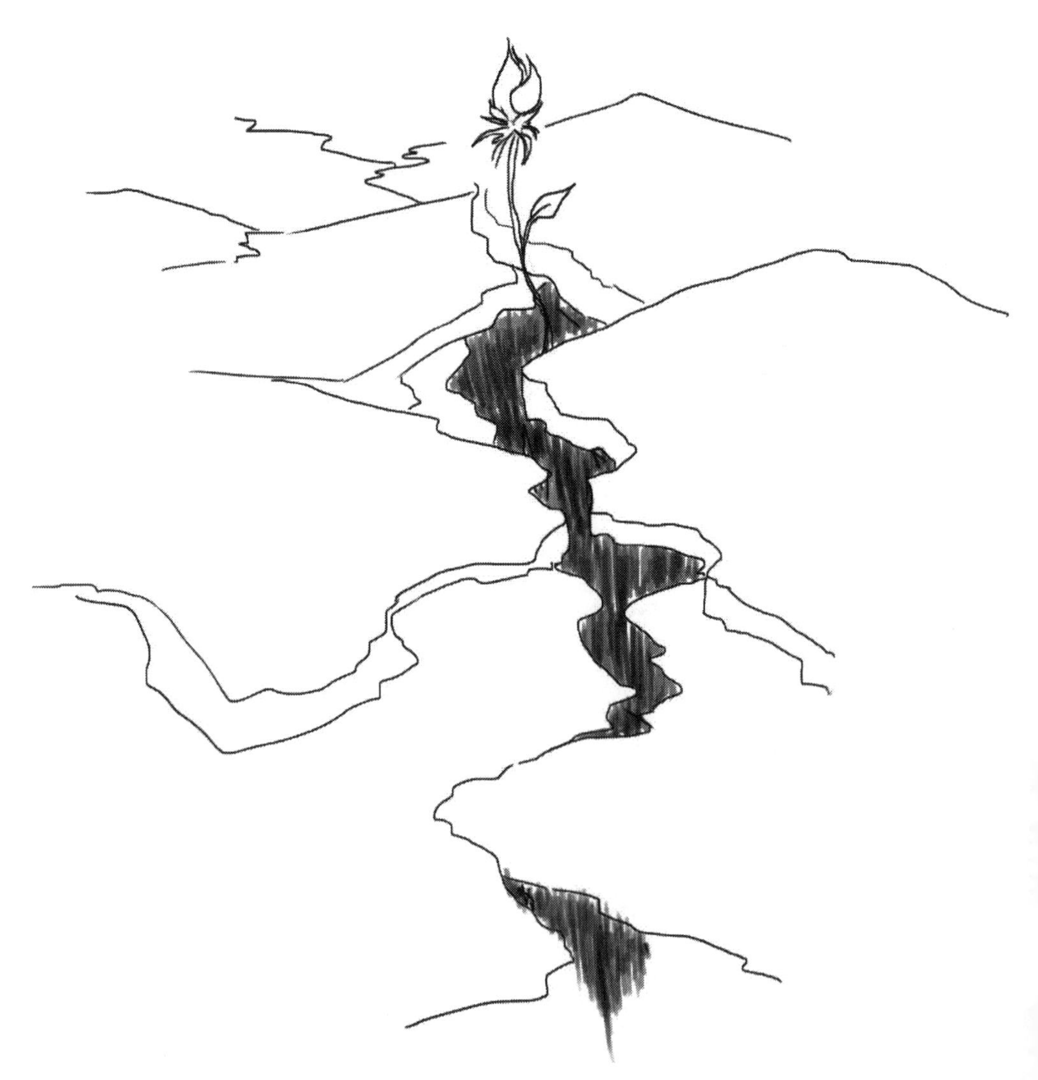

# April

## Writing to Renew

Let the words flow through you, Like the water flowing in the stream Place no dam over your words, Do not ask them to slow down, Do not hasten them forward Allow them to move freely As they are. Let the words pass through you, Peaceful and pleasant Temperamental and raging Sweet or bitter. They are not yours, They never were. Remember that all they want Is to reach their

# April 1st

## All the Lies

Many countries around the world celebrate April Fool's Day by telling lies and playing tricks on family and friends.

Celebrate this day by writing a whole text about yourself and your life that is nothing but lies. Make up your name, your age, your profession and your entire life story. Invent whatever lies you want. Set truth free, and make sure your text has no truth in it whatsoever! You may write anything you want, and remember to have fun while you do.

### April 2nd

## Renewal

Turn over the word **renewal** in your mind and let it roll down your pen onto the journal page.

How does this word make you feel? Do you experience renewal in your life? Do you want to?

Write what renewal means to you, and when you really feel renewed.

Begin by writing the word **Renewal...** and continue on a quest to investigate it in depth.

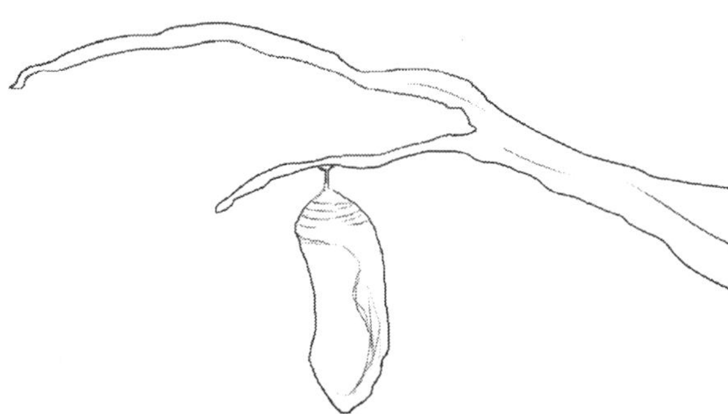

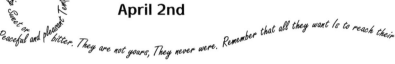

With the sea. Do not over flow, Do not hang on words. Learn from the river: Its only designation is To carry water

## Walking and Writing

Take the journal and go out for a 10-minute walk on the street near your home. As you walk, look for as many new things as you can find - things you have never noticed before. Pay close attention to everything around you. Write down all that you see, documenting your surroundings. Now find a comfortable place to sit, and continue recording every movement or object your eyes are drawn to.

Do not let anything slip past you - people, animals, trees, leaves, stones, thoughts and sensations.

Put it all in words on the page.

## April 4th

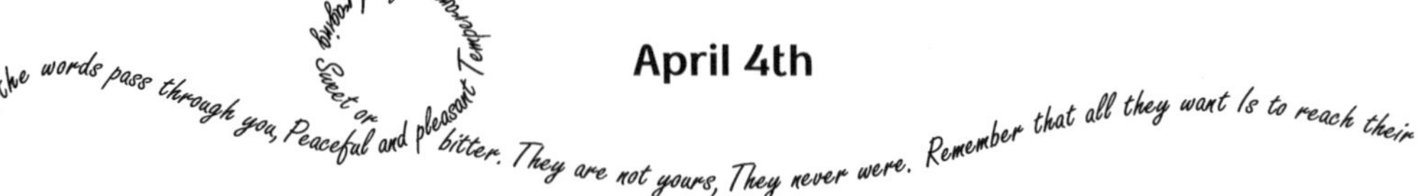
Let the words pass through you, Peaceful and pleasant Temperamental and raging Sweet or bitter. They are not yours, They never were. Remember that all they want Is to reach their

Let the words flow through you, Like the water flowing in the stream Place no dam over your words, Do not ask them to slow down, Do not hasten them forward Allow them to move freely As they are. Let the words pass through you,

# Abnormal

This is the birthday of poet **Maya Angelou**, born in 1928.

"If you are always trying to be normal, you will never know how amazing you can be," said Angelou.

This exercise is inspired by her words. Connect to the "abnormal" person inside you and meet that person here, in writing. Agree to be abnormal. Agree to be different. Unusual. Not one of the crowd.

What is it in you that makes you abnormal? Begin with the words **I am abnormal...** and continue from there.

"Nothing is more liberating than joy; it frees your mind and creates peace."
**Rabbi Nachman of Breslov,** also born on this day in 1772.

With the sea. Do not over flow, Do not hang on words. Learn from the river: Its only designation is To carry water

## My Muse

What is a muse to you? When does she visit you? When do you experience her presence? Do you call her when you hope she will come, or does she simply appear? Are you attentive in her presence? What are your expectations of your muse?

Write freely about your muse, her character and your relationship with her.

**April 6th**

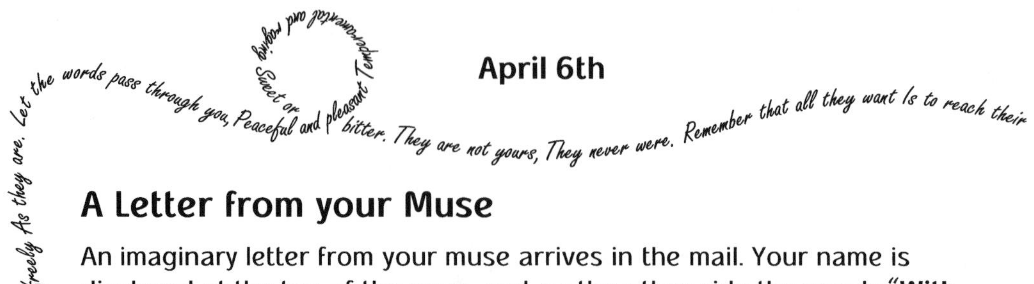
Let the words flow through you, Like the water flowing in the stream Place no dam over your words, Do not ask them to slow down, Do not hasten them forward Allow them to move freely As they are. Let the words pass through you, Peaceful and pleasant Temperamental and raging Sweet or bitter. They are not yours, They never were. Remember that all they want Is to reach their

## A Letter from your Muse

An imaginary letter from your muse arrives in the mail. Your name is displayed at the top of the page, and on the other side the words "**With love, your Muse**" are written.

What does this letter say? What is your muse telling you? What is she explaining? Is she asking you for something? Copy her letter here.

## Writing the Breathings of the Heart

This is the birthday of poet **William Wordsworth**, born in 1770.

In his autobiographical poem "The Prelude" he wrote, "Fill your paper with the breathings of your heart."

This exercise is inspired by Wordsworth. Write what your breathing heart is telling you right now. Are its breaths short or long, deep or shallow? What does your heart want to tell you? Feel and write the breathings of your heart.

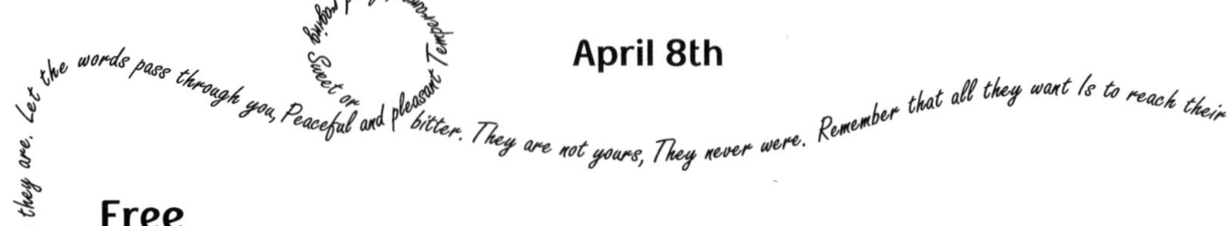
Let the words flow through you, Like the water flowing in the stream Place no dam over your words, Do not ask them to slow down, Do not hasten them forward Allow them to move freely As they are. Let the words pass through you, Peaceful and pleasant Temperamental and raging Sweet or bitter. They are not yours, They never were. Remember that all they want Is to reach their

**April 8th**

## Free

What does liberty mean to you? When do you feel truly liberated to be who you are, express yourself, and do what you long to do? Are you free to love? Create? Think? Dance?

Write your freedom. Write about all the places where you feel free.

Begin with the words **I am free ...**

With the sea. Do not over flow, Do not hang on words. Learn from the river: Its only designation is To carry water

## Now, of all Times

Write a text that begins with the words **Now, of all times...**

Write these words again and again, and see what they free within you, now, at this moment.

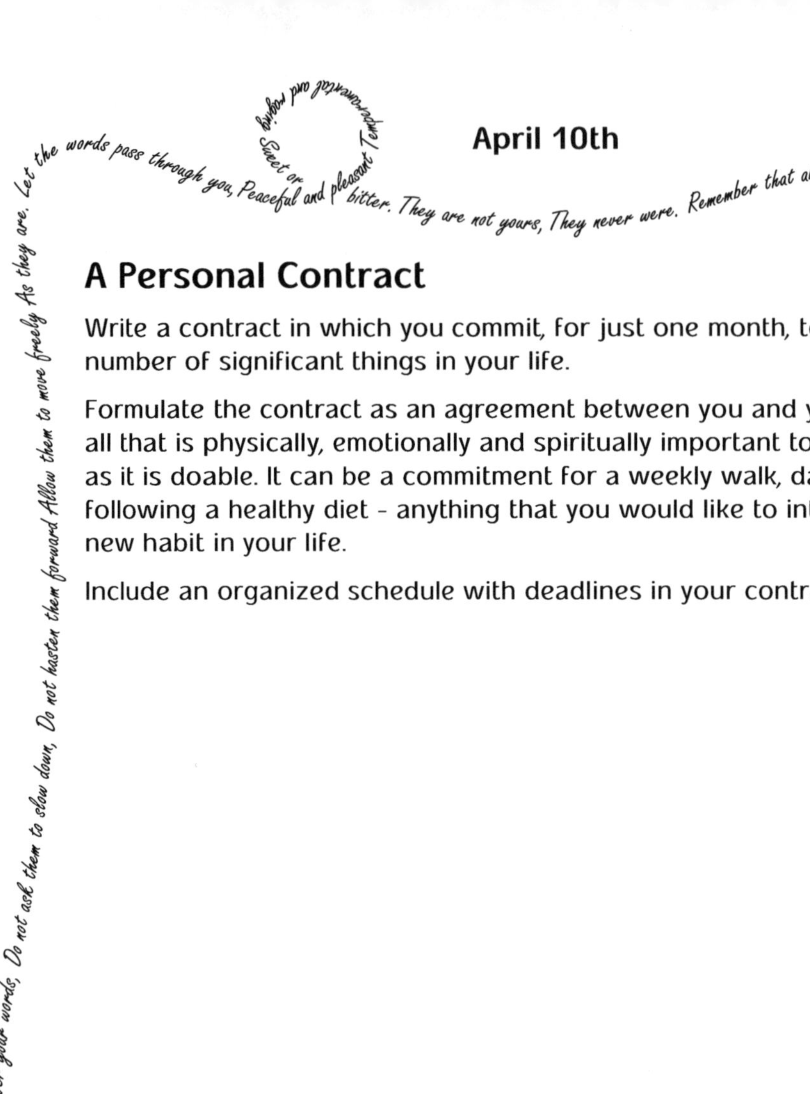
Let the words flow through you, Like the water flowing in the stream Place no dam over your words, Do not ask them to slow down, Do not hasten them forward Allow them to move freely As they are. Let the words pass through you, Peaceful and pleasant Temperamental and raging Sweet or bitter. They are not yours, They never were. Remember that all they want Is to reach their

## April 10th

# A Personal Contract

Write a contract in which you commit, for just one month, to doing a number of significant things in your life.

Formulate the contract as an agreement between you and yourself. Include all that is physically, emotionally and spiritually important to you, as long as it is doable. It can be a commitment for a weekly walk, daily writing or following a healthy diet - anything that you would like to introduce as a new habit in your life.

Include an organized schedule with deadlines in your contract, then sign it.

## April 11th

*With the sea. Do not over flow, Do not hang on words. Learn from the river: Its only designation is To carry water*

# Giving Birth

What does **birth** mean to you? What do you wish to **give life to** from within your soul?

Perhaps you are not the one doing the wishing. Perhaps something that wants to be born from deep inside you is speaking?

Write about something within your very soul, your womb, that is asking to be born. Write the **story of its birth**.

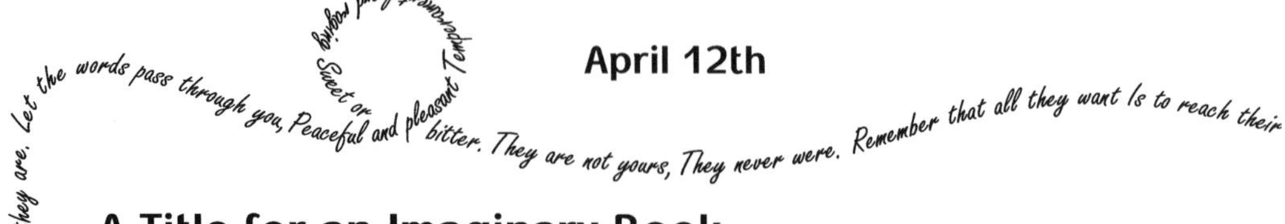
Let the words pass through you, Peaceful and pleasant Temperamental and raging Sweet or bitter. They are not yours, They never were. Remember that all they want Is to reach their

Let the words flow through you, Like the water flowing in the stream Place no dam over your words, Do not ask them to slow down, Do not hasten them forward Allow them to move freely As they are.

## April 12th

# A Title for an Imaginary Book

Were you to write a book, what would its title be? Write your chosen title on the page, and continue writing its story.

April 13th

## Erotic Writing

Erotic writing deals with many aspects, much more than sexuality.

This exercise encourages you to investigate what erotic writing is **to you**. Write freely about everything you consider to be erotic, even if it is not what is normally called erotic. You can write, for example, about a strand of hair blowing in the wind, the gentle touch of someone's palm, a garment, a mango, a pineapple.

Then, put all the words you have written together, and integrate them in a poem. Let your poem drip with eroticism.

April 14th

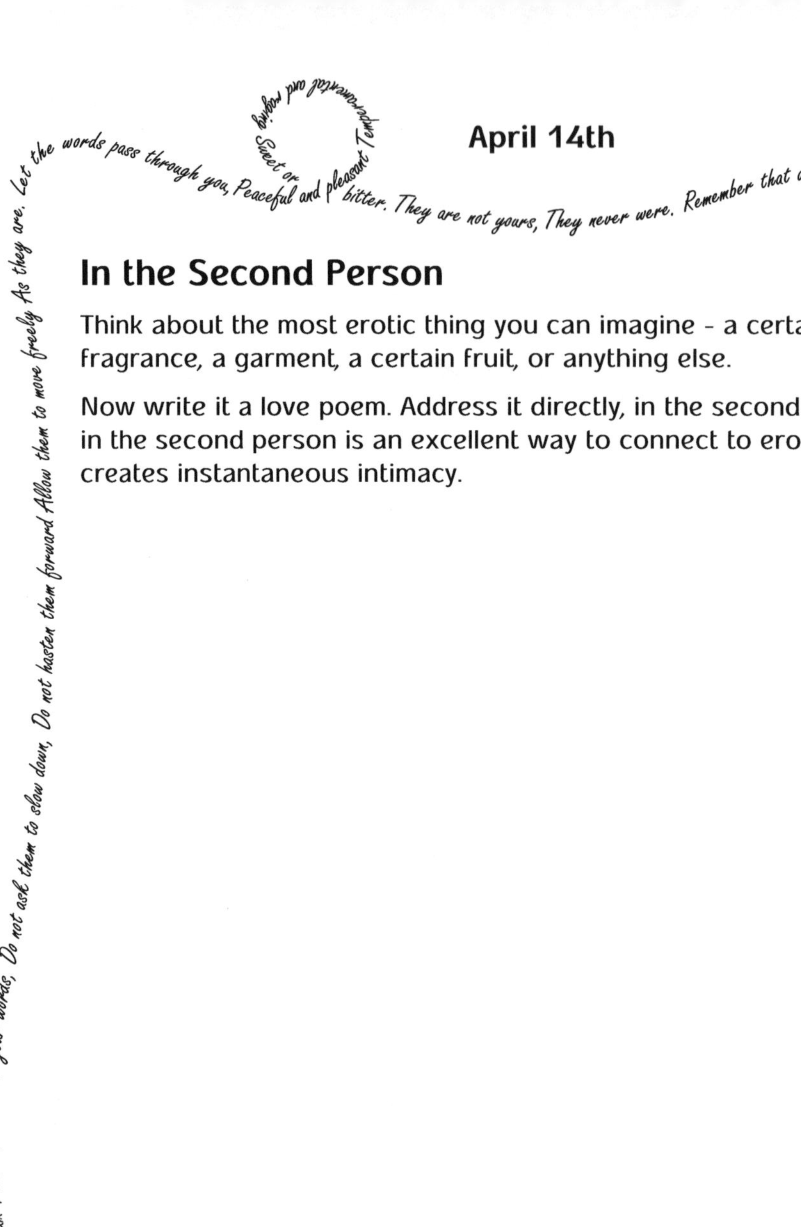
Let the words flow through you, Like the water flowing in the stream Place no dam over your words, Do not ask them to slow down, Do not hasten them forward Allow them to move freely As they are.
Let the words pass through you, Peaceful and pleasant Temperamental and raging Sweet or bitter. They are not yours, They never were. Remember that all they want Is to reach their

## In the Second Person

Think about the most erotic thing you can imagine - a certain person, a fragrance, a garment, a certain fruit, or anything else.

Now write it a love poem. Address it directly, in the second person. Writing in the second person is an excellent way to connect to eroticism - it creates instantaneous intimacy.

## April 15th

# Collecting Words at a Bookstore

Take your journal with you and go into a big bookstore you love, or to the local library. Wander around the bookshelves, randomly open books, and start writing titles, words, sentences, perhaps even complete sections that inspire you.

Compile your writing ideas on this page using the notes you made - titles you found interesting, or suggestions for writing new stories or poems, inspired by your bookstore harvest.

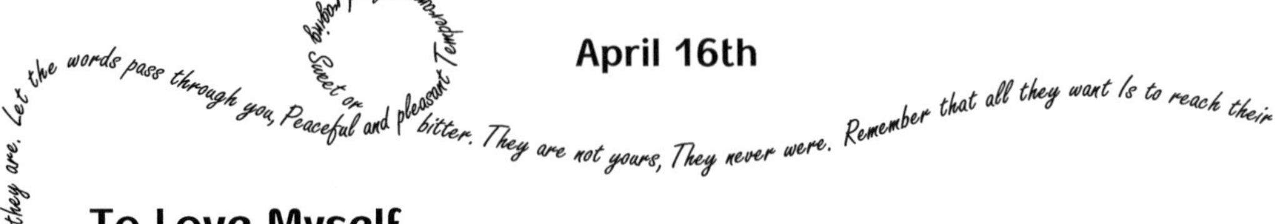
Let the words flow through you, Like the water flowing in the stream Place no dam over your words, Do not ask them to slow down, Do not hasten them forward Allow them to move freely As they are. Let the words pass through you, Peaceful and pleasant Temperamental and raging Sweet or bitter. They are not yours, They never were. Remember that all they want Is to reach their

**April 16th**

# To Love Myself

Write a text that starts with the words **When I love myself**... Remember the moments when you truly loved yourself in your life. What was special about these moments? What did you do that made you realize that you truly loved yourself?

With the sea. Do not over flow, Do not hang on words. Learn from the river: Its only designation is To carry water

## A Stolen Story

Do you know the feeling when you identify with someone's story so deeply that it leaves its mark on you, and when you share it with others, even experience it as if it actually happened to you?

Well, you are free to do this any time you want!

Tell a story here that is not your own, as if it happened to you.

Let the words flow through you, Like the water flowing in the stream Place no dam over your words, Do not ask them to slow down, Do not hasten them forward Allow them to move freely As they are. Let the words pass through you, Peaceful and pleasant Temperamental and raging Sweet or bitter. They are not yours, They never were. Remember that all they want Is to reach their

April 18th

## Words in the Middle

Select a song or poem you love. Copy the opening and closing lines, and write your own words in between. How does it feel writing within a defined framework, with the beginning and ending clearly defined for you? How much freedom do you have inside this framework?

# April 19th

*With the sea. Do not over flow, Do not hang on words. Learn from the river: Its only designation is To carry water*

## Sing the Day

Select a song that you love. Use it to describe something that happened to you this week - an event, an emotion, a conversation.  Sing your song to that same rhythm, style and language.

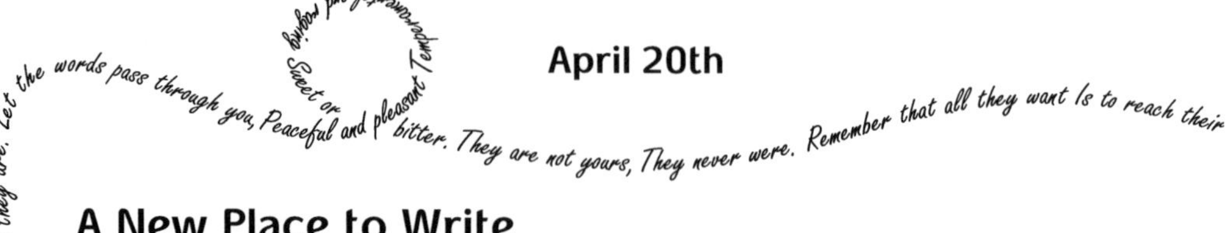
Let the words flow through you, Like the water flowing in the stream Place no dam over your words, Do not ask them to slow down, Do not hasten them forward Allow them to move freely As they are. Let the words pass through you, Peaceful and pleasant Temperamental and raging Sweet or bitter. They are not yours, They never were. Remember that all they want Is to reach their

**April 20th**

## A New Place to Write

Write a list of interesting places you would be happy to take your journal to in order to write - your parents' house, a train station, the airport, an empty bench on the street, playground or park, your yard or even a room inside your house where you do not usually write. Where do you feel like writing?

Now select one of these places and actually go there to write. What within you desires to be written in that place?

## April 21st

# Writing the Sky

This exercise invites you to lie down on the ground, relax your body, breathe to the rhythm of the earth and look up at the sky. Follow the movement of the clouds and try to feel connected to the universe.

Write about the feelings arising in you now. Write about the sky, infinity, freedom and space.

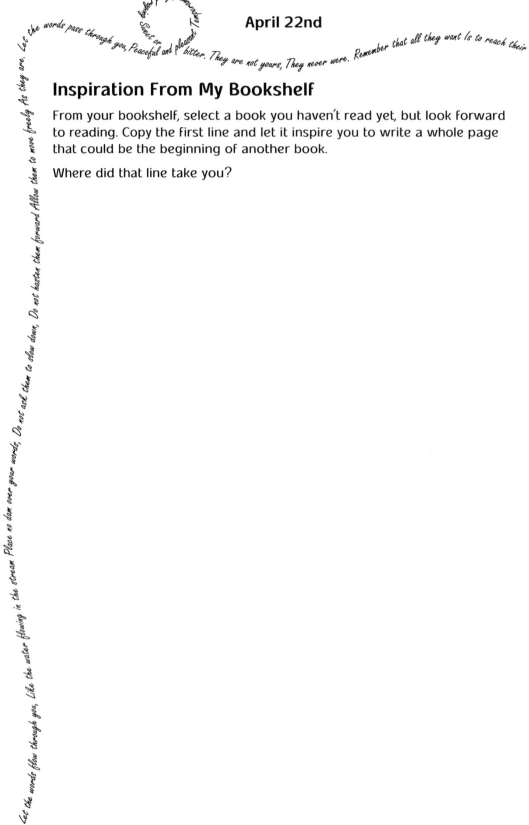

Let the words flow through you, Like the water flowing in the stream Place no dam over your words, Do not ask them to slow down, Do not hasten them forward Allow them to move freely As they are.

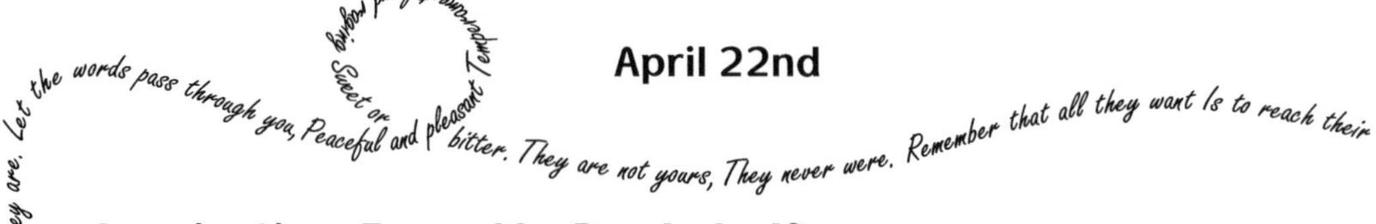
Let the words pass through you, Peaceful and pleasant Temperamental and raging Sweet or bitter. They are not yours, They never were. Remember that all they want Is to reach their

## April 22nd

# Inspiration From My Bookshelf

From your bookshelf, select a book you haven't read yet, but look forward to reading. Copy the first line and let it inspire you to write a whole page that could be the beginning of another book.

Where did that line take you?

*With the sea. Do not over flow, Do not hang on words. Learn from the river: Its only designation is To carry water*

## A Poem Expressed My Way

Select a poem you love – what is its topic? Write it down. Then write the theme of the poem in your own words, in your unique voice. Delve into its theme, but articulate it your way. Where does it take you?

April 24th

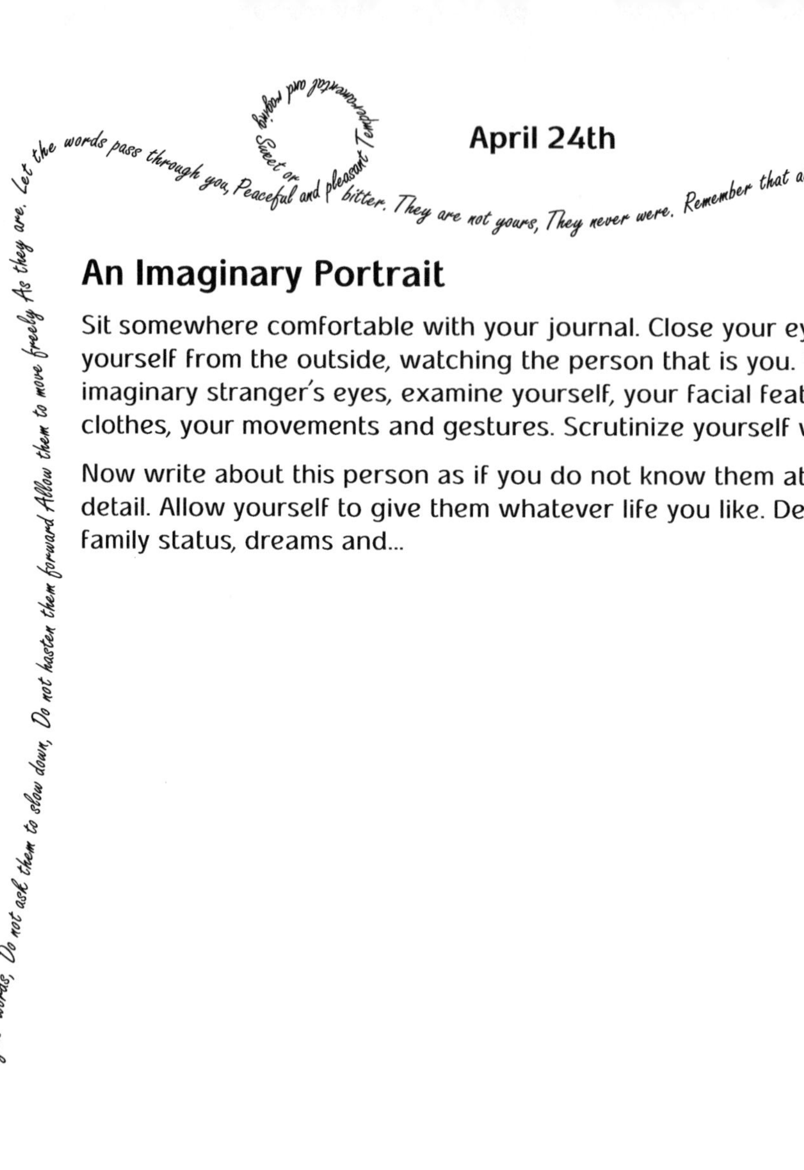
Let the words flow through you, Like the water flowing in the stream Place no dam over your words, Do not ask them to slow down, Do not hasten them forward Allow them to move freely As they are. Let the words pass through you, Peaceful and pleasant Temperamental and raging Sweet or bitter. They are not yours, They never were. Remember that all they want Is to reach their

## An Imaginary Portrait

Sit somewhere comfortable with your journal. Close your eyes and observe yourself from the outside, watching the person that is you. With those imaginary stranger's eyes, examine yourself, your facial features, your clothes, your movements and gestures. Scrutinize yourself with new eyes.

Now write about this person as if you do not know them at all, not a single detail. Allow yourself to give them whatever life you like. Describe their job, family status, dreams and...

*With the sea. Do not over flow, Do not hang on words. Learn from the river: Its only designation is To carry water*

## Anything is Possible

Turn the word **possible** over in your mind and let it roll down your pen onto this page.

What does the word arouse within you? Do you feel that anything is possible for you? Try, even for a few moments, to connect to the sensation that anything really is possible, that you are free of any limits or obstacles.

Begin your text with the words **Anything is possible...** and let writing carry you into new realms of freedom.

Let the words flow through you, Like the water flowing in the stream Place no dam over your words, Do not ask them to slow down, Do not hasten them forward Allow them to move freely As they are. Let the words pass through you, Peaceful and pleasant Temperamental and raging Sweet or bitter. They are not yours, They never were. Remember that all they want Is to reach their

**April 26th**

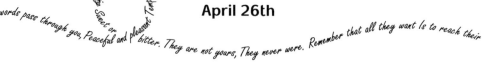

## The Role of my Life

On this date, in the year 1564, playwright and poet, **William Shakespeare**, was baptized.

"All the world's a stage,  
And all the men and women merely players;  
They have their exits and their entrances;  
And one man in his time plays many parts"

he wrote in *As You Like It*.

This exercise is inspired by Shakespeare. If you were an actor, what role would you choose for yourself on the stage? And what would this role be on the stage of your own life, here and now? Write it.

## April 27th

# May You Never Grow Accustomed

This is the birthday of poet **Racheli Reuven**, born in 1972.

"May you never grow accustomed," she writes in one of her wonderful poems.

This exercise is inspired by Reuven. We tend to lose ourselves in the race of life, and we do not stop to admire things that have become a habit for us. List your habits here: drinking coffee in the morning, brushing your teeth, kissing your child or spouse, going to work, watering the plants, walking the dog, calling a friend, etc. etc.

Now, turn your habits into a poem. Begin with the words **May you never grow accustomed...** and weave all your habits into the text. When you are done, promise yourself never to grow accustomed to the simple and beautiful things in life.

"May you never grow accustomed To the way life happens through you
To how a wound heals And to how children are born
May it never happen That you stop being amazed at How a leaf falls And a bird flies
And how a man lives and dies and is born again
May you never grow accustomed to The miracle That is you"

**Racheli Reuven**, "Never", **2017**.

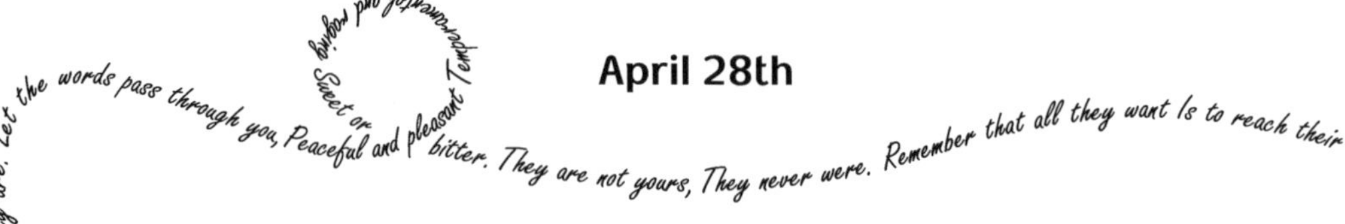
Let the words flow through you, Like the water flowing in the stream Place no dam over your words, Do not ask them to slow down, Do not hasten them forward Allow them to move freely As they are. Let the words pass through you, Peaceful and pleasant Temperamental and raging Sweet or bitter. They are not yours, They never were. Remember that all they want Is to reach their

**April 28th**

## Learn Something New

Write about something new you have learned to do or make, where the learning itself gave you pure pleasure. Write about the process, about the will to learn, about the fear of trying and then failing, up to the moment when something happened. Something was born. Something transpired. Write about a bench you have built, a cake you have baked, a picture you have drawn or any other new thing you have learned to do. Recall the sensation that suffused you the moment you saw the final product in front of you. Write it.

# April 29th

## Advice from a Tree

Choose a tree you love. Sit beside it and describe it in words. Focus on the details. Investigate it in depth.

Then let the tree speak to you. Listen to its wisdom. The tree has very important advice to give you. Devote yourself to its words and write them here. Compose the tree's monologue.

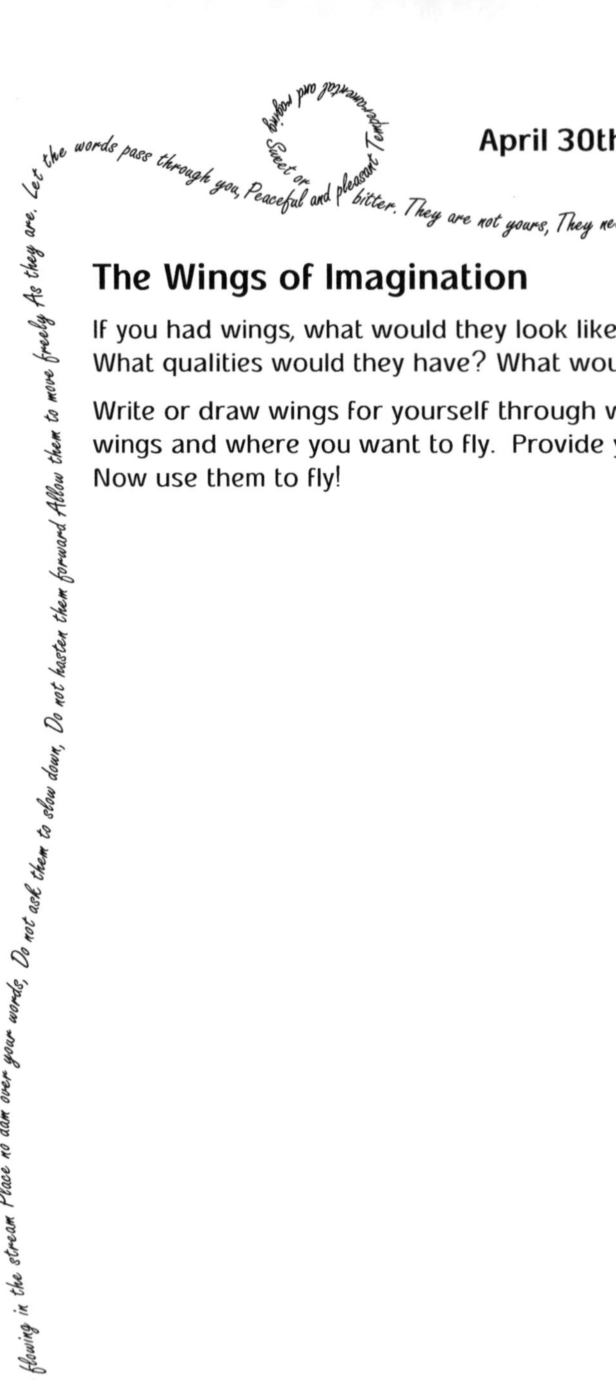
Let the words flow through you, Like the water flowing in the stream Place no dam over your words, Do not ask them to slow down, Do not hasten them forward Allow them to move freely As they are. Let the words pass through you, Peaceful and pleasant Temperamental and raging Sweet or bitter. They are not yours, They never were. Remember that all they want Is to reach their

## The Wings of Imagination

If you had wings, what would they look like? What would they be made of? What qualities would they have? What would you use them for?

Write or draw wings for yourself through words. Write why you need wings and where you want to fly. Provide yourself with the best of wings. Now use them to fly!

With the sea. Do not over flow, Do not hang on words. Learn from the river: Its only designation is To carry water

# May

## Writing to Love

Let the words flow through you, Like the water flowing in the stream Place no dam over your words, Do not ask them to slow down, Do not hasten them forward Allow them to move freely As they are. Let the words pass through you, Peaceful and pleasant Temperamental and raging Sweet or bitter. They are not yours, They never were. Remember that all they want Is to reach their

With the sea. Do not over flow, Do not hang on words. Learn from the river: Its only designation is To carry water

## The Things I Love

Write a list of all the things, people and experiences you love.

Begin with the words **I love...** and give voice to all that you love.

**May 2nd**

## An Interview with Love

If you could meet Love, what would you say to it? What would you ask it? Would you wish to make a request?

Imagine that Love is with you right now, and agrees to let you "interview" it. Converse with Love in writing, as you listen attentively. You have the opportunity to understand what makes the world go round.

*Let the words flow through you, Like the water flowing in the stream Place no dam over your words, Do not ask them to slow down, Do not hasten them forward Allow them to move freely As they are. Let the words pass through you, Peaceful and pleasant Temperamental and raging Sweet or bitter. They are not yours, They never were. Remember that all they want Is to reach their*

May 3rd

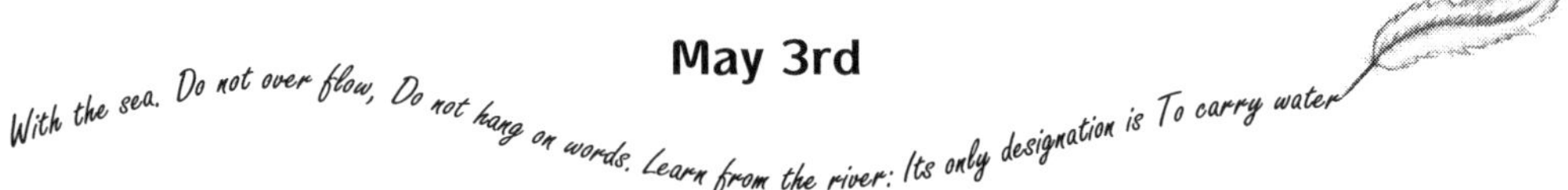
With the sea. Do not over flow, Do not hang on words. Learn from the river: Its only designation is To carry water

## With Our Love

This is the birthday of poet **Yehuda Amichai**, born in 1924.

"With our love - a body became a place," he wrote in one of his love poems.

This is an exercise inspired by Amichai. Think back about one of the greatest romantic loves you have ever experienced. What happened there - within you, in your body, in your heart? What went on between the two of you? What happened to you when you agreed to truly love?

Begin with the words **Our love...** and describe the greatest love of your life.

"My bounty is as boundless as the sea,
My love as deep; the more I give to thee,
The more I have, for both are infinite." **William Shakespeare**

May 4th

# I Will Never Love

Write a text that begins with the words **I will never love...**

*Let the words flow through you, Like the water flowing in the stream Place no dam over your words, Do not ask them to slow down, Do not hasten them forward Allow them to move freely As they are. Let the words pass through you, Peaceful and pleasant Temperamental and raging Sweet or bitter. They are not yours, They never were. Remember that all they want Is to reach their*

# May 5th

## Love Speaks

Could you write your love rather than **about** your love?

This is an invitation to try and do just that: let Love speak from within you and write its words, let them flow through you.

Write Love's monologue.

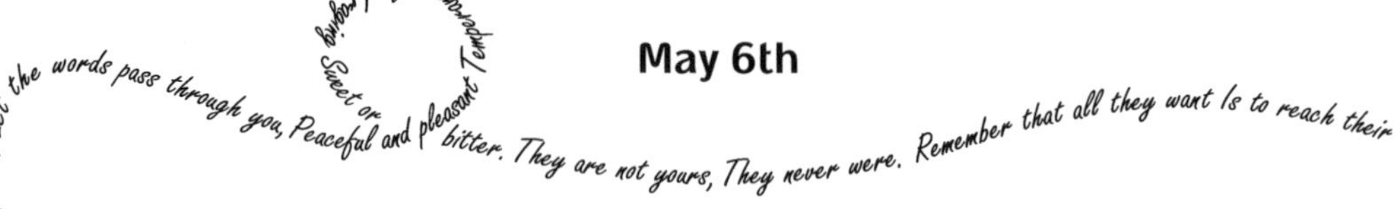
Let the words flow through you, Like the water flowing in the stream Place no dam over your words, Do not ask them to slow down, Do not hasten them forward Allow them to move freely As they are. Let the words pass through you, Peaceful and pleasant Temperamental and raging Sweet or bitter. They are not yours, They never were. Remember that all they want Is to reach their

**May 6th**

## My God

Who is God to you? What do you have to say about the essence called God?

Where does she or he reside? Within you or outside of you? Do you communicate with that essence? And if so, do you talk to him or her face to face, or from a distance?

Write the characteristics and qualities of your God, if you have one. Alternatively, allow yourself to imagine what kind of God she or he would be, if they existed.

Begin with the words **My God...**

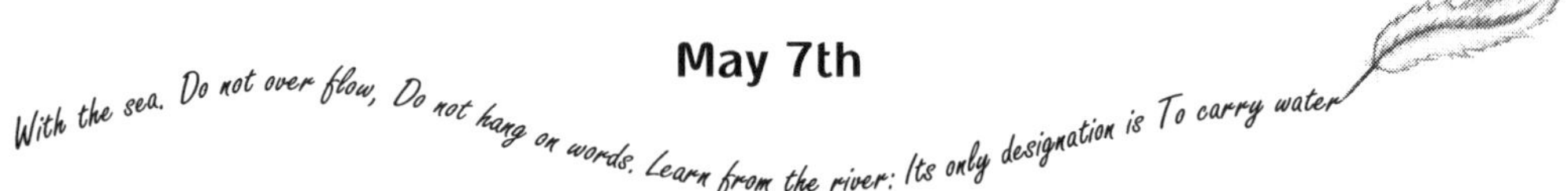
With the sea. Do not over flow, Do not hang on words. Learn from the river: Its only designation is To carry water

**May 7th**

## Living In God

Today is the birthday of poet **Rabindranath Tagore**, born in 1861.

"With the breath we draw we must always feel this truth that we are living in God,*" he wrote.

This exercise is inspired by Tagore. Write about a quality you possess that you consider godly. Something within you that is part of your behavior, a heavenly spark. Is it, perhaps, your grace, your generosity, your love?  Your creativity, or your aspiration for beauty and harmony?

Write about the divine residing within you.

"Love is the highest bliss that man can attain." **Tagore**

* *The English Writings of Rabindranath Tagore: Essays: Vol. 4.* Introduction by Mohit Kumar Ray, Atlantic, 2007, p. 407; 291

*Let the words flow through you, Like the water flowing in the stream Place no dam over your words, Do not ask them to slow down, Do not hasten them forward Allow them to move freely As they are. Let the words pass through you, Peaceful and pleasant Temperamental and raging Sweet or bitter. They are not yours, They never were. Remember that all they want Is to reach their*

**May 8th**

## Longing

Write about the longing in your life. What is longing to you? What or who do you long for? What does that longing awaken in you?

Begin with the words **I long for...**

## May 9th

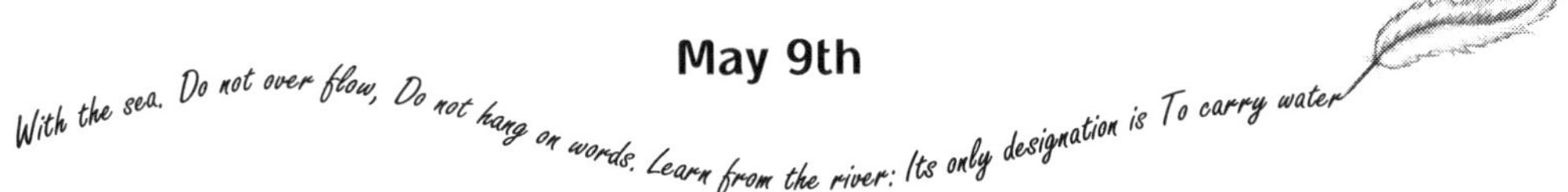
With the sea. Do not over flow, Do not hang on words. Learn from the river: Its only designation is To carry water

# If I were God

Ask yourself: if I were God and I could create an ideal world, what world would I create? What would it look like?

Imagine that you are God for a moment and that you have the opportunity to create the world any way you want. Describe in writing the world you would construct. Let yourself go wild on the page.

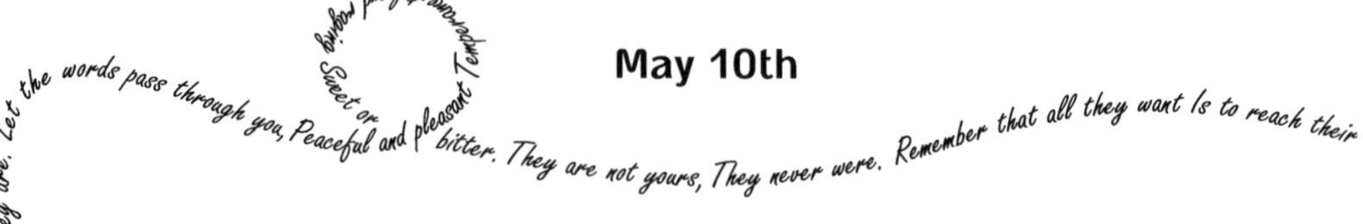
Let the words flow through you, Like the water flowing in the stream Place no dam over your words, Do not ask them to slow down, Do not hasten them forward Allow them to move freely As they are.
Let the words pass through you, Peaceful and pleasant Temperamental and raging Sweet or bitter. They are not yours, They never were. Remember that all they want Is to reach their

**May 10th**

## God Came to Me

When did God reveal Himself/Herself to you? When have you experienced divine moments in your life, moments of miracle and wonder?

Write 20 sentences to God that begin with the words **You have revealed yourself to me...**

If you prefer, you can write to Love, Compassion or any other quality that is divine in your eyes.

# May 11th

## A Love Poem

What person, animal or object do you love most in the world, to which your heart goes out?

Write a love poem to them. You can also address a hobby, a way of life or a value close to your heart.

Anything you choose is fine, as long as you allow yourself to compose your love in poetry.

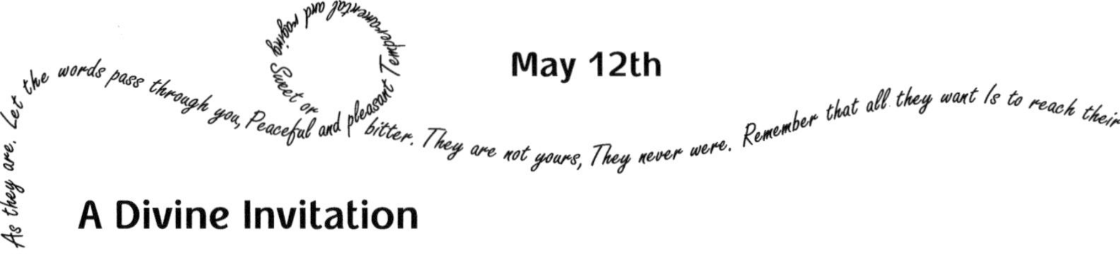
Let the words flow through you, Like the water flowing in the stream Place no dam over your words, Do not ask them to slow down, Do not hasten them forward Allow them to move freely As they are. Let the words pass through you, Peaceful and pleasant Temperamental and raging Sweet or bitter. They are not yours, They never were. Remember that all they want Is to reach their

**May 12th**

## A Divine Invitation

Today is the birthday of Persian poet **Hafiz**, born in 1320.

This is an exercise inspired by his poem "Divine Invitation". Imagine that you receive an invitation to meet God. What does this invitation say? Copy it here.

"No one can prevent us from carrying God wherever we go.
No one can rob His name from our hearts,...

We must not leave Him in the mosque, or the synagogue, alone at night." **Hafiz**

*The Subject Tonight is Love: 60 Wild and Sweet Poems of Hafiz.* Translated by Daniel Ladinsky, Penguin, 2003.

## May 13th

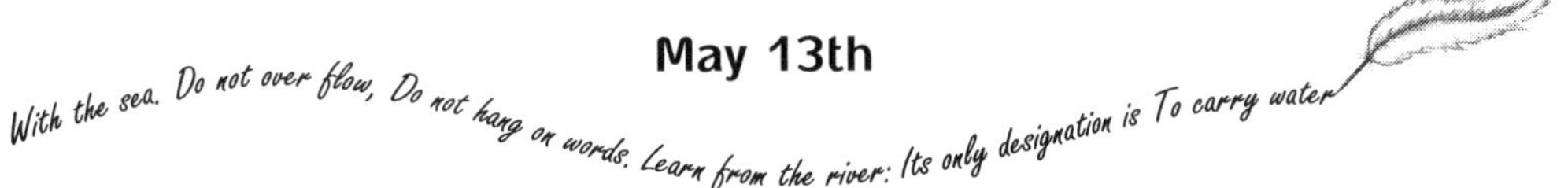
With the sea. Do not over flow, Do not hang on words. Learn from the river: Its only designation is To carry water

# Drinking Coffee with God

You have the opportunity to meet God face to face, to talk to Him/Her about anything, ask any question, and try to understand some aspects of your own life, with Their help. This is an invitation for you to open the door and sit down with God over a cup of coffee or tea.

Write about your imaginary meeting with God. Allow yourself to fly on the wings of your imagination. Anything is possible.

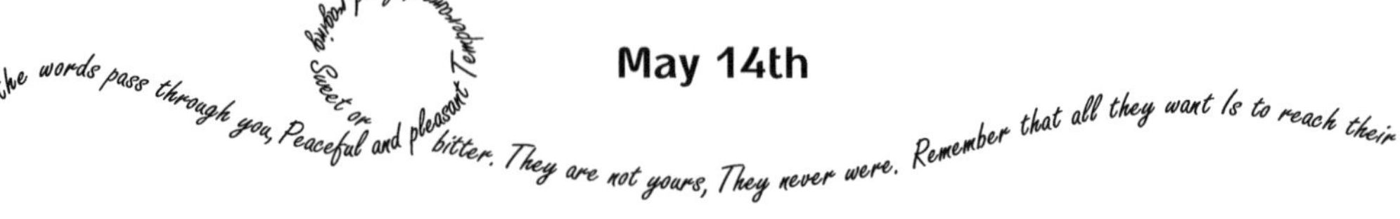
Let the words flow through you, Like the water flowing in the stream Place no dam over your words, Do not ask them to slow down, Do not hasten them forward Allow them to move freely As they are. Let the words pass through you, Peaceful and pleasant Temperamental and raging Sweet or bitter. They are not yours, They never were. Remember that all they want Is to reach their

**May 14th**

# Writing Love that Broke the Rules

Remember a moment in your life when love crossed every boundary, leaped over hurdles and broke through walls. Write that moment of your love. Give it space.

Let your words burst out like love. Let them be love.

## May 15th

# A Pure Heart

Today is the birthday of novelist **Frank L. Baum**, the author of *The Wizard of Oz*, born 1856.

"I have no heart, and so I must be very careful," says the Tin Man in this wonderful story.

This exercise is inspired by the Tin Man. Write what you must be careful about, in order to protect your heart. What must you avoid? What must you be strict about? Write these things as they are, so you can remember them.

Start with the words **I must be careful...**

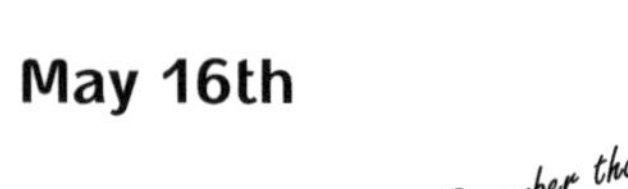

May 16th

## Writing the Truth

Today is the birthday of poet and feminist novelist **Adrienne Rich**, born in 1929.

"When a woman tells the truth she is creating the possibility for more truth around her,*" she wrote.

This exercise is inspired by Rich. Write the truth. What is your truth? When you speak or write your truth, what happens within you? Around you? Is it important to you that you live and express your truth? Must you express the truth?

Start with **When I am truthful...** and continue from these words to explore in writing what truth brings into your life.

"You must write, and read, as if your life depended on it." **Adrienne Rich**
*What Is Found There: Notebooks on Poetry and Politics*, Norton, 2003.

* *On Lies, Secrets, and Silence: Selected Prose* 1966–1978, Norton, 1995.

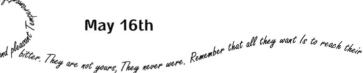

## May 17th

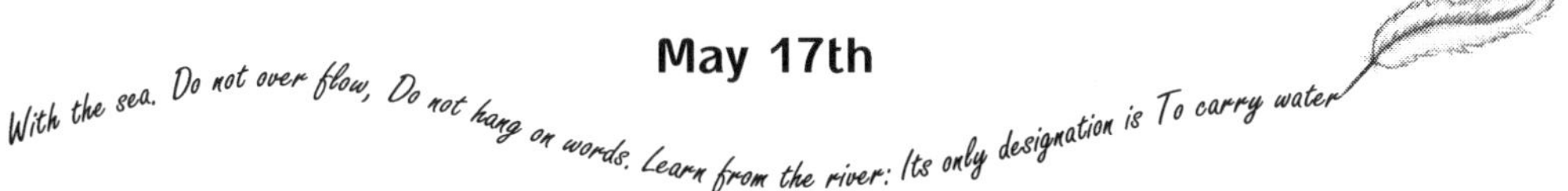
With the sea. Do not over flow, Do not hang on words. Learn from the river: Its only designation is To carry water

# The Heart-Shrine

This exercise is inspired by Cashmere poet **Lalla**, born in 1320.

In one of her poems*, Lalla discovers within the walls of her body, in the shrine of her heart, the love of her life.

Write about the shrine of your heart. What is inside that shrine? Who is inside it? Is the shrine exposed or guarded? What does it contain?

* *Naked Song*. Translated by Coleman Barks, Maypop, 1992.

**May 18th**

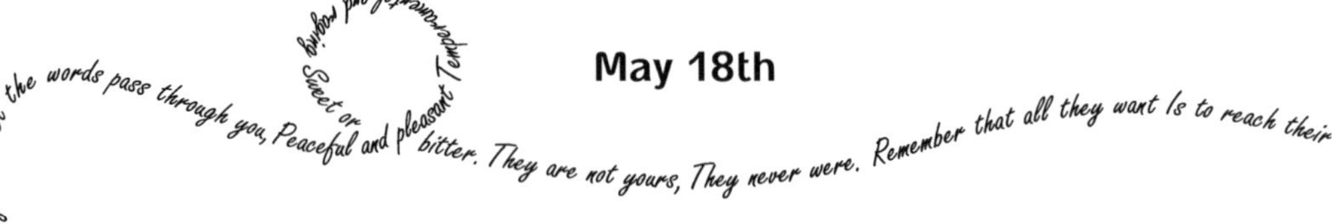
Let the words pass through you, Peaceful and pleasant Temperamental and raging Sweet or bitter. They are not yours, They never were. Remember that all they want Is to reach their

Let the words flow through you, Like the water flowing in the stream Place no dam over your words, Do not ask them to slow down, Do not hasten them forward Allow them to move freely As they are.

## A Love Letter to a Part of Me

Write a list of things you do not like about yourself: patterns, behaviors, beliefs, characteristics, parts of your physical body - anything that comes to mind.

Then choose the one item from this list you **like the least**, and write a love letter to it. Write about all the good you can possibly see in it. Write to it with profound understanding, acceptance and compassion. Find all that is good within it. Fill it with happiness, and learn to love that part of you as if there were nothing more precious.

Finally, I invite you to write that part of you a poem of love and acceptance, a true hymn of praise!

# May 19th

*With the sea. Do not over flow, Do not hang on words. Learn from the river: Its only designation is To carry water*

## Love thy Neighbor as Thyself

What kind of love do you need in your life?

Write the love you would like to have in your life. Describe it in detail.

When you finish writing, find a way to give someone else the exact love you need.

May 20th

## On the Way to Myself

Write a text with the title **On the Way to Myself**.

Where are these words leading you? Follow them.

*Let the words flow through you, Like the water flowing in the stream Place no dam over your words, Do not ask them to slow down, Do not hasten them forward Allow them to move freely As they are. Let the words pass through you, Peaceful and pleasant Temperamental and raging Sweet or bitter. They are not yours, They never were. Remember that all they want Is to reach their*

## May 21st

*With the sea. Do not over flow, Do not hang on words. Learn from the river: Its only designation is To carry water*

# Movement

What makes you move in your life? What leads you forward, propels you in the right direction?

Do you like being in motion? Explore what motivates you to move in life.

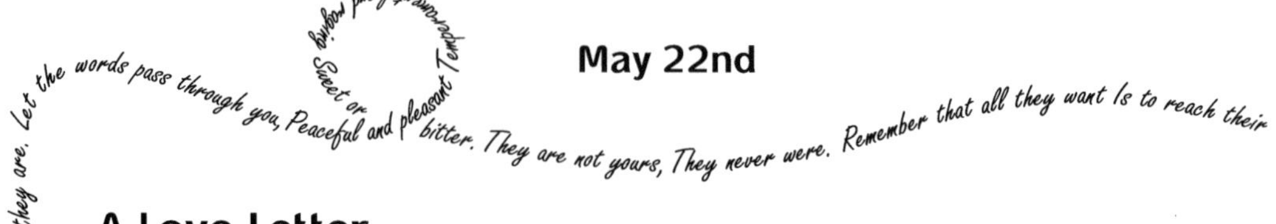
Let the words flow through you, Like the water flowing in the stream Place no dam over your words, Do not ask them to slow down, Do not hasten them forward Allow them to move freely As they are, Let the words pass through you, Peaceful and pleasant Temperamental and raging Sweet or bitter. They are not yours, They never were. Remember that all they want Is to reach their

**May 22nd**

## A Love Letter

Think of a person you love very much, but you don't think you express your love for them often or well enough. This is your chance to tell them how much you love him or her, and what it is about them that you love.

Write your love for this person with no holds barred. You are welcome to write similar love letters to other people in your life as well.

## May 23rd

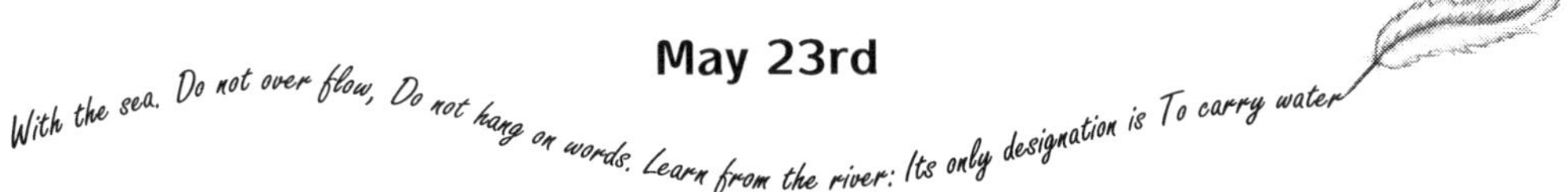
With the sea. Do not over flow, Do not hang on words. Learn from the river: Its only designation is To carry water

# What is the Story of Your Heart?

Write the story of the journey of your heart throughout your life. What has it gone through from the moment you were born until this day? Take a journey with your heart through meaningful moments when it opened up, fell in love, broke, closed down and healed. Your heart has been through a lot. Write **the journey of your heart**.

**May 24th**

## My Pen: The Monologue

Your writing tool is always accessible. It enables you to express yourself, create your words, stories and poems. Will you be there for it in return?

Close your eyes. Hold your pen or pencil, the utensil that connects you and your writing. Feel it as a living, beating object, flowing and full of soul. What role does it fulfill in your life?

Now open your eyes and allow the pen to "speak" to you. What does it have to say to you, ask of you? What does it need? What is its message to you? Listen to its words and write them. Let it tell you one thing that you do not know, from its point of view. Devote yourself to it. This time, your pen is the one controlling your writing.

## May 25th

*With the sea. Do not over flow, Do not hang on words. Learn from the river: Its only designation is To carry water*

# Words of Honey

What would you like to write in honey? What would you like to sweeten?

Write a text that is as sweet as honey. Start with the words **Writing with honey...** and let them carry you on a sweet little journey.

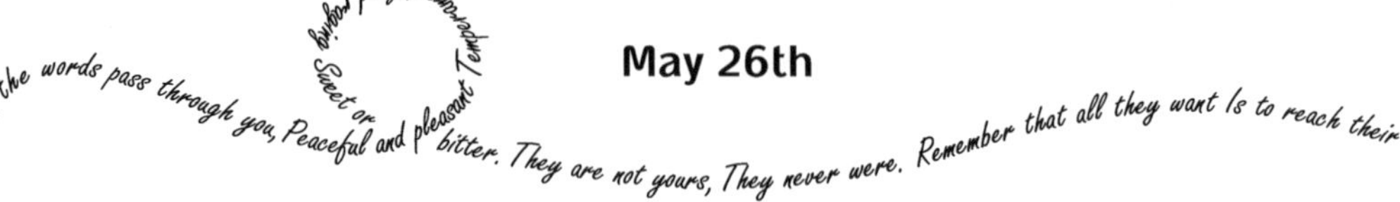
Let the words flow through you, Like the water flowing in the stream Place no dam over your words, Do not ask them to slow down, Do not hasten them forward Allow them to move freely As they are. Let the words pass through you, Peaceful and pleasant Temperamental and raging Sweet or bitter. They are not yours, They never were. Remember that all they want Is to reach their

**May 26th**

## Home

Write about your home. What is home for you? What qualities are in your home? What do you experience when you are at home? When and where do you feel at home, and who do you feel at home with?

Let yourself come back home through writing.

"Build a House for men and birds.
Sit with them and play music.
For a day, for just one day,
talk about that which disturbs no one
and bring some peace,
my friend,
into your beautiful eyes." **Hâfiz**

*The Subject Tonight Is Love: 60 Wild and Sweet Poems of Hafiz.* Translated by Daniel Ladinsky, Penguin, 2003.

With the sea. Do not over flow, Do not hang on words. Learn from the river: Its only designation is To carry water

## An Autobiography of Love

Happy birthday to poet and writer **Portia Nelson**, born in 1920.

This exercise is inspired by one of her most powerful poems, "Autobiography in Five Short Chapters" that describes a process of development, a process of change and especially the cyclicity of life.

Write a short text, as though it were a chapter from your own imaginary autobiography that describes the process **of loving yourself** from the moment you were born until this day.

"To love oneself is the beginning of a lifelong romance." **Oscar Wilde**

Let the words flow through you, Like the water flowing in the stream Place no dam over your words, Do not ask them to slow down, Do not hasten them forward Allow them to move freely As they are. Let the words pass through you, Peaceful and pleasant Temperamental and raging Sweet or bitter. They are not yours, They never were. Remember that all they want Is to reach their

**May 28th**

## Words From Outside and Inside the House

Out all the houses you have lived in over the course of your life, choose the one you loved the most, a place where you felt at home in every sense of the word. A home you wish to return to, perhaps in order to achieve closure, to find inspiration, or simply because you miss it.

Now imagine you are standing in front of that house, on the doorstep or in the garden, and write from that place. Then open the door, go inside and write from there. What do you find inside? Detail all the senses and impressions you find: smells, flavors, sounds, touch. When you have finished writing, consider what you would like to take from that house to yours.

With the sea. Do not over flow, Do not hang on words. Learn from the river: Its only designation is To carry water

## Teach Me, My Lord

Today is the birthday of poet **Leah Goldberg**, born in 1911.

In "End of the Road Poems" Goldberg asks God to teach her "to breathe, to sense, to see, to know, to wish, to fail."

This exercise is inspired by Goldberg. Write a poem that starts with the words **Teach me, my Lord...** What do you wish to learn?

May 30th

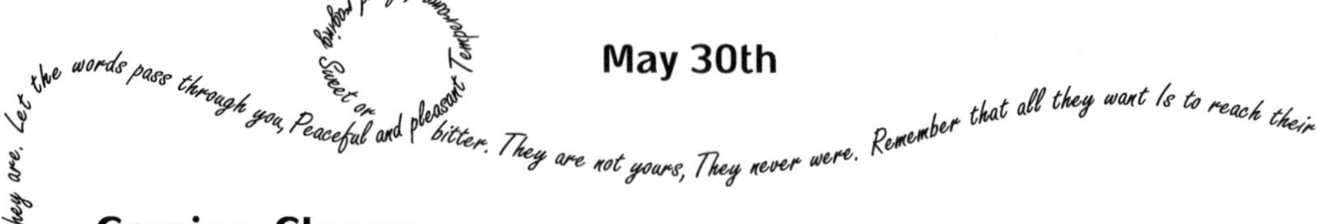
Let the words flow through you, Like the water flowing in the stream Place no dam over your words, Do not ask them to slow down, Do not hasten them forward Allow them to move freely As they are. Let the words pass through you, Peaceful and pleasant Temperamental and raging Sweet or bitter. They are not yours, They never were. Remember that all they want Is to reach their

## Coming Closer

Turn the words **come closer** over in your mind and let them roll down your pen onto your journal.

What do these words awaken in you? Do you experience more closeness or distance in your life? What would you be happy to get closer to in your life?

Write a text that invites you to come closer. Allow writing to draw you in.

## May 31st



# A Love Letter to Myself

This is the birthday of poet **Walt Whitman**, born in 1819.

"Nor do I understand who there can be more wonderful than myself," he wrote.

This exercise is inspired by Whitman. Write a love letter or poem to yourself, describing all the wonderful things you love about yourself. Write about all the characteristics, the qualities and the gifts you bring to the world. Look back at everything you have been through, and let yourself be enchanted by your journey and cherish yourself for it. Love yourself with your words. You are worthy.

# Summer
## BAREFOOT WORDS

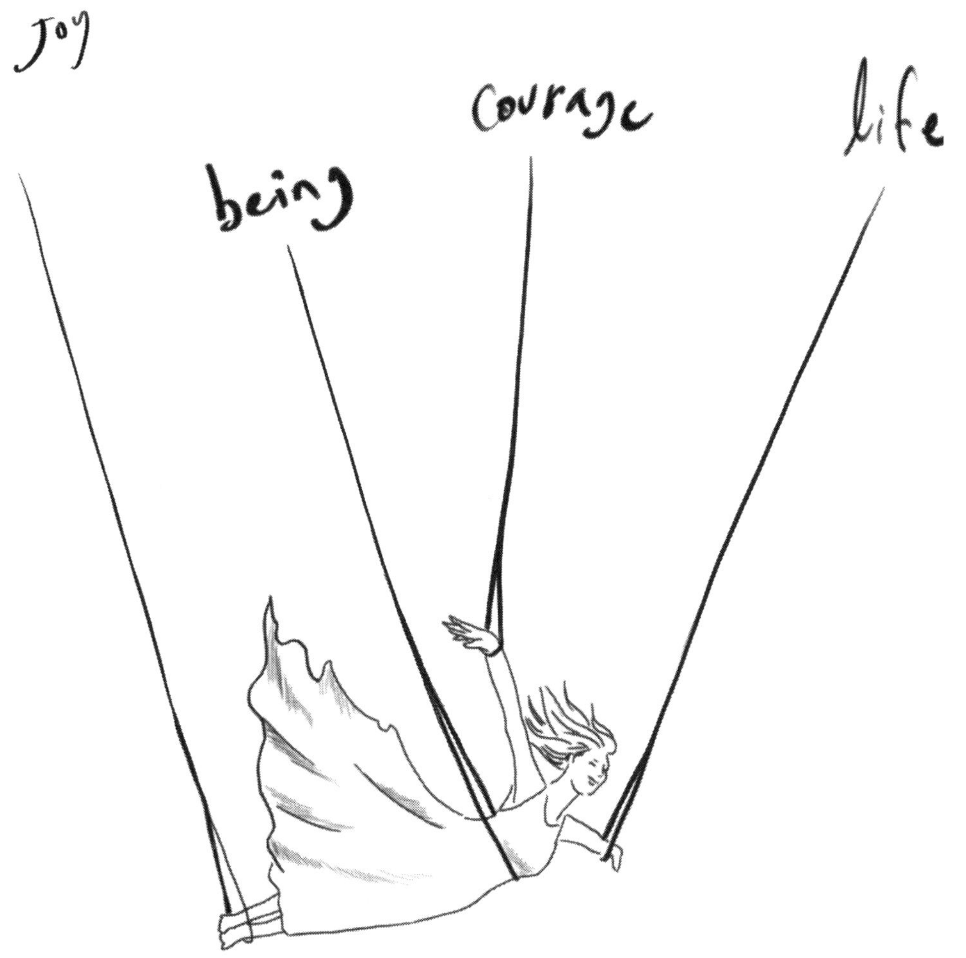

## Writing in Summer

Summer is the time to come out into the light. This is the season symbolizing the sun, the fire of recognition. On summer days, the sun's energy and presence is very strong. Everything is outdoors, brightly colored and potent.

Summer is the time the fruit of our labor from the passing year ripens. As in nature, this is the time when we harvest and enjoy that fruit. If we sow in the fall, water and nurture in winter, while contemplating both our deficiencies and our virtues throughout the year, then our rewards will arrive during the summer, and we can take delight in and celebrate the fruits of our labor.

So this is a wonderful time to sit back and enjoy all that there is to enjoy. Rest is also an important part of the process. Real rest is not laziness; rather, it can be expressed in strengthening friendships, reading fascinating books, creativity, hiking, tidying up the house and much, much more. All these activities comprise genuine rest that does not put us to sleep.

We should use summer days to truly rest and recharge, in order to arrive renewed and refreshed for the cycle in the coming new year.

**This portal invites you to shed all your familiar vocabulary and walk with barefoot words. Write the good, write to be happy, write your gratitude, and write to simply** be.

# June

## Writing the Good

Let the words flow through you, Like the water flowing in the stream Place no dam over your words, Do not ask them to slow down, Do not hasten them forward Allow them to move freely As they are. Let the words pass through you, Peaceful and pleasant Temperamental and raging Sweet or bitter. They are not yours, They never were. Remember that all they want Is to reach their

June 1st

*With the sea. Do not over flow, Do not hang on words. Learn from the river: Its only designation is To carry water*

## An Invitation to the Party of Your Life

The early days of summer invite you to come out into the light and celebrate life. Write an invitation to the "party of your life".

In this invitation, describe what the greatest party of your life is going to be like, and invite your loved ones to participate. Create your party without boundaries or limitations, anywhere and with whomever you wish. Anything is possible at the party of your life.

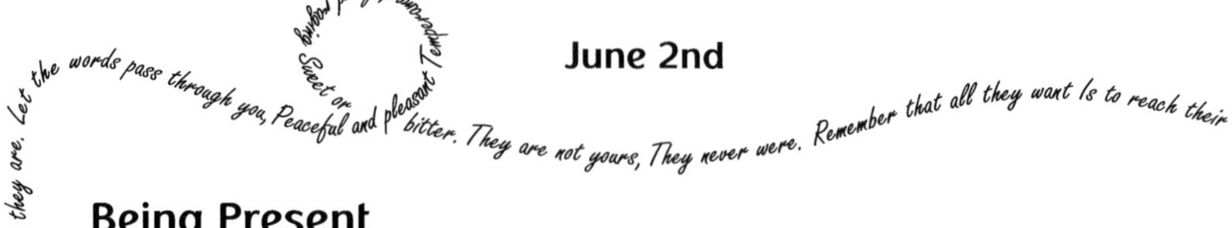
words pass through you, Peaceful and pleasant Temperamental and raging Sweet or bitter. They are not yours, They never were. Remember that all they want Is to reach their

## June 2nd

Let the words flow through you, Like the water flowing in the stream Place no dam over your words, Do not ask them to slow down, Do not hasten them forward Allow them to move freely As they are. Let the

# Being Present

Go for a short walk close to home. Be aware of everything around you. Listen to the sounds – let nature permeate your being and speak to you in its wonderful language.

Allow yourself to merge with nature, linger, take your time, marvel at everything that rises from within, become one with it. Now is the time to simply be. Write yourself present, here and now.

## June 3rd

*With the sea. Do not over flow, Do not hang on words. Learn from the river: Its only designation is To carry water*

# One Line a Day

Visit your bookshelf at home and choose a book that is calling out to you: "Take me!" Open it randomly, put your finger somewhere on the page and copy just one sentence from where your finger is.

Keep writing without knowing where this sentence is taking you.

Explore the sentence you've selected; notice if it brings up any memories, feelings, sensations or thoughts. Correspond with it, make love to it.

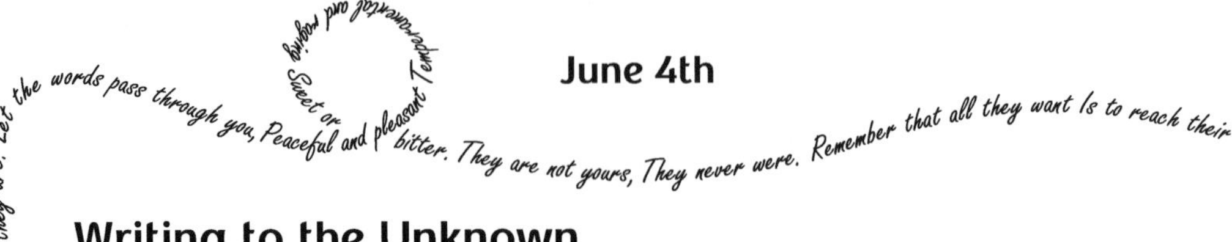


## June 4th

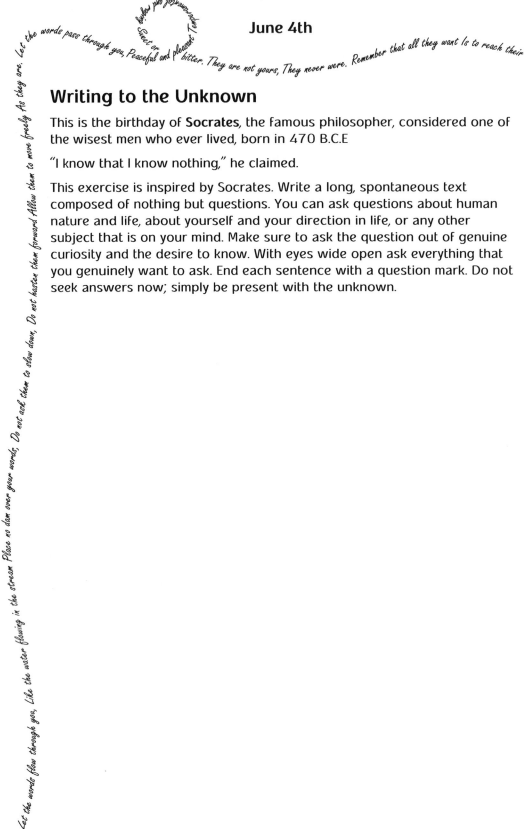

# Writing to the Unknown

This is the birthday of **Socrates**, the famous philosopher, considered one of the wisest men who ever lived, born in 470 B.C.E

"I know that I know nothing," he claimed.

This exercise is inspired by Socrates. Write a long, spontaneous text composed of nothing but questions. You can ask questions about human nature and life, about yourself and your direction in life, or any other subject that is on your mind. Make sure to ask the question out of genuine curiosity and the desire to know. With eyes wide open ask everything that you genuinely want to ask. End each sentence with a question mark. Do not seek answers now; simply be present with the unknown.

## Do Not Ask Me

Are there questions that bother you? Questions you do not like to be asked?

Write all the questions that you do not want to be asked. Start with the words: **Do not ask me...**

You may address the text to everyone around you or to someone in particular.

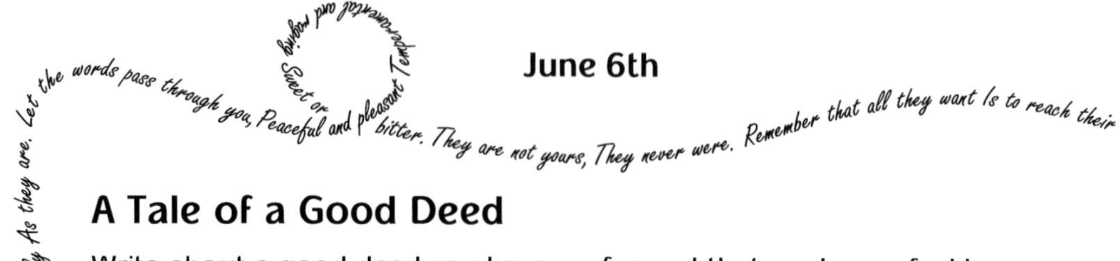
Let the words flow through you, Like the water flowing in the stream Place no dam over your words, Do not ask them to slow down, Do not hasten them forward Allow them to move freely As they are.
Let the words pass through you, Peaceful and pleasant Temperamental and raging Sweet or bitter. They are not yours, They never were. Remember that all they want Is to reach their

**June 6th**

## A Tale of a Good Deed

Write about a good deed you have performed that made you feel happy and content.

Tell this story from an external perspective, as if you were not a part of it.

What can you say about the person who did that good deed?

June 7th

*With the sea. Do not over flow, Do not hang on words. Learn from the river: Its only designation is To carry water*

## The Legend of a Tree

Sit and rest by your favorite tree. Write a short imaginary legend inspired by the tree you chose.

Allow the story to evolve from within, line by line, as though the plot created itself through the act of writing.

Let the words flow through you, Like the water flowing in the stream Place no dam over your words, Do not ask them to slow down, Do not hasten them forward Allow them to move freely As they are.

Let the words pass through you, Peaceful and pleasant Temperamental and raging Sweet or bitter. They are not yours, They never were. Remember that all they want Is to reach their



## Too Late?

Many times we live with the feeling of missing out, that it is too late to make an old dream come true. We think that it is too late for us to start dancing, singing, exercising, to learn something new. That it is too late to go on the stage, to surf in the sea, to bungee jump or to publish a book of poems.

Write ten sentences that start with the words **If it weren't too late, I would...**

Write quickly, without stopping, thinking as little as possible.

Then write another text that starts with the words **It is not too late...**

## June 9th

# The Child I Used to Be

This is your chance to go back in time to the child you used to be, to a particularly significant moment in your life.

What moment would you choose to go back to in your past? In this exercise you return to that moment and talk to the child you used to be.

Write everything here you would tell that child. Start with the words **My beloved child ...**

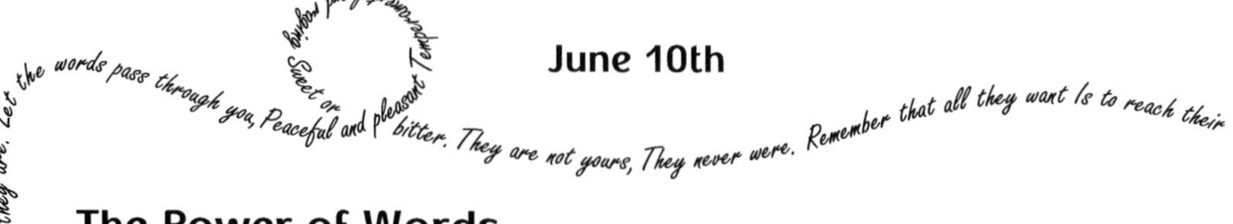
Let the words flow through you, Like the water flowing in the stream Place no dam over your words, Do not ask them to slow down, Do not hasten them forward Allow them to move freely As they are. Let the words pass through you, Peaceful and pleasant Temperamental and raging Sweet or bitter. They are not yours, They never were. Remember that all they want Is to reach their

## June 10th

# The Power of Words

Words have a creative force, the power to create life. Words are nature itself, the entire world was created with words. If we connect to the divine part inside us, we will find that our whole life is an act of writing and creating.

Recall a significant experience in your life that demonstrated the creative force of words. Have you ever said something that immediately happened? Do you remember words you said, or were said to you, at a turning point in your life that led to change? Have you ever saved someone, or have been saved, through words?

Describe this experience in writing. Start with the words that were meaningful for you, and continue writing about what the power of words is to you.

# June 11th



## Elementary Writing

Write about the four elements that function within you:

**Fire** (willpower), **Water** (emotion), **Air** (thought), **Earth** (realization).

Explore, in writing, your connection to each element, and describe its expression in your life.

Then ask yourself to which of these elements you feel most connected, and write a text expressing you as this element: "**I am earth**" or "**I am water**" or "**I am fire**" or "**I am air**".

Let the words pass through you, Peaceful and pleasant Temperamental and raging Sweet or bitter. They are not yours, They never were. Remember that all they want Is to reach their

**June 12th**

Let the words flow through you, Like the water flowing in the stream Place no dam over your words, Do not ask them to slow down, Do not hasten them forward Allow them to move freely As they are.

## Dear Diary

Today is the birthday of **Anne Frank**, born in 1929.

"I want this diary itself to be my friend, and I shall call my friend Kitty," she wrote in her personal diary, which, over the years since its publication, became the most-read personal journal in the world.

This exercise – **Dear Diary** – is inspired by Anne Frank. Give the diary you write in every day a name. Now write a personal letter to your diary. Tell it everything, as if you are writing to your best friend.

# June 13th

*With the sea. Do not over flow, Do not hang on words. Learn from the river: Its only designation is To carry water*

## Be Kind to Yourself

Write a text in the second person that starts with these words: **Be kind to yourself.**

Treat yourself with love and compassion. Immerse yourself in the words you need to hear.

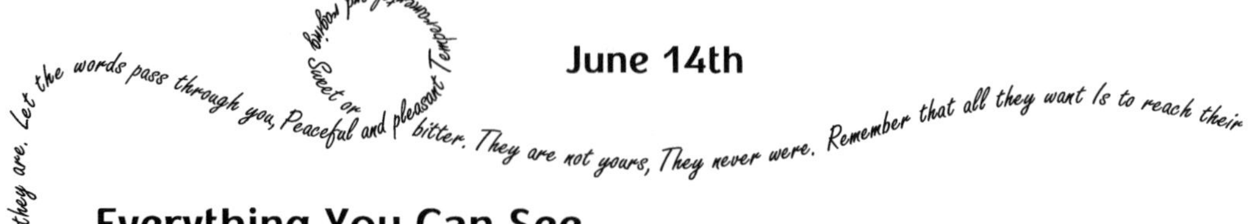
Let the words flow through you, Like the water flowing in the stream Place no dam over your words, Do not ask them to slow down, Do not hasten them forward Allow them to move freely As they are. Let the words pass through you, Peaceful and pleasant Temperamental and raging Sweet or bitter. They are not yours, They never were. Remember that all they want Is to reach their

**June 14th**

## Everything You Can See

Dedicate a minute or two to looking around. Now write everything you see in front of you at this moment. Include the minutest details: colors, shapes, composition, light and shade. Don't skip anything.

Be attentive to your sense of vision and everything that your eyes can see.

With the sea. Do not over flow, Do not hang on words. Learn from the river: Its only designation is To carry water

## Everything You Cannot See

Write everything that you cannot actually see now. Allow your imagination to guide your writing and fill the page.

## June 16th

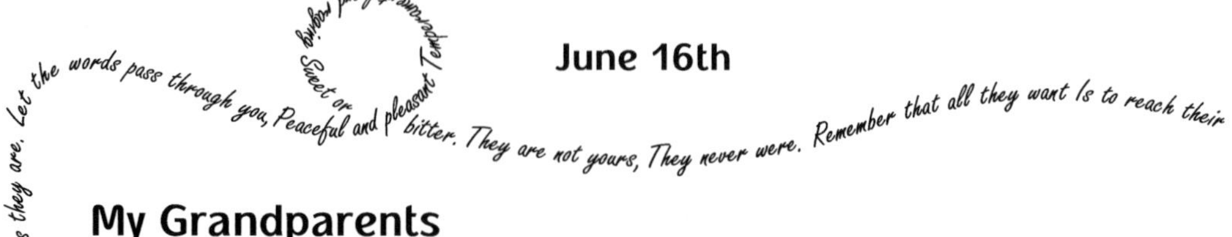
Let the words pass through you, Peaceful and pleasant Temperamental and raging Sweet or bitter. They are not yours, They never were. Remember that all they want Is to reach their

Let the words flow through you, Like the water flowing in the stream Place no dam over your words, Do not ask them to slow down, Do not hasten them forward Allow them to move freely As they are.

# My Grandparents

What did your grandmother or grandfather like to tell you about your life? Whether they are alive or not, whether you knew each other well, or whether you never met, write a text from their perspective that expresses who you are today. Let them speak to you as a loving grandparent who wishes the very best for you.

You may also write as the ideal grandmother or grandfather you never had.

## June 17th

*With the sea. Do not over flow, Do not hang on words. Learn from the river: Its only designation is To carry water*

# Impel or Inhibit?

Write two lists: one a list of all the things that **inhibit** you from writing, and the other a list of all the things that **impel** you to write.

Now write which of the lists you empower to guide you.

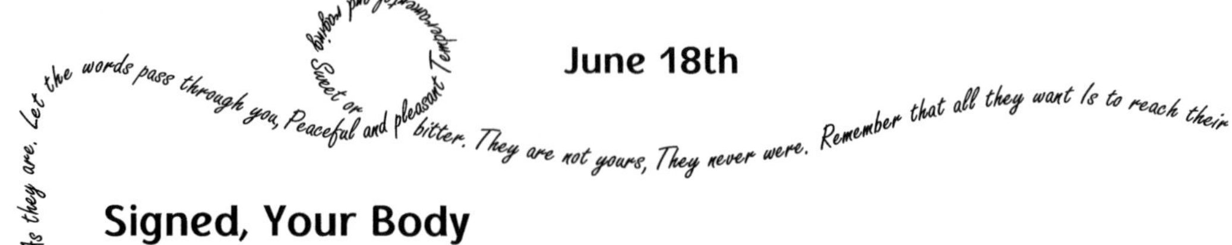
Let the words flow through you, Like the water flowing in the stream Place no dam over your words, Do not ask them to slow down, Do not hasten them forward Allow them to move freely As they are. Let the words pass through you, Peaceful and pleasant Temperamental and raging Sweet or bitter. They are not yours, They never were. Remember that all they want Is to reach their

June 18th

## Signed, Your Body

Imagine there is a letter from your body waiting in your mailbox. It turns out that for a long time it has wanted to tell you something.

Open it and copy that imaginary letter here, signed by your body.

# June 19th

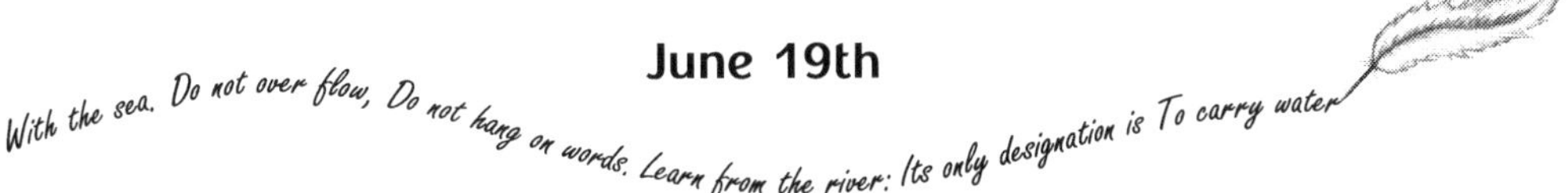
With the sea. Do not over flow, Do not hang on words. Learn from the river: Its only designation is To carry water

## Leisure

Today is the birthday of the poet **Zelda**, born in 1914.

In her poem, "Leisure"* Zelda wrote:

"We had a hidden treasure of leisure, – / gentle as the morning air, leisure of stories, tears, kisses – / leisure of holidays."

This exercise is inspired by Zelda. Do you have leisure time? Do you know how to fill your free time with things that expand your heart and spirit? Write about the "hidden treasure" of your leisure. What is it made of?

* *The Spectacular Difference: Selected Poems of Zelda*. Translated by Marcia Falk, Hebrew Union College Press, 2004.

June 20th

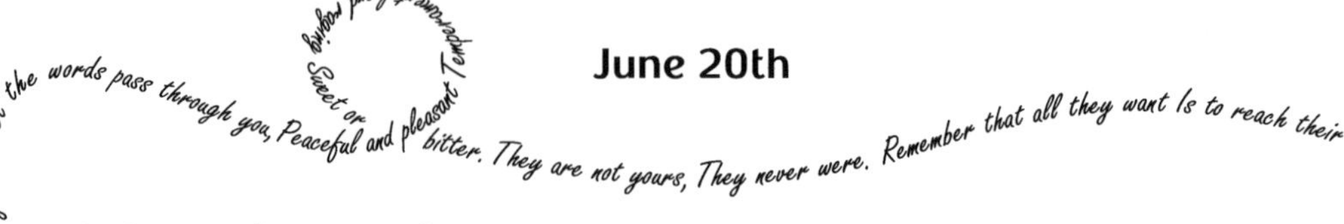
Let the words flow through you, Like the water flowing in the stream Place no dam over your words, Do not ask them to slow down, Do not hasten them forward Allow them to move freely As they are.
Let the words pass through you, Peaceful and pleasant Temperamental and raging Sweet or bitter. They are not yours, They never were. Remember that all they want Is to reach their

## A Story in the Light

Today is your chance to touch a story that empowers and strengthens you, a story that lights your way. It can be an experience you have had, kind and meaningful words said to you, or a tale that, every time you think about it, fills you with inspiration. When times are tough, it reminds you that there is light at the end of the tunnel, instilling joy, hope and beauty in you.

What is it? Write it.

## June 21st

*With the sea. Do not over flow, Do not hang on words. Learn from the river: Its only designation is To carry water*

# Going Out into the Light

This exercise is inspired by **the longest day of the year.** Write a text that expresses your coming into the light. What within you is asking to come out into light right now?

Perhaps something within you is asking to "come out" and express itself. Perhaps a song or story, your voice, or some other hidden talent that revealed itself to you on your journey in life. Agree to meet it – agree to be in the light. Start with the words **I go out into the light...**

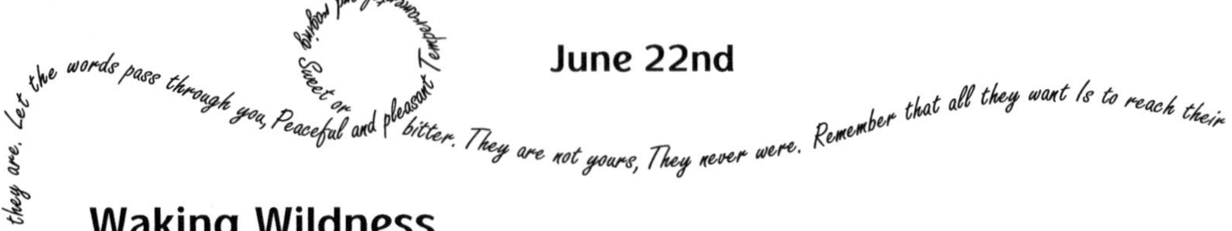
Let the words flow through you, Like the water flowing in the stream Place no dam over your words, Do not ask them to slow down, Do not hasten them forward Allow them to move freely As they are. Let the words pass through you, Peaceful and pleasant Temperamental and raging Sweet or bitter. They are not yours, They never were. Remember that all they want Is to reach their

**June 22nd**

## Waking Wildness

What is it that "turns off" the wild person living and breathing inside you? Can you identify what makes you keep quiet, belittle yourself, disappear, lose yourself?

In contrast, what is it that ignites and awakens you from within? What lights you and empowers your presence, freedom and expression?

Write about these contradicting forces inside you.

June 23rd

*With the sea. Do not over flow, Do not hang on words. Learn from the river: Its only designation is To carry water*

## I Have Learned to Live

Today is the birthday of poet **Anna Akhmatova**, born in 1889.

"I taught myself to live simply and wisely, to look at the sky and pray to God,*" she wrote in one of her beautiful poems.

This exercise is inspired by Akhmatova. Write how you have learned to live your life, to be kind to yourself and your surroundings. What have you learned about how to live life? What is the right way for you? Write the learning process from your life experience.

Start with the words **I have learned to live...** and let them lead you.

* first published in *Russkaia mysl'* (*Russian Thought*), in 1913

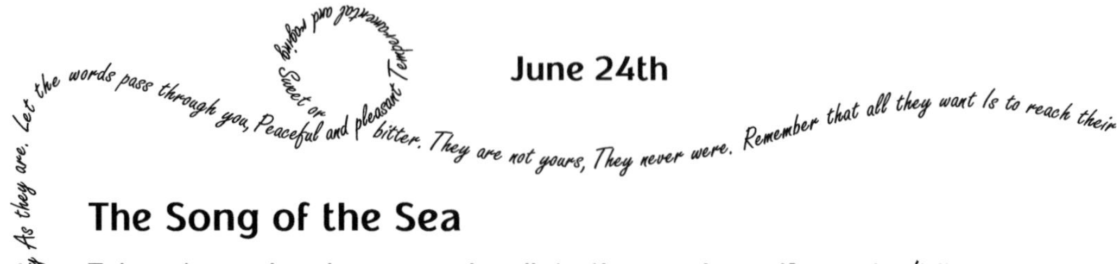
Let the words flow through you, Like the water flowing in the stream Place no dam over your words, Do not ask them to slow down, Do not hasten them forward Allow them to move freely As they are.
Let the words pass through you, Peaceful and pleasant Temperamental and raging Sweet or bitter. They are not yours, They never were. Remember that all they want Is to reach their

June 24th

## The Song of the Sea

Take a journal and a pen and walk to the seashore. If you don't live near the sea, use your imagination. Dip your feet in the water, and let the words come to you.

Write with the waves while you move your feet in the water, wave after wave, word after word. Let the words come to touch you, and then let them go, until new words appear.

Thus, echoing the movement of waves in the water, write your own sea song.

## June 25th

# One Day It Will Happen

Write a text that starts with the words **One day it will happen.**

Surrender yourself to this sentence and follow where it leads you.

What will happen one day?

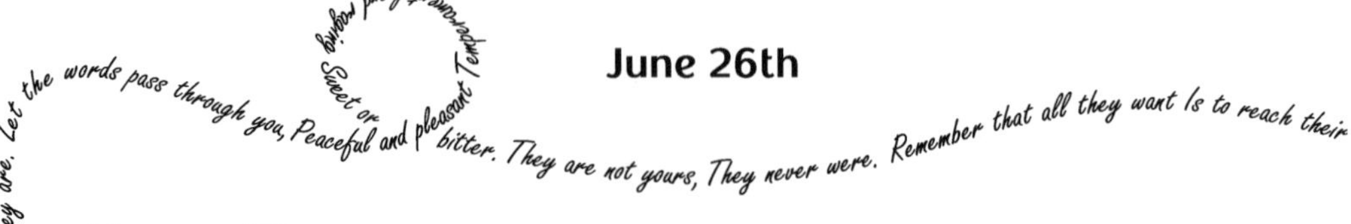
Let the words flow through you, Like the water flowing in the stream Place no dam over your words, Do not ask them to slow down, Do not hasten them forward Allow them to move freely As they are. Let the words pass through you, Peaceful and pleasant Temperamental and raging Sweet or bitter. They are not yours, They never were. Remember that all they want Is to reach their

**June 26th**

## Happy Rhymes

This exercise is inspired by your favorite children's poet. Write a poem with happy rhymes. Have fun, write lightheartedly, and rhyme like a child exploring language – its sounds, voices, words and letters.

With the sea. Do not over flow, Do not hang on words. Learn from the river: Its only designation is To carry water

## Blind Writing

This is the birthday of author and activist **Helen Keller**, who was born in 1880. When she was two years old, an illness left her deaf and blind.

This exercise is inspired by her: **sensory writing**. Close your eyes for five minutes and be attentive to your five senses: sight, sound, taste, smell and touch. Then sit in the dark for about five minutes. Allow these senses to awaken and grow stronger within.

Now start writing with your eyes closed. Do not flinch at the thought that the writing will not be readable but devote yourself to the writing. Open your eyes only when the process is complete.

"Keep your face to the sun and you will never see the shadows." **Helen Keller**

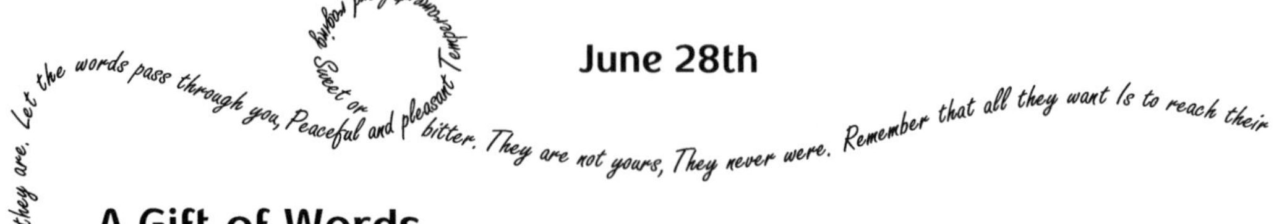
Let the words pass through you, Peaceful and pleasant Temperamental and raging Sweet or bitter. They are not yours, They never were. Remember that all they want Is to reach their

June 28th

Let the words flow through you, Like the water flowing in the stream Place no dam over your words, Do not ask them to slow down, Do not hasten them forward Allow them to move freely As they are.

## A Gift of Words

Think about someone in your life who is presently coping with a challenge. Write him or her a letter of support in their difficult time. Share your wisdom and experience with them. Tell them how you handled a difficult period in your life.

With the sea. Do not over flow, Do not hang on words. Learn from the river: Its only designation is To carry water

## The Eyes of the Heart

Today is the birthday of author **Antoine de Saint-Exupéry**, born in 1900, who wrote *The Little Prince*.

This exercise is inspired by Saint-Exupéry. Write a text that corresponds with his famous sentence: "It is only with the heart that one can see rightly; what is essential is invisible to the eye."

Reflect upon this sentence in writing. What does it mean to you, to see things with the heart?

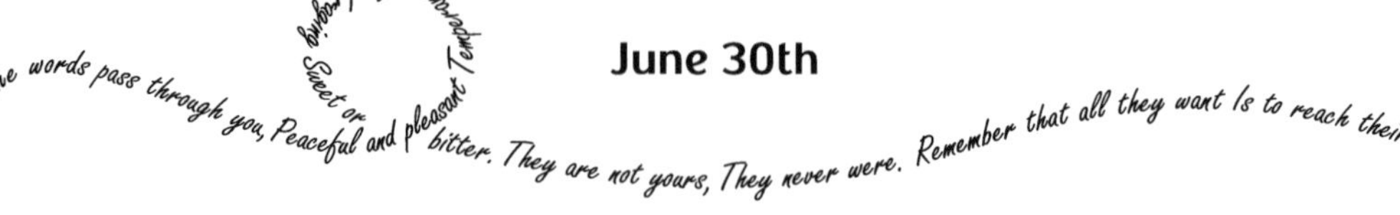
Let the words flow through you, Like the water flowing in the stream Place no dam over your words, Do not ask them to slow down, Do not hasten them forward Allow them to move freely As they are. Let the words pass through you, Peaceful and pleasant Temperamental and raging Sweet or bitter. They are not yours, They never were. Remember that all they want Is to reach their

**June 30th**

## The Gift of a Day

This is the birthday of poet **Czeslaw Milosz**, born in 1911.

"A day so happy.... / There was nothing on earth I wanted to possess," wrote Milosz in his poem "Gift"*.

This exercise is inspired by his poem. Write a day in your life that has been a gift to you. A day when you were happy to be who you are, doing what you do. Describe this day in your own words.

* *New and Collected Poems (1931-2001).* Ecco (HarperCollins), 2003.

With the sea. Do not over flow, Do not hang on words. Learn from the river: Its only designation is To carry water

# July

## Writing to be Happy

Let the words flow through you, Like the water flowing in the stream Place no dam over your words, Do not ask them to slow down, Do not hasten them forward Allow them to move freely As they are. Let the words pass through you, Peaceful and pleasant Temperamental and raging Sweet or bitter. They are not yours, They never were. Remember that all they want Is to reach their

## July 1st



# Open the Door to Happiness

What is happiness to you? What makes you truly happy?

Open the doors of your heart and your home (as well as all the windows) and let the joy of summer in. Today, connect to the natural, childish, pure happiness within you.

Write a text that starts with the words **When I open the door to happiness...**

Let the words flow through you, Like the water flowing in the stream Place no dam over your words, Do not ask them to slow down, Do not hasten them forward Allow them to move freely As they are. Let the words pass through you, Peaceful and pleasant Temperamental and raging Sweet or bitter. They are not yours, They never were. Remember that all they want Is to reach their

**July 2nd**

## The Joy of Writing

This is the birthday of poet **Wisława Szymborska**, born in 1923.

This exercise is inspired by one of her wonderful poems, "The Joy of Writing".

How does writing make you feel? Do you feel happy after writing? Or perhaps for you, writing and joy don't connect at all? Write about that.

If the joy of writing exists within you, let yourself rejoice in your own words.

And if writing evokes a different feeling inside of you, express it.

"To achieve the possible, the impossible must be tried again and again."
**Hermann Hesse**, also born on this day in 1877.

## July 3rd

# A Prayer

This is the birthday of novelist **Franz Kafka**, born in 1883.

According to Kafka, "Writing is a form of prayer."

This exercise is inspired by his words. Give yourself permission to pray in writing on this page. Pray sincerely in your own words.

Let the words flow through you, Like the water flowing in the stream Place no dam over your words, Do not ask them to slow down, Do not hasten them forward Allow them to move freely As they are.

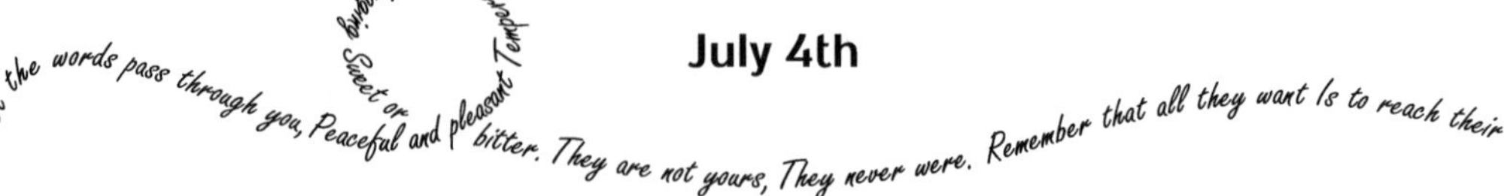
Let the words pass through you, Peaceful and pleasant Temperamental and raging Sweet or bitter. They are not yours, They never were. Remember that all they want Is to reach their

**July 4th**

## A Prescription for Myself

What prescription will empower you to be yourself? How can you be most authentic and genuine?

Write a prescription that will lead you into yourself, a compass to show you the way – the right amount, the desired doses and the exact times to take your prescription. Write what it is you must do, and how you should live, in order to be your best self.

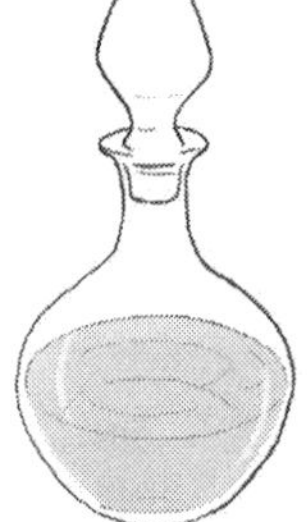

## That Day

Today is the birthday of novelist **George Sand,** born in 1804.

"Nature is an artistic masterpiece, and God Himself is the only great artist," she wrote.

Think about a day in your life when you felt a part of nature's artistic masterpiece. Now write a text that expresses that day and its importance.

Start with the words **That day**... and let your writing take you from there. What happened that day that left an impression on you?

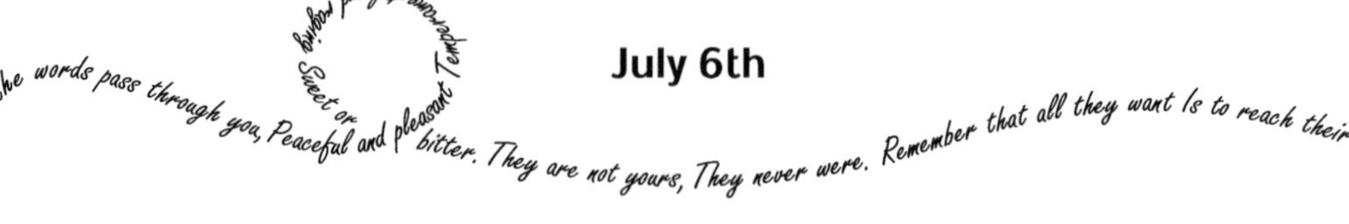
Let the words flow through you, Like the water flowing in the stream Place no dam over your words, Do not ask them to slow down, Do not hasten them forward Allow them to move freely As they are. Let the words pass through you, Peaceful and pleasant Temperamental and raging Sweet or bitter. They are not yours, They never were. Remember that all they want Is to reach their

**July 6th**

## Cultivating the Power of Joy

Today is the birthday of the **Dalai Lama**, born in 1935.

"The more we turn toward others, the more joy we experience, and the more joy we experience, the more we can bring joy to others,"* he wrote.

This exercise is inspired by the Dalai Lama. Write what cultivates joy within you. Describe what fills you with joy and delight when you do them.

* Bstan-dzin-rgya-mtsho, Dalai Lama XIV and Desmond Tutu. *The Book of Joy: Lasting Happiness in a Changing World.* Avery, 2016.

With the sea. Do not over flow, Do not hang on words. Learn from the river: Its only designation is To carry water

## The Greatest Joy in my Life

What is the happiest thing that ever happened to you, something that caused your heart to overflow with delight?

Write in great detail about this event. Remember the joy that entered your life then.

Let the words flow through you, Like the water flowing in the stream Place no dam over your words, Do not ask them to slow down, Do not hasten them forward Allow them to move freely As they are. Let the words pass through you, Peaceful and pleasant Temperamental and raging Sweet or bitter. They are not yours, They never were. Remember that all they want Is to reach their

**July 8th**

## Worthwhile

Turn the word **worthwhile** over in your mind and let it roll down your pen onto your journal. What does it evoke in you? What is worth your while? When? Under what circumstances?

Start with the word **Worthwhile...** and write freely. Let the writing carry you to new realms. It's worth your while!

## July 9th

# Write a Story for Children

Select a children's book that you especially love. Read it, and consider how it relates to your life story – does it remind you of something or evoke feelings in you?

Now, think about the story of your life, or certain events from your life, as a source of for a children's story. Draw inspiration from the book you love (from its content, illustrations, rhythm, repetitiveness or anything else that comes to mind), and write a simple, lighthearted children's book, one page long.

*Let the words flow through you, Like the water flowing in the stream Place no dam over your words, Do not ask them to slow down, Do not hasten them forward Allow them to move freely As they are. Let the words pass through you, Peaceful and pleasant Temperamental and raging Sweet or bitter. They are not yours, They never were. Remember that all they want Is to reach their*

**July 10th**

## In Search of Lost Time

This is the birthday of author **Marcel Proust**, born in 1871.

This exercise is inspired by his great creation *In Search of Lost Time.*

It is human nature to put emphasis on traumatic and unpleasant events, but our life is also full of joy, moments of laughter, love and happiness.

Set out on a writing journey in search of your lost happy time. Browse through your photo albums and look for pictures from the past that express joy. Select a picture where you are laughing or playful. It might be a photo taken on a happy occasion you may have forgotten and has faded over the years. Remember this occasion in as much detail as possible, and follow this lost memory. Give it new life within you. Write as if it is happening now.

You can select more than one photograph that makes you happy and revive those lost memories in your words.

# July 11th

*With the sea. Do not over flow, Do not hang on words. Learn from the river: Its only designation is To carry water*

## Proud of Yourself

Write a list of 20 things in your life that you are very proud of.

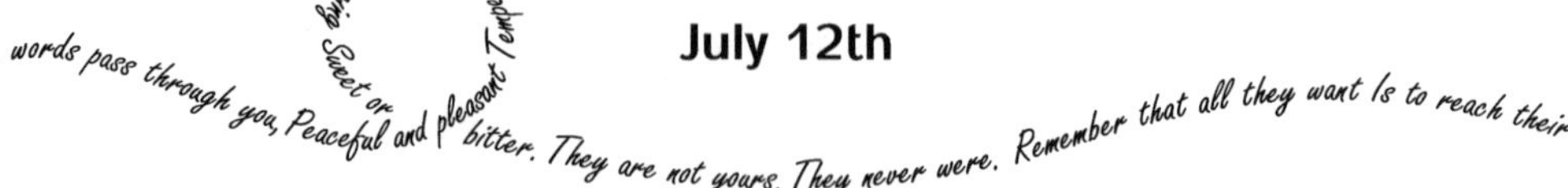
Let the words pass through you, Peaceful and pleasant Temperamental and raging Sweet or bitter. They are not yours, They never were. Remember that all they want Is to reach their

## July 12th

Let the words flow through you, Like the water flowing in the stream Place no dam over your words, Do not ask them to slow down, Do not hasten them forward Allow them to move freely As they are. Let the

# To Live Deliberately

Today is the birthday of author and philosopher, **Henry David Thoreau**, born in 1817.

"I went to the woods because I wished to front only the essential facts of life, and see if I could not learn what it had to teach, and not, when I came to die, discover that I had not lived," he wrote in his book *Walden*.

Write what it means to you to "live deliberately" or to prioritize "the essential facts of life".

Where do you need to go or what do you need to do to live a life of intent and essence? Who do you think lives that way? When do you?

Start with the words **To live deliberately...** and let your words express the spirit of the life you seek.

"You must live in the present, launch yourself on every wave, find your eternity in each moment." **Henry David Thoreau**

*The Writings of Henry D. Thoreau: Journal, Volume 7: 1853-1854.* Edited by Nancy Craig Simmons and Ron Thomas, Princeton UP, 2009.

With the sea. Do not over flow, Do not hang on words. Learn from the river: Its only designation is To carry water

## All that I am Not

Write a text that includes all that you are not.

**July 14th**

## All that I am

Write a text that includes all that you are.

*Let the words flow through you, Like the water flowing in the stream Place no dam over your words, Do not ask them to slow down, Do not hasten them forward Allow them to move freely As they are. Let the words pass through you, Peaceful and pleasant Temperamental and raging Sweet or bitter. They are not yours, They never were. Remember that all they want Is to reach their*

With the sea. Do not over flow, Do not hang on words. Learn from the river: Its only designation is To carry water

## Precision

What does being precise mean to you? Why do you need precision in your life? Do you aspire to it? When do you experience precision? How does it feel when you are precise? Start writing spontaneously, and then more precisely.

Start with the words **When I am precise...**

## July 16th

# Writing Happiness

Write a happy poem about happiness, without using the word "happiness", or any variations of it, even once. Instead of talking about it, become happiness – through your words.

*Let the words flow through you, Like the water flowing in the stream Place no dam over your words, Do not ask them to slow down, Do not hasten them forward Allow them to move freely As they are. Let the words pass through you, Peaceful and pleasant Temperamental and raging Sweet or bitter. They are not yours, They never were. Remember that all they want Is to reach their*

**July 17th**

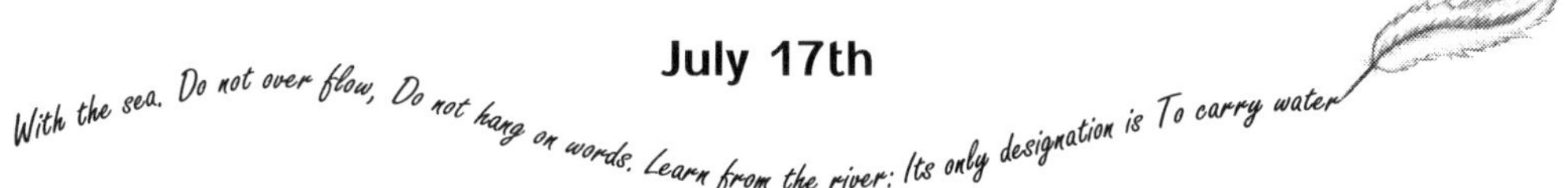
With the sea. Do not over flow, Do not hang on words. Learn from the river: Its only designation is To carry water

## Gathering Together

Write about everything that would make you happy to collect onto this page, into this day and into your life.

Perhaps you want to gather yourself? Or gather strength? Gather the pieces together, or gather your child into your arms? Imagine that you are a collector who gathers the very best, a collector of words that create life. Gather them together into you, word by word, line by line. Let them be collected one on top of the other.

Start with the words **I am gathering ...**

**July 18th**

*Let the words flow through you, Like the water flowing in the stream Place no dam over your words, Do not ask them to slow down, Do not hasten them forward Allow them to move freely As they are. Let the words pass through you, Peaceful and pleasant Temperamental and raging Sweet or bitter. They are not yours, They never were. Remember that all they want Is to reach their*

## Impossible

Today is the birthday of **Nelson Mandela**, born in 1918.

"It always seems impossible until it is done," he said.

This exercise is inspired by Mandela – agree to face the impossible. Write about all the impossible things in your life. Write a list of all the things that are inaccessible to you.

Now reassess your lists and rewrite; ask yourself as you do if what you wrote is really impossible for you. Are you prepared to try to make the impossible possible?

July 19th

With the sea. Do not over flow, Do not hang on words. Learn from the river: Its only designation is To carry water

## Getting Closer

Think about someone close or distant to you, who makes you uncomfortable. Write about this person "from the outside"– describe what they wear and what they do, their facial expressions, the way they speak, and other details that describe **how you perceive this person.**

Now, write about this person "from the inside"– describe what drives them in life, their story, where they come from and where they are going. Write about them intimately, empathetically as if you know them very well.

Put your opinion, criticism and judgement aside, so you can see this person **for who they really are.**

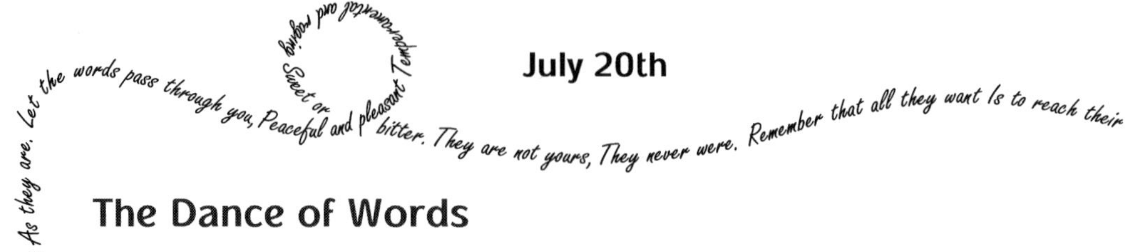
Let the words flow through you, Like the water flowing in the stream Place no dam over your words, Do not ask them to slow down, Do not hasten them forward Allow them to move freely As they are. Let the words pass through you, Peaceful and pleasant Temperamental and raging Sweet or bitter. They are not yours, They never were. Remember that all they want Is to reach their

**July 20th**

## The Dance of Words

Think of one word that you love very much, a word that creates joy inside you. Write a sequence of thoughts and reflections about the word you choose. Now flirt in writing with the words that your chosen word evokes.

Let more and more words and sentences come to you – they might be stories or moments in time. Let everything that comes from within you be present in this mutual dance of pleasure and happiness.

## July 21st

*With the sea. Do not over flow, Do not hang on words. Learn from the river: Its only designation is To carry water*

# Inspiration

Write a list of all the things that inspire you, and that you need to be part of your way of life: people, poetry, nature, music, movies, colors, thoughts, paintings, quotes, walking, hiking, design, and whatever else comes to mind.

Flood your consciousness with these sources of inspiration so they can become, more and more, a part of your life.

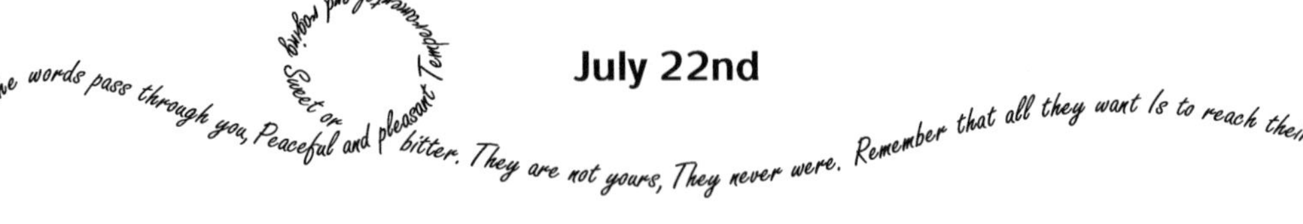
Let the words flow through you, Like the water flowing in the stream Place no dam over your words, Do not ask them to slow down, Do not hasten them forward Allow them to move freely As they are. Let the words pass through you, Peaceful and pleasant Temperamental and raging Sweet or bitter. They are not yours, They never were. Remember that all they want Is to reach their

**July 22nd**

## Giving Instead of Receiving

This is the birthday of **Janusz Korczak**, born in 1878.

"I exist not to be loved and admired, but to love and act. It is not the duty of those around me to love me. Rather, it is my duty to be concerned about the world, about man,"* he wrote.

This exercise is inspired by Korczak. Write a list of all the places and people in your life in which and from whom you seek love, appreciation, recognition and assistance. Write without stopping or judging. Claim your profound need for these things.

Now do the opposite. For every part of your life you want someone to recognize or love, write how you can recognize and love it yourself. Is it possible for you to actively give instead of receive?

* *The Warsaw Ghetto Memoirs of Janusz Korczak*. Translated with an introduction and notes by E.P. Kulawiec, University Press of America, 1978.

## July 23rd

*With the sea. Do not over flow, Do not hang on words. Learn from the river: Its only designation is To carry water*

# The Color I Am

If you had to describe yourself only in color, what color would you choose?

Write about your color. Write about your qualities this color expresses.

Let the color write itself from within you, painting all of you. Discover your color as you move, in your words. Be the color that you bring into this world – with all its value.

Let the words flow through you, Like the water flowing in the stream Place no dam over your words, Do not ask them to slow down, Do not hasten them forward Allow them to move freely As they are. Let the words pass through you, Peaceful and pleasant Temperamental and raging Sweet or bitter. They are not yours, They never were. Remember that all they want Is to reach their

July 24th

## Do not Forget

Write your "Do not forget" list. What are the things you never want to forget? What are the things, big or small, that you must not forget?

Write a text that starts with the words **Do not forget**... and don't forget a thing!

*With the sea. Do not over flow, Do not hang on words. Learn from the river: Its only designation is To carry water*

## I Insist

What do you insist on in your life? Write a list of the things you are not prepared to give up – values, qualities, people, animals, objects.
Write them all.

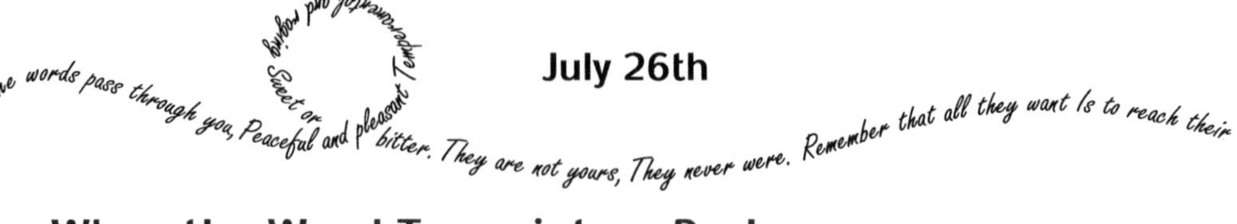
Let the words flow through you, Like the water flowing in the stream Place no dam over your words, Do not ask them to slow down, Do not hasten them forward Allow them to move freely As they are. Let the words pass through you, Peaceful and pleasant Temperamental and raging Sweet or bitter. They are not yours, They never were. Remember that all they want Is to reach their

**July 26th**

## When the Word Turns into a Body

Today is the birthday of poet **Hezy Leskly**, born in 1952.

"When the word turns into a body.../ I will embrace this body" writes Leskly in his poem "Lessons E-I" that deals with the creative power of words and the cyclicity of life.

This is an exercise inspired by Leskly's poem. Close your eyes and begin scanning the parts of your body. Feel your body. Slowly let it "speak itself" through your writing. As in Leskly's poem, let your "body open its mouth and say the word" that created it. Let your body speak. Listen to it. What is it saying?

*With the sea. Do not over flow, Do not hang on words. Learn from the river: Its only designation is To carry water*

## The Heart's Desire

What is your heart's greatest desire? Write it here.

Do not overthink; just write everything that comes to you from your heart.

July 28th

*Let the words flow through you, Like the water flowing in the stream Place no dam over your words, Do not ask them to slow down, Do not hasten them forward Allow them to move freely As they are. Let the words pass through you, Peaceful and pleasant Temperamental and raging Sweet or bitter. They are not yours, They never were. Remember that all they want Is to reach their*

## Bringing Joy into Daily Life

Write about the possibility of introducing joy and love into each simple action in your daily life: washing dishes, doing laundry, drawing, a phone call, going to the bank, driving.

Write about the possibility of doing all these things with a loving heart and a wide smile. Describe what each day looks like when you actively bring joy into everything you do, from morning till night. Put this idea into practice, and explore what it brings into your life.

July 29th

*With the sea. Do not over flow, Do not hang on words. Learn from the river: Its only designation is To carry water*

## The Most Important Thing I Have Learned

Write about the most important thing you have learned in your life. Where did you learn it? What does it mean to you? And are you passing on your experience and wisdom to others?

**July 30th**

*Let the words flow through you, Like the water flowing in the stream Place no dam over your words, Do not ask them to slow down, Do not hasten them forward Allow them to move freely As they are. Let the words pass through you, Peaceful and pleasant Temperamental and raging Sweet or bitter. They are not yours, They never were. Remember that all they want Is to reach their*

## Drawing with Words

In this exercise, write or draw a painting with your words. Let the words glide freely on the page through your pen, and carry you wherever they want to go, until they become a drawing.

Do not think about the choice of words. Let them come to you spontaneously. Allow them to pour themselves into any shape created by your writing. Enjoy every moment!

With the sea. Do not over flow, Do not hang on words. Learn from the river: Its only designation is To carry water

# July 31st

## Collecting Words

Wander through your writing journal. Stroll among the texts, the poems, and the letters. Go through everything that you have written since you started your journey. Choose sentences that are significant to you, gather them together and turn them into a poem or a simple text. Allow yourself to rediscover the materials you have written, have fun with them, make unexpected connections among the texts and enjoy yourself!

If you have only recently started writing in this journal, come back to this page in a few weeks – or next year.

"If they had shut my mouth after the liberation, I wouldn't have stayed alive."
Author **Primo Levi**, born this day in 1919.

# August

## Writing to be

Let the words flow through you, Like the water flowing in the stream Place no dam over your words, Do not ask them to slow down, Do not hasten them forward Allow them to move freely As they are. Let the words pass through you, Peaceful and pleasant Temperamental and raging Sweet or bitter. They are not yours, They never were. Remember that all they want Is to reach their

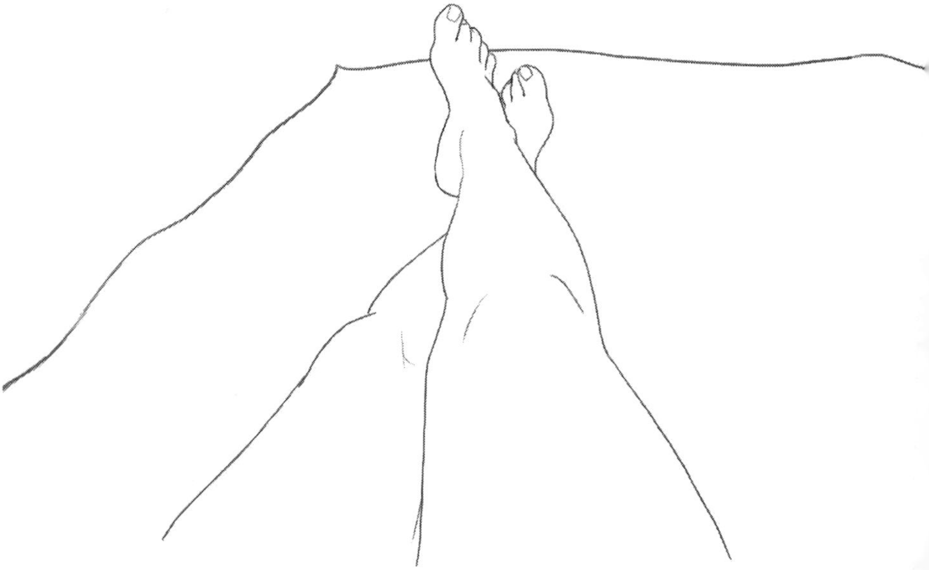

With the sea. Do not over flow, Do not hang on words. Learn from the river: Its only designation is To carry water

## Simply Being

Write about what it means to you to be. When do you feel you are simply being? When do you feel you are truly present?

What is the connection between "to be" and "to live"?

Write about being. Start with **To be...** and simply begin to explore what that means. Let it be. Let yourself be in the writing, just as you are.

*Let the words flow through you, Like the water flowing in the stream Place no dam over your words, Do not ask them to slow down, Do not hasten them forward Allow them to move freely As they are. Let the words pass through you, Peaceful and pleasant Temperamental and raging Sweet or bitter. They are not yours, They never were. Remember that all they want Is to reach their*

**August 2nd**

## A Time for Myself

Do you dedicate time for yourself? Do you value your time?

What does it mean to "dedicate time for you"?

Write a text about the private time you esteem and dedicate for yourself.

# August 3rd



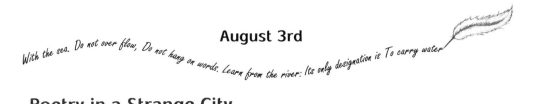

## Poetry in a Strange City

Walk around your neighborhood. Observe the people, the places and the scenery through the eyes of a stranger visiting a foreign, unfamiliar place for the first time.

What do you see around you? What can you smell? What do you feel inside? Perhaps you want to meet the locals, taste their food? Come closer and be excited by the beauty, the new and the unfamiliar.

Describe all that unfamiliarity in your journal, and then write a poem about your experience.

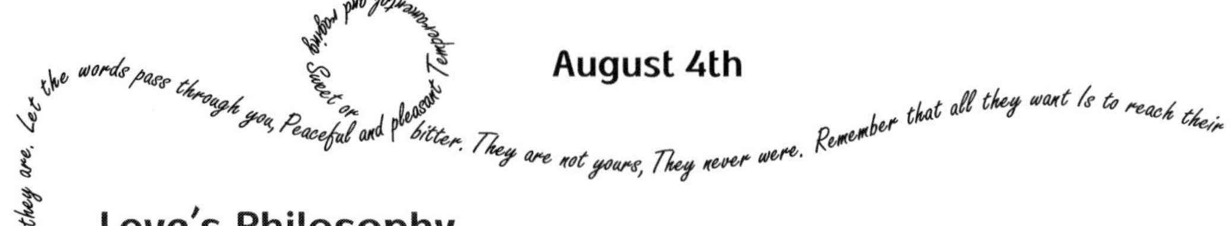
Let the words flow through you, Like the water flowing in the stream Place no dam over your words, Do not ask them to slow down, Do not hasten them forward Allow them to move freely As they are. Let the words pass through you, Peaceful and pleasant Temperamental and raging Sweet or bitter. They are not yours, They never were. Remember that all they want Is to reach their

## August 4th

# Love's Philosophy

Today is the birthday of poet **Percy Bysshe Shelley**, born in 1792.

"Nothing in the world is single," wrote Percy in his poem "Love's Philosophy".

This exercise is inspired by his poem. Write about the philosophy of your love. What do you believe in, when it comes to love? Write your convictions, your musings and your thoughts about love.

## Talking Eyes

Close your eyes and focus your attention on them. Breathe into them and sense their presence.

Now open your eyes and write from their point of view. Use the words: **We see you.**

Explore what your eyes see through writing. Is there a curtain between them and the world? What can be done to raise this veil, so your eyes are able to see things as they are?

Is there something your eyes see that you don't? Write it.

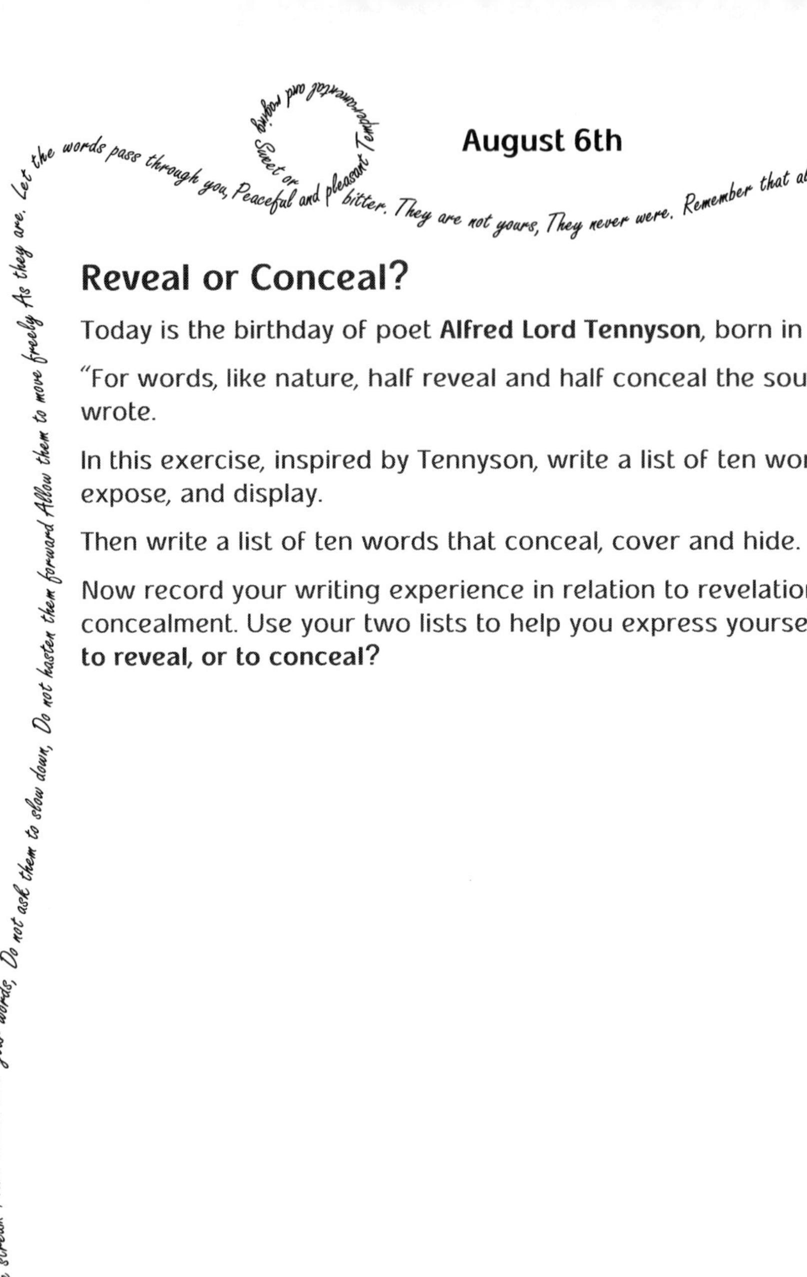
Let the words flow through you, Like the water flowing in the stream Place no dam over your words, Do not ask them to slow down, Do not hasten them forward Allow them to move freely As they are. Let the words pass through you, Peaceful and pleasant Temperamental and raging Sweet or bitter. They are not yours, They never were. Remember that all they want Is to reach their

## August 6th

# Reveal or Conceal?

Today is the birthday of poet **Alfred Lord Tennyson**, born in 1809.

"For words, like nature, half reveal and half conceal the soul within," he wrote.

In this exercise, inspired by Tennyson, write a list of ten words that reveal, expose, and display.

Then write a list of ten words that conceal, cover and hide.

Now record your writing experience in relation to revelation and concealment. Use your two lists to help you express yourself. **Do you write to reveal, or to conceal?**

# August 7th

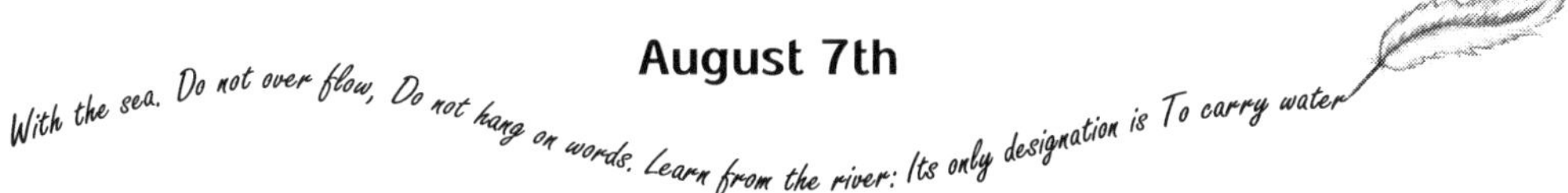
With the sea. Do not over flow, Do not hang on words. Learn from the river: Its only designation is To carry water

## A Writing Break

Think of a recent event that you would like to reflect on, to understand your insights better, from which you can extract a kernel of experience and wisdom.

First, describe what happened. Then, choose a moment within the event you would like to pause. Freeze that moment in writing. Delve into this moment, and describe what happens when time stands still.

Let the words write themselves, without any movement forward within the event. Enjoy taking a breath, slowing down and being present. Connect to how time stretches, and how long you can linger in the moment.

Use this pause to record everything your senses absorb: colors, smells, shapes, sights, the weather, tastes, emotions and memories. Write from a deep contemplation of the moment.

Let the words flow through you, Like the water flowing in the stream Place no dam over your words, Do not ask them to slow down, Do not hasten them forward Allow them to move freely As they are. Let

the words pass through you, Peaceful and pleasant Temperamental and raging Sweet or bitter. They are not yours, They never were. Remember that all they want Is to reach their

**August 8th**

## A Simple Tale

This is the birthday of author **Shmuel Yosef Agnon**, born in 1887.

"When a person's world is dark for him, he reads a book and sees the world differently," he wrote in his book *A Simple Tale**.

This exercise is inspired by Agnon. Write about a world you discovered in a book that shed light on your life, and gave you strength, inspiration, joy and hope. Write the simple tale of that book, how it opened a new world for you.

* The Toby Press; Revised edition, 2014.

August 9th

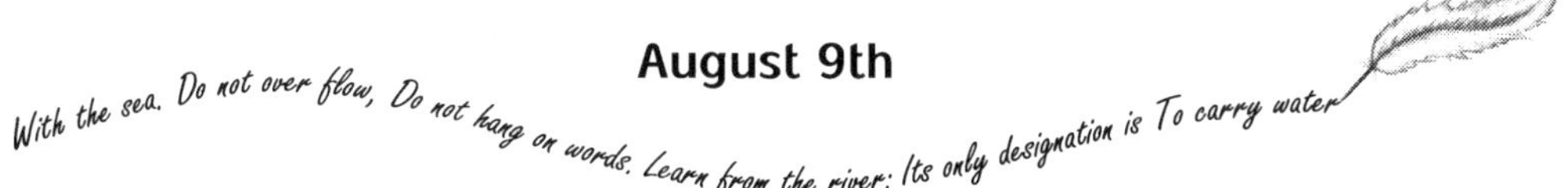
With the sea. Do not over flow, Do not hang on words. Learn from the river: Its only designation is To carry water

## An Island of Certainty

This is the birthday of children's writer **Tove Jansson**, born in 1914.

"All things are so very uncertain, and that's exactly what makes me feel reassured," she wrote in her book, *The Moomins*.

This exercise is inspired by Jansson. Write about all the things in this world that you are not sure about and that you feel are unsafe and won't necessarily be here tomorrow.

Can you find an island of certainty in all this uncertainty?

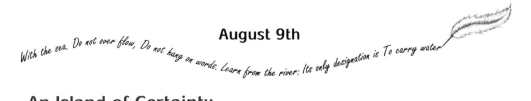

## August 10th

# Decisions

Write about a decision you have to make that you are putting off. Let's assume you are sitting on the fence, torn between options. What needs to happen in order for you to make a decision? What is stopping you?

Write about it. You do not have to make any decisions, of course. But it is a good idea to reflect.

It takes courage to cross to the other side.

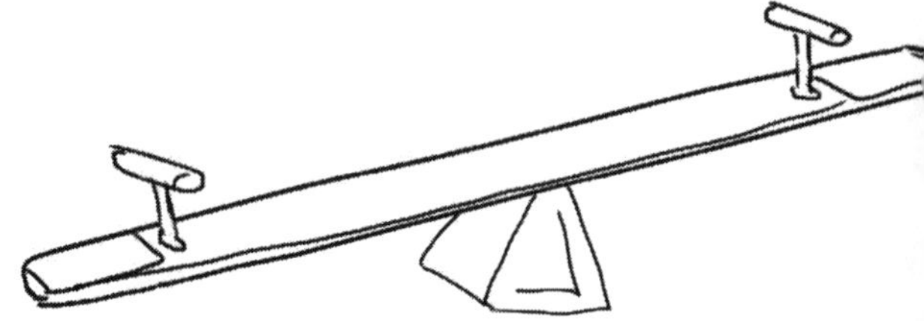

*With the sea. Do not over flow, Do not hang on words. Learn from the river: Its only designation is To carry water*

## Home and Away

Write about a place that is far away from you, as far as can be.

Write about it as if it is nearby. As close as it can be.

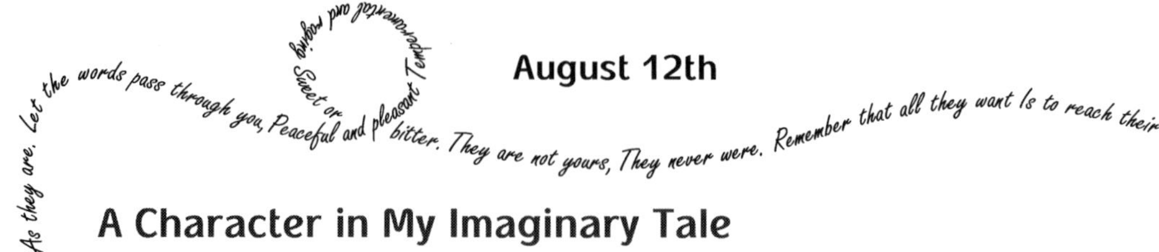
Let the words flow through you, Like the water flowing in the stream Place no dam over your words, Do not ask them to slow down, Do not hasten them forward Allow them to move freely As they are. Let the words pass through you, Peaceful and pleasant Temperamental and raging Sweet or bitter. They are not yours, They never were. Remember that all they want Is to reach their

## August 12th

# A Character in My Imaginary Tale

If you wrote a story, who would your main character be? Invent the protagonist in your imaginary book. Describe your hero and give them life. Who is that person? What is their life story? How old are they? What do they do? Where do they live? What is his or her family status?

In writing about your protagonist, include an event that changed their life, their quirky habits, their greatest moments of pain and joy, their qualities and flaws. Write everything there is to know about your character, what kind of person they are and what they look like – within and without.

*With the sea. Do not over flow, Do not hang on words. Learn from the river: Its only designation is To carry water*

## Without Saying a Word

Choose a word that is meaningful to you, a word you love and feel connected to. Now write a text that expresses it and its profound meaning for you, without once using the word itself.

Let the words flow through you, Like the water flowing in the stream Place no dam over your words, Do not ask them to slow down, Do not hasten them forward Allow them to move freely As they are. Let the words pass through you,

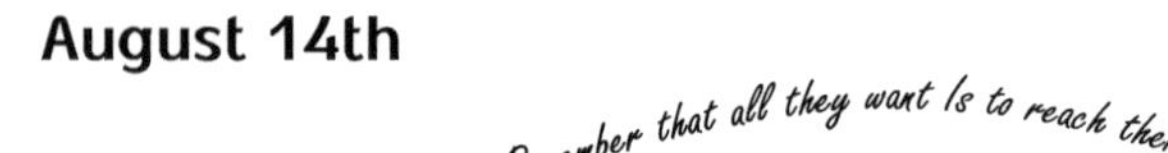
Peaceful and pleasant Temperamental and raging Sweet or bitter. They are not yours, They never were. Remember that all they want Is to reach their

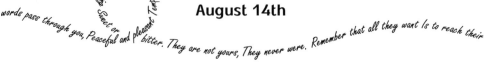

## August 14th

# A Summer Night

This is the birthday of poet **Nathan Alterman**, born in 1910.

"Summer breeze floats, vague, stormy," Alterman wrote in his poem "A Summer Night"*.

This exercise is inspired by his poem. Write about your summer night, about the summer breeze you feel, about the stars that come into view, about time and about silence. What is your summer night composed of?

* *Selected Poems, Bilingual Edition*. Translated by Robert Friend, Hakibbutz Hameuchad Publishing House, 1978.

## Two Minutes

Write a text that extensively describes an event that lasted only two minutes. Describe every single second within those two minutes.

Allow your words to stop time and express those moments completely.

## August 16th

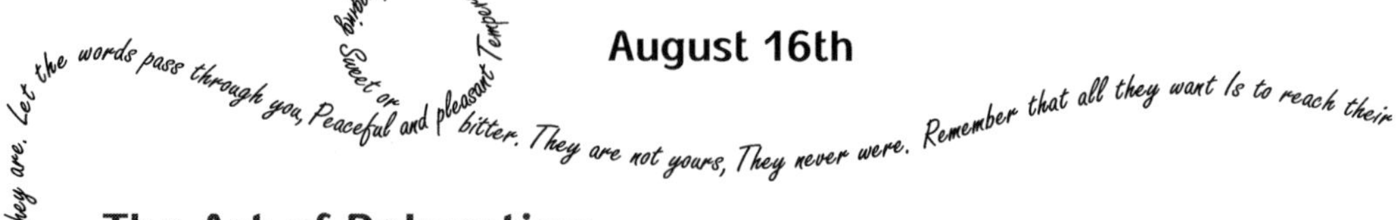
Let the words flow through you, Like the water flowing in the stream Place no dam over your words, Do not ask them to slow down, Do not hasten them forward Allow them to move freely As they are. Let the words pass through you, Peaceful and pleasant Temperamental and raging Sweet or bitter. They are not yours, They never were. Remember that all they want Is to reach their

# The Art of Relaxation

Write what true relaxation means to you. Describe when you feel truly rested, when you let everything go and can just *be*. Linger over what enables you to relax.

*With the sea. Do not over flow, Do not hang on words. Learn from the river: Its only designation is To carry water*

## The Monologue of a Portrait

Choose a portrait you feel connected to. It can be an image you find in a magazine or on the internet – one that captures your attention. Study it patiently, until it starts to talk to you. As you listen, write its monologue.

Let the words flow through you, Like the water flowing in the stream Place no dam over your words, Do not ask them to slow down, Do not hasten them forward Allow them to move freely As they are. Let the words pass through you, Peaceful and pleasant Temperamental and raging Sweet or bitter. They are not yours, They never were. Remember that all they want Is to reach their

**August 18th**

## Writing in Good taste

What is the food you most love to eat? Indulge yourself and eat it.

Close your eyes and eat slowly. Pay attention to every bite. Chew gently and softly. Notice your breathing as you eat.

Now, slowly take your journal, and write about your experience. Express the taste, the texture, the feeling, and the process in your words. Let each bite become a line in a poem. Let your sense of taste become poetry.

## Curiosity

Are you curious? What are you curious about? How truly curious are you?

Does curiosity help you, or perhaps the opposite?

Write about your curiosity. Would you like to increase it or reduce it?

Let the words flow through you, Like the water flowing in the stream Place no dam over your words, Do not ask them to slow down, Do not hasten them forward Allow them to move freely As they are. Let the words pass through you, Peaceful and pleasant Temperamental and raging Sweet or bitter. They are not yours, They never were. Remember that all they want Is to reach their

August 20th

## My Word Bridge

Sometimes, we need a bridge to connect us to the world, to the sky and earth, or bring us closer to another person. Where in your life do you need a bridge? What bridge will help you fulfill yourself?

Build your bridge with words; write a bridge that leads you wherever you want to go, over existing barriers, that spans the gap between your real life and the life you wish you had.

## What Can You Expect?

What are your expectations of yourself? Of others? Are you often disappointed?

Write everything you expect of yourself, the people around you, the whole world.

Start with the words **I expect...** .Then review what you have written, and consider if you are prepared to give up some of your expectations. If you do, how will that affect your life?

*Let the words flow through you, Like the water flowing in the stream Place no dam over your words, Do not ask them to slow down, Do not hasten them forward Allow them to move freely As they are. Let the words pass through you, Peaceful and pleasant Temperamental and raging Sweet or bitter. They are not yours, They never were. Remember that all they want Is to reach their*

**August 22nd**

## Do not Tell Me

Write a text that starts with the words **Do not tell me...**

## August 23rd

*With the sea. Do not over flow, Do not hang on words. Learn from the river: Its only designation is To carry water*

# Letting Go

Where is the safest place for you to let go? Where do you feel secure?

When and with whom do you allow yourself to truly let go?

What should you let go of at this moment in your life? Write about this.

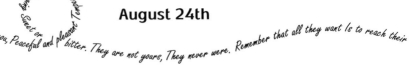

Let the words flow through you, Like the water flowing in the stream Place no dam over your words, Do not ask them to slow down, Do not hasten them forward Allow them to move freely As they are. Let the words pass through you, Peaceful and pleasant Temperamental and raging Sweet or bitter. They are not yours, They never were. Remember that all they want Is to reach their

**August 24th**

## Enjoying

This is the birthday of poet **Jorge Luis Borges**, born in 1899.

"I have spent my life reading, analyzing, writing... and enjoying," he said. "I found the last to be the most important thing of all."*

This is an exercise inspired by Borges. Explore the word **Enjoying**. What does it mean to you? When do you enjoy yourself? What makes you feel pure pleasure more than anything else? Write a text that expresses everything that you enjoy in life – about the things, big and small, that fill your life with pleasure. Start your writing with the word **Enjoying** ...

* *This Craft of Verse*. Harvard UP, 2000, p.1.

# August 25th

*With the sea. Do not over flow, Do not hang on words. Learn from the river: Its only designation is To carry water*

## Your Breakthrough

What is your next breakthrough? Explore, as you write, the next rung you must climb on the ladder of your personal development. What will facilitate your growth?

Open the door to whatever that may be, and the path you need to follow will begin to pave itself.

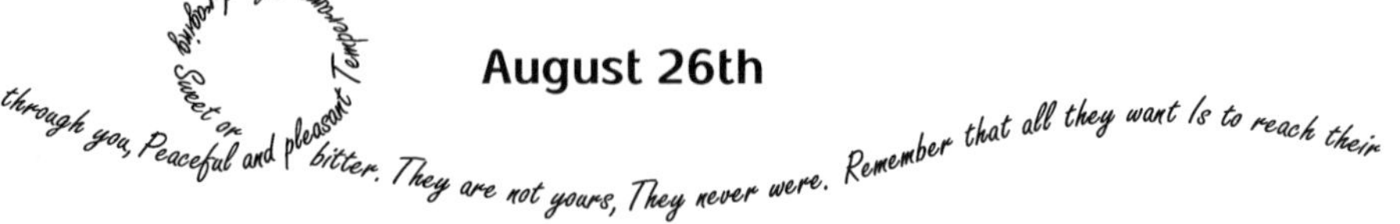
Let the words pass through you, Peaceful and pleasant Temperamental and raging Sweet or bitter. They are not yours, They never were. Remember that all they want Is to reach their

## August 26th

Let the words flow through you, Like the water flowing in the stream Place no dam over your words, Do not ask them to slow down, Do not hasten them forward Allow them to move freely As they are. Let

# The Small Things

This is the birthday of **Mother Theresa**, born in 1910.

"Not all of us can do great things. But we can do small things with great love," she said.

This exercise is inspired by Mother Theresa. Do you find satisfaction in the small things you do regularly and routinely?

Write the small things you do each and every day that satisfy you and bring you joy, pleasure and inspiration.

"Be faithful in small things because it is in them that your strength lies." **Mother Theresa**

## August 27th

# I Knew, I Always Knew

Write a text that ends with the words **I knew, I always knew.** Assume that you do not know while you write. At the end of the text, let these words come to you. Trust yourself. You know.

Let the words flow through you, Like the water flowing in the stream Place no dam over your words, Do not ask them to slow down, Do not hasten them forward Allow them to move freely As they are. Let the words pass through you, Peaceful and pleasant Temperamental and raging Sweet or bitter. They are not yours, They never were. Remember that all they want Is to reach their

**August 28th**

## After the Story Ends

Choose a book you really loved, and read its ending again. Now write beyond the end. Use your imagination to create a story that continues after the story ends.

"Only after the end of the story
Can I finally write the end" **Yael Tzivoni**

*After the End of the Story*. Tzivonim, 2012

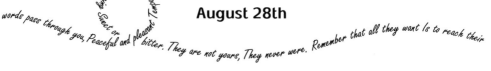

# August 29th

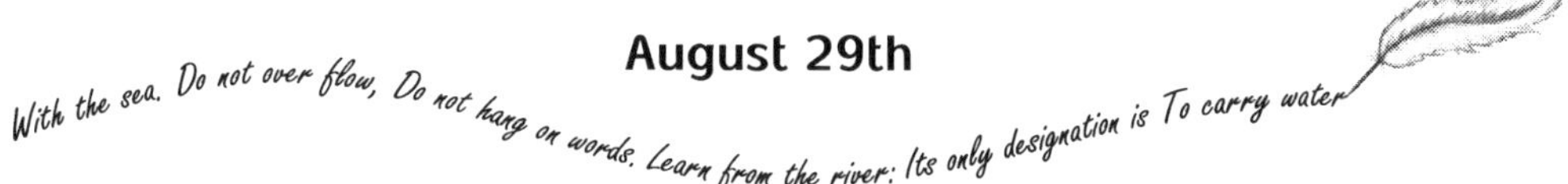
With the sea. Do not over flow, Do not hang on words. Learn from the river: Its only designation is To carry water

## An Opportunity

Turn the word **Opportunity** over in your mind and let it roll down your pen onto your journal.

What does this word evoke within you? Do you recognize opportunities when they appear at your door?

What opportunities do you think often come your way, and which have not ever presented themselves?

Write about the opportunities in your life and the way you harvest them – or don't. This is **your opportunity**!

Let the words flow through you, Like the water flowing in the stream Place no dam over your words, Do not ask them to slow down, Do not hasten them forward Allow them to move freely As they are. Let the words pass through you, Peaceful and pleasant Temperamental and raging Sweet or bitter. They are not yours, They never were. Remember that all they want Is to reach their

**August 30th**

## The Journey of Four Seasons

Today, just before summer ends, write a list of the meaningful instances in your life over the past year – the times of light and times of darkness, revelations, changes, new experiences, people you met, memories you recovered, stories that affected you, presents you were given, new qualities you found within yourself, special moments to cherish.

Gather all these moments together, and look compassionately at how far you have come.

Write a text about the journey you have taken, about what you have achieved, and all you have experienced along the way.

Write your **four-season journey**.

## August 31st

*With the sea. Do not over flow, Do not hang on words. Learn from the river: Its only designation is To carry water*

# The End of Summer

The summer has ended and autumn lies ahead. The cycle of four seasons is coming to a close.

Write the music of your summer. The words permit you to savor the whole process of coming full circle. Cherish yourself for the journey you have taken over the past four seasons.

## Some Final Words

There are so many more writing exercises that wanted to enter this journal, but were unable to do so.
Many words within are still waiting to be written, to be expressed on paper, dreamed, and realized.
This is your time.
Open a new, blank journal, and simply write yourself.
Write yourself, like you have never written before.
Allow yourself to be who you are, on paper and in your life.
With or without writing exercises.
You can always come back here for inspiration.
You can always come back here to start...
From the beginning

## My sources of inspiration

My first writing workshop, **Writing from Instinct**, was born in early 2006. At that time, I was a journalist and I felt I had found the way to express myself in the world of writing. One night, as I was filled with anger towards a woman who was very close to me, I assaulted the paper, pouring out all the rage that had built up inside me toward her. After the anger had subsided, I felt great pain and sadness, and then, suddenly, there was compassion, and even love.

When the tide receded, it suddenly occurred to me that what I had gone through intuitively needed to go out into the world, that I must pass it on to as many people as I possibly can.

This was not the first time I experienced the power of writing. For me, writing is like a long-time "secret friend" who has been with me since my childhood. However, this time I realized that I must share her existence with others.

With the help of my good friend **Nili Dor Ha'Elah**, I embarked on a journey, which is not yet over.

At the beginning, I drew my inspiration from the simple, accessible and intuitive knowledge that I possess. As the workshops developed, I was exposed to new content and ideas that sharpened and deepened the writing processes I was guiding. Close friends I have met over the years shared their wisdom and personal experiences with me. I met some of these friends through the books they have written.

In recent years, another huge source of inspiration has become available to me, one which is also the home of my personal development - I became a student at the school of practical philosophy, **The New Acropolis**. During my studies, I rediscovered my natural connection to the annual cycle of the seasons in nature. Over and above the influence my studies have had on my personal life and my work with the seasons, I wanted to create a writing process that follows the rhythm of nature.
Everything I have mentioned above has affected, either directly or indirectly, my way of writing, as well as influenced the exercises I provide in this journal.

I feel privileged to have this opportunity to thank all the people who have accompanied me, and express my deep gratitude to them. I sincerely recommend you add their books to your private library:

**Natalie Goldberg,** *Writing Down the Bones*. Shambala Publications, 2010.

**Julia Cameron,** *The Artist's Way,* 1992. and *The Right To Write,* 1999, both published by Jeremy P. Tarcher/Putnam.

**Yael Tzivoni,** A dear friend and colleague, who established a school of creative writing.

**Tlalit Cohen Asna**, my bibliotherapy teacher, who provided me with an important additional tool for my private toolbox. She also introduced me to the books of **Prof. Adir Cohen,** which deal with the power of writing as a therapeutic tool.

**Shez**, author and poet, dear friend and colleague, who led the first writing workshop I participated in.

## Acknowledgements from the bottom of my heart

A special thanks to you, **dear writer**, for embarking on this journey through words with me, and with yourself, for agreeing to commit, to meet yourself, to discover and create from the core of your being.

Thank you, **Ido**, my beloved partner and friend on this journey of life, for your never-ending belief and confidence in me, your vision, your patience, and your help every step of the way. You are always here for me, my beacon of light.

Thank you sisters of my heart, for holding the sky and the earth for me during this creative process:

To **Tali Cohen Zion**, for editing the original Hebrew version of the journal with her professionalism and exceptional talent, for supporting the idea and myself all the way, for putting abundant attention and love into each word, comma and full stop.

To **Gali Gonen**, the graphic artist who has been with me over the past few years, and who has worked day and night to ensure that this journal is published as completely and aesthetically as possible.

To **Yael Herzog**, the talented illustrator, who has been working with me from the start, and whose illustrations have inspired me to continue evolving in the creative process.

To **Mali Ben-Simon**, for her devoted and accurate proofreading in Hebrew.

To **Racheli Reuven**, for her keen eye and constructive words, for her encouragement to give birth to this journal, and for reminding me of all the individuals who are waiting for it.

To **Rika Or Lev**, for holding my dream in her two hands and seeing it come to light even before it was ready.

To **Yael Tzivoni**, for the personal and professional support, for the willingness to share, and for her wise counsel and our mutual inspiration.

Thanks to **Nili Dor Ha'Elah**, for being the first to open the door for me into the world of writing workshops, and who continues to connect women to their dreams.

Thanks to **Adva Webber** who offered to translate this book out of her love and connection to the words and the exercises it holds, to bring it to light in English for the first time. And thanks to **Tanya Rosenblit**, who continued the complex task of translating this book with great commitment and love

Thanks to **Nancy Peled**, my dearest editor, who happily invested her time, skill and great love of both words and writing to create a reader-friendly English version of this journal. Thanks for the solid, endless cooperation you offered along the way.

A huge thank you to all the **participants** of my workshops, who I have been privileged to meet in recent years, who were the first to experience the diverse exercises and processes, and especially for putting their trust in me along the way.

Thanks to my incredible **parents and my family**, for being a part of my life. I love you beyond time and nature's cycles.

Thanks to the school of philosophy, **The New Acropolis**, for the home I have found there and for being a space of spiritual nourishment to me, a place where I am learning to know myself and to give to the world.

Thank you, **God**.

This page
Will never remain
White
For long
Under my galloping pen

Made in the USA
Las Vegas, NV
18 December 2023

83086925R00252